MW01122228

Corporate Social Responsibility, Sustainability and Public Relations

While public relations offers numerous assets for organization–stakeholder relationship building and for ethical corporate social responsibility and sustainability communication, it also faces challenges linked to negative perceptions of the profession which can lead to accusations of "greenwashing." This innovative book critically explores the growing, complex, and sometimes contradictory connections among public relations, corporate social responsibility, and sustainability.

This book advocates a postmodern insider-activist role for public relations which can transform organizations into moral places committed to people, planet, and profit. By amplifying voices of nearly one hundred for-profit and nonprofit professionals, and using hermeneutic phenomenological theme analyses of CSR/Sustainability reports and websites, this book invokes public relations, postmodern, and critical theories to empower public relations professionals to transform organizations into ethical, authentic, and transparent actors in the public sphere. It is essential reading for scholars, educators, and enquiring professionals working in public relations, corporate communication, sustainability, and corporate social responsibility.

Donnalyn Pompper is Associate Professor of Strategic Communication at Temple University, USA. She also has extensive corporate PR experience with Campbell's Soup Company, Tasty Baking Company, and Lewis, Gilman & Kynett, once the largest public relations/advertising firm in Philadelphia.

Routledge New Directions in Public Relations and Communication Research

Edited by Kevin Moloney

Routledge New Directions in Public Relations and Communication Research is a new forum for the publication of books of original research in PR and related types of communication. Its remit is to publish critical and challenging responses to continuities and fractures in contemporary PR thinking and practice, and its essential yet contested role in market-orientated, capitalist, liberal democracies around the world. The series reflects the multiple and inter-disciplinary forms PR takes in a post-Grunigian world; the expanding roles which it performs; and the increasing number of countries in which it is practised.

The series will examine current trends and explore new thinking on the key questions which impact upon PR and communications including:

- Is the evolution of persuasive communications in Central and Eastern Europe, China, Latin America, Japan, the Middle East and South East Asia developing new forms or following Western models?
- What has been the impact of postmodern sociologies, cultural studies and methodologies which are often critical of the traditional, conservative role of PR in capitalist political economies, and in patriarchy, gender and ethnic roles?
- What is the impact of digital social media on politics, individual privacy and PR practice? Is new technology changing the nature of content communicated, or simply reaching bigger audiences faster? Is digital PR a cause or a consequence of political and cultural change?

Books in this series will be of interest to academics and researchers involved in these expanding fields of study, as well as students undertaking advanced studies in this area.

Public Relations and Nation Building
Influencing Israel
Margalit Toledano and David McKie

Gender and Public Relations
Critical perspectives on voice, image and identity
Edited by Christine Daymon and Kristin Demetrious

Corporate Social Responsibility, Sustainability and Public Relations

Negotiating multiple complex challenges

Donnalyn Pompper

Routledge
Taylor & Francis Group

LONDON AND NEW YORK

First published 2015
by Routledge
2 Park Square, Milton Park, Abingdon, Oxon OX14 4RN

and by Routledge
711 Third Avenue, New York, NY 10017

Routledge is an imprint of the Taylor & Francis Group, an informa business

© 2015 Donnalyn Pompper

The right of Donnalyn Pompper to be identified as author of this work has
been asserted by her in accordance with sections 77 and 78 of the
Copyright, Designs and Patents Act 1988.

All rights reserved. No part of this book may be reprinted or reproduced or
utilised in any form or by any electronic, mechanical, or other means, now
known or hereafter invented, including photocopying and recording, or in
any information storage or retrieval system, without permission in writing
from the publishers.

Trademark notice: Product or corporate names may be trademarks or
registered trademarks, and are used only for identification and explanation
without intent to infringe.

British Library Cataloguing in Publication Data
A catalogue record for this book is available from the British Library

Library of Congress Cataloging in Publication Data
Pompper, Donnalyn, 1960-
Corporate social responsibility, sustainability and public relations :
negotiating multiple complex challenges / Donnalyn Pompper.
    pages cm. -- (Routledge new directions in public relations and
communication research)
Includes bibliographical references and index.
1. Social responsibility of business. 2. Corporations--Public relations.
3. Sustainable development. I. Title.
    HD60.P66 2015
    658.4'08--dc23
        2014038938

ISBN: 978-0-415-85591-4 (hbk)
ISBN: 978-0-203-73387-5 (ebk)

Typeset in Times New Roman
by Taylor & Francis Books

To public relations and CSR/Sustainability students and researchers everywhere: Acting as an organization's conscience is courageous work.

Contents

List of figures

Foreword

This text unflinchingly puts the critical perspectives about the role of public relations in CSR/Sustainability on the table and makes the argument that public relations practitioners not only have a role to play but bring a unique perspective to CSR/Sustainability practice that will eventually benefit the organization through transparent practices and relationship management.

The role of public relations in CSR/Sustainability has been challenged and even mocked for many years. Part of the problem is the fact that public relations and media relations are often viewed as synonymous, thus bringing the practice into disrepute among organizational stakeholders, particularly the media. Pompper consistently argues that CSR/Sustainability practice should not be used as a publicity tool, but that CSR/Sustainability reporting should be extensive, transparent, and accessible. Following Lyotard (1984) she argues for making all information available so that stakeholders can find any of the information they require. Today that is easily accomplished by using an organization's own media for this. Pompper consistently argues that authenticity and sincerity in CSR/Sustainability efforts are crucial. Making information widely available and easily accessible contributes to transparency of CSR/Sustainability efforts, which will prevent accusations of greenwashing.

The reality of all practice is that it can be put to good or bad use. CSR/Sustainability is no exception and it is the role of the internal-activist to speak up for what is good. It is hard not to become cynical about organizations' abuse of CSR/Sustainability mechanisms to greenwash or hide their lack of social responsibility. Internal activists will guard against this cynicism. Arguing for CSR as sustainable practice will help them make the argument that an organization cannot be financially sustainable if it is not socially and environmentally sustainable as well. Language matters and raising questions about CSR/Sustainability practice is already action on the part of the public relations practitioner.

It is doubtful that CSR/Sustainability is the sole responsibility of the public relations professional. It is clear from the text that successful CSR/Sustainability is a collective effort involving governments, stakeholders, and shareholders, and actively enforced by the public through consumer and other actions. For organizations, CSR/Sustainability is a complex process often requiring extensive and complicated compliance procedures involving multiple internal participants. Public relations practice is particularly suited to be part of such a collective effort within the organization and undeniably deserves a seat at the CSR/Sustainability table. Public relations practitioners should use their understanding of organizational processes, their networking and communication skills, and their knowledge of the organizational environment to ensure that seat.

This text also has great heuristic value. The practitioner interviews raised additional questions and lay the foundation for expanding research in the field. One of the issues that can be further explored in the future is the relationship between values, norms, and the law, particularly because of legal compliance requirements with administrative procedures, such as accounting practices, audits, and the US Sarbanes–Oxley Act. To this is linked the much neglected concept of agency, which this text touches on as well. It raises the question of the legal contract between the public relations practitioner and employer or client, which requires specific outcomes, versus the concept of agency as the ability of practitioners to resist unethical practices and to deal reflexively with their employment environment.

Yet another question this text raises is whether CSR/Sustainability can or should be strategic. This issue is raised particularly in the context of corporate philanthropy. The concept of philanthropy is intimately tied to giving money to what organizations perceive as good causes. When does a good cause become a strategic focus for an organization and will it lose its philanthropic value if it is so named? The link between CSR and sustainability provides a better perspective. Linking CSR to sustainable practices makes it possible to argue that the practice can, and in fact should, be strategic. If sustainability efforts do not address the social and environmental footprints of the organization, they are random rather than strategic and quite useless.

This thoughtful text, based on the actual words of practitioners, addresses other important issues. Pompper applies the work of Levinas and his concept of the *Other* to the ethical practice of CSR/Sustainability. This is an important contribution to the CSR/Sustainability debate because it raises the fundamental question of who the Other is and whether CSR/Sustainability practices lead to what Bauman (1993) calls pastoral power, that is, using good actions to control the behavior of others. This is indeed one of the paradoxes or aporiae of the practice that Pompper refers to consistently. One can never be sure that what one views as ethical might in the long term have negative consequences.

At this time it is important to accept that life is full of aporiae. This is exacerbated by the fact that there is no single understanding of definition of what CSR/Sustainability practice is. As Pompper shows, the understanding of CSR/Sustainability is highly situational and differs between organization type, region, culture, social practices, and nation states. The European response to CSR/Sustainability is clearly very different from that in the USA, where the financial bottom line is viewed as a value system and often viewed as the only value system. Bauman argues that all ethical arguments crumble when faced with "the acid test of usefulness or profit" (Bauman 1993: 36), which explains why CSR/Sustainability practices in the USA have not risen to the same levels as in Europe. I wish to argue that it is a very good thing that no single definition of CSR/Sustainability exists because it should be implemented thoughtfully and with specific concern for the organization's unique economic, social, and environmental footprint.

In the final instance it is good to remember that life is a messy business. Any public relations practitioner looking for clear-cut answers and definitions of CSR/Sustainability practices in a fragmented world will be disappointed. This is why an ethic of personal responsibility is so important and why we can and should no longer hold others responsible for our own actions. We have to muddle through every day and we can only do that when we live consciously, reflexively, thoughtfully, and fully engaged in our practice.

Derina Holtzhausen
Professor and Director
School of Media and Strategic Communications
Oklahoma State University
Author of *Public Relations as Activism:*
Postmodern Approaches to Theory and Practice (2014, Routledge)

Preface

Writing this book has enabled me to enjoin an early passion for study of environmental risk journalism with a commitment to critique of power and public relations dynamics as they play out in organizations and impact the larger public sphere. The aim of the book is to open new space for critically examining connections between the public relations function and increasing attention to CSR/Sustainability, globally. A normative lens is employed which calls for public relations managers to embrace the insider-activist role as a postmodern and ethical commitment to social responsibility and sustainability. This book's aims include critically exploring the interplay among public relations, communication, and CSR/Sustainability; navigating ethical dilemmas in CSR/sustainability work; and moving beyond the business case—how the public relations profession contributes to CSR/Sustainability. Overall, it seeks to inspire public relations agents to transform organizations and make them ethical, responsible, sustainable, authentic, and transparent.

To avoid excluding those who uniquely define CSR, sustainability, corporate citizenship, or any of the other comparable concepts, I enjoin CSR/Sustainability throughout the book—knowing full well that certain terms resonate more with some than with others. Often, I rely on definitions offered by the many professionals from around the world who were interviewed for this book and amplify their voices using their own words. About a hundred interviews were conducted for this book and the content of about as many CSR and Sustainability reports and links on corporate and nonprofit websites were analyzed. Extensive hermeneutic phenomenological theme analyses (Van Manen, 1990) were conducted upon statements, phrases, and photographic representations of CSR/Sustainability that were particularly revealing, essential, or remarkable to identify patterns or themes of meaning embedded in data sets of interview transcripts, websites, CSR/Sustainability reports, and Facebook pages. For interviews, some research participants were comfortable being named, but many asked that their identity remain confidential and I have respected that. A multi-paradigmatic perspective guided reviews of multiple literature sets and theories from business management, communication, public relations, social and environmental accounting, marketing, and more.

Thanks to research participants for sharing your stories and voices. Much appreciation to the Temple University Summer Research Grant program and inspiration from graduate students eager to shape a future where organizations are committed to profit and fundraising goals on par with social goals impacting people and the planet. Special acknowledgement to graduate students Erin Kuhl and Lauren Bradford for classroom engagement with CSR/Sustainability as it affects millennials, communities, and partnerships with nonprofits. Thanks also to friends at Routledge for expert support and guidance, including Kevin Moloney, Sinead Waldron, Jacqueline Curthoys, Rosalind Wall, Penny Brown. Indeed, book publishing is a team effort.

1 Forging public relations and CSR/Sustainability connections

Perhaps no concept has gained greater popularity—or notoriety—in business management circles than corporate social responsibility (CSR) and related discourses of sustainability and corporate citizenship. CSR has grown in importance with practitioners and scholars even though it remains a "contested issue" (O'Riordan and Fairbrass 2008: 746). This chapter critically explores the interplay between public relations and CSR/Sustainability as viewed through lenses of culture, economics, and politics. A philosophy increasingly interrogated since the mid-1990s, social responsibility puts corporations squarely in economic and social spaces (Brown 2008). On the one hand, CSR has been heralded as an ideological panacea response to the dot.com collapse and a prescription for reversing Worldcom and Enron-sized ethics lapses which robbed stockholders of billions (Verschoor 2005). On the other hand, some call CSR a smokescreen for masking poor accountability and camouflage for exorbitant profit making while carrying on with business as usual. Some researchers warn that overuse of the CSR term threatens its utility (Cheney, Roper, and May 2007). The concept of *green*, similarly, is contested. Carrie Christopher, Co-owner of the Albuquerque-based consulting firm in the USA, Concept Green, explained: "We really went back and forth about the use of the word *green* because it's very overused. It means everything and nothing…"

Links between CSR/Sustainability and public relations have been uneasy ones. In fact, CSR has been called an *invention* of public relations (Frankental 2001, italics added); a tool used for communication, image/reputation management, and relationship-building (Sagar and Singla, 2004). More critically, public relations is considered by some to be a strategy "for complacency and control" (Cheney, Roper, and May 2007: 3) and an instrument for propaganda (Beder 2000). As perceived by Scott Dille, Group Leader at Denmark-based healthcare provider, Novo Nordisk, the public relations profession has lost significant credibility since being paired with CSR/Sustainability:

> The true definition of PR is building and maintaining relationships. Where I think CSR has suffered some credibility, globally, is that when it is so aligned with PR when PR is defined as publicity… just corporate

advertising trying to squeeze additionally out of CSR efforts. It's also very one-way and you don't get that level of engagement … PR can be helpful and supportive of CSR when we're talking about stakeholder relationship building and maintenance – and as a research component, finding out where stakeholder perceptions are and how to educate them. It's a bit of a double edged sword is where I am now.

Because interplay between public relations and CSR has yielded over-whelmingly negative critique, some organizations opt instead to use the term *sustainability*. Fundamentally, the sustainability narrative refers to reactions to unintended consequences of natural resource consumption and commerce (Millar, Hind, and Magala, 2012). Public relations practitioners and scholars use the sustainability narrative to enhance corporate image/reputation, which ultimately supports bottom-line profits. Less plentiful are critical scholars urging for public relations practitioners to act normatively from inside organizations; as a means for inspiring organizations' authentic, ethical commitment to a wide number of stakeholders (people), while also being respectful of natural environments (planet) and earnings (profit) as illustrated by Elkington's (1999) triple bottom-line model. This book is written from such a standpoint.

Examining interplay between public relations and CSR/Sustainability exposes disparities among operationalizations of the term and raises concerns. Public relations' involvement in CSR/Sustainability arenas has dominated academic conference papers and journals since the mid-1990s. This book examines these issues and exposes behind-the-scenes perspectives of CSR/Sustainability space professionals as they ponder Friedman's (1970) critique that in a capitalist system corporations primarily are responsible to stock-holders—so, to do otherwise constitutes theft and *ir*responsibility. Also explored are public relations and CSR/Sustainability managers' perceptions of triple bottom-line thinking and business case arguments.

Primary aims of this book are: 1) to examine overlap of public relations and CSR/Sustainability by comparing/contrasting origins, theories, and attention to stakeholders; 2) to build upon relevant bodies of literature and to reveal empirical findings for the purpose of better understanding CSR/Sustainability's ethics and communicative components; 3) to interrogate the broader scope of the public relations industry for contributing to public communication involving culture, economics, and politics; 4) to enjoin several theory frameworks in order to closely critique public relations; and 5) to examine how/if it is possible for public relations practitioners to navigate CSR/Sustainability even when outcomes may be inconsistent with organizational self-interest. This first chapter addresses connections between public relations and CSR/Sustainability in these contexts: CSR/Sustainability's roots and scope of the field, defining CSR and sustainability, and public relations' stewardship role in navigating CSR/Sustainability.

CSR/Sustainability's roots and scope of the field

By the end of the twentieth century, big business had earned significant disapproval—especially corporations associated with highly publicized corruption, environmental degradation, and human rights and labor abuses. Holding corporations accountable to more than just profits was inspired by the Earth Charter Initiative, drawn in 2000 following the United Nations World Commission on Environment and Development in 1987. It called for a cross-cultural discussion about shared values and common goals:

> The Earth Charter is a declaration of fundamental ethical principles for building a just, sustainable, and peaceful global society in the 21st century. It seeks to inspire in all people a new sense of global interdependence and shared responsibility for the well-being of the whole human family, the greater community of life, and future generations. It is a vision of hope and a call to action.
>
> (Earth Charter n.d.)

Also, the United Nations Framework Convention on Climate Change's Kyoto Protocol in 1997 emphasized "internationally binding emission reduction targets" (United Nations n.d.) and the United Nations Global Compact in 1999 turned worldwide attention to corporations' impact on the planet. Criticized corporations included Arthur Andersen, Enron, Nestlé, Nike, Parmalat, Shell, and Union Carbide (O'Higgins 2005). The United Nations Global Impact of Ten Principles was a non-legally-binding plea for businesses worldwide to adopt socially responsible and sustainable policies ("Overview" 2013). Particular industries, such as pharmaceuticals, have undergone intense scrutiny (Clark 2000) and the petrochemical industry has experienced widely publicized incidences of catastrophic spills and pollution at various phases of petroleum exploration, production, transportation, and refining (e.g., Unocal Corp. off Santa Barbara, CA, USA in 1969; Texaco/Chevron Corporation in the Amazon rainforest region, Ecuador, since the 1960s). More recently, however, Frynas (2005) ranked "the oil and gas sector" among "the leading industries championing CSR" (p. 581) in moves attributed to international CSR initiatives and the Global Reporting Initiative (GRI) which was established by the Coalition for Environmentally Responsible Economies (CERES)—as well as efforts by the US Agency for International Development (USAID) and the United Nations Development Programme (UNDP).

Possibly the most persistent critique of CSR practice is that it lacks in authenticity. Doane (2005) called CSR an oxymoron. Frankental (2001) identified a paradox "inherent in the phrase" (p. 18), and other skeptics hold that *responsibility* is a nebulous concept since corporations are profit centric and unmotivated to do anything which could detract from bottom-line earnings. *The Economist* characterized CSR as "pernicious" and "delusional" (Anonymous 2005). When CSR efforts are voluntary, public relations and environmental image advertising (CorpWatch 2001) are used to spread disinformation and "sinister corporate agendas" (Brown and Fraser 2006: 111). Non-governmental organizations (NGOs) remain highly critical of CSR, too, considering it to be "corporate PR or regulation-dodging" (Heath and Ni 2009).

Academic research on CSR/Sustainability also features shortcomings. Carroll (1994) called it "an eclectic field with loose boundaries, multiple memberships, and differing training/perspectives; broadly rather than narrowly focused, multidisciplinary… " (p. 14). Some analyses have shown how poorly the literature is mapped, revealing significant opportunities for enhancing knowledge and building theory about CSR. Multiple variables impacting CSR/Sustainability include: culture, size of organization (employees, sales, distribution, etc.), business-to-business and business-to-consumer orientations, national and local government regulations, for-profit versus nonprofit settings, regional/national/ global footprint, union versus non-union shops, external and internal stakeholders, and more. A content analysis of academic journals and books dating back to the 1970s in fields of administration, ethics, management, psychology, marketing, and organizational behavior, exposed themes of CSR's utility with regard to financial outcomes, and its normativity for "doing the right thing" (De Bakker, Groenewegen, and den Hond 2005: 943). Garriga and Melé (2004) resolved that the main CSR theories cluster into one of four groups based on economic instrumentality, politics, satisfying social demands, and ethically demonstrating responsibility to society—and concluded that new theory is needed to integrate all four orientations. Recommendations include greater attention to internal CSR impacts and research methods that promote multi-level analyses (Aguinis and Glavas 2012).

Some researchers have responded to negative critique of public relations' interplay with CSR/Sustainability by advancing an eventual reward of risk aversion and competitive advantage. Some academics have argued that public relations managers must serve as an organizational conscience (Holtzhausen 2014), while Heath and Ni (2009) advocated for a "triangle of reputation, relationship, and responsive rectitude" in order to strategically and measurably engage corporations in the CSR movement. CSR/Sustainability paradigm shortcomings published in other fields call for public relations expertise without actually invoking the term. For example, Frynas' (2005) critique of false promises implied in CSR as practiced by multinational oil companies speaks to the need for authentic relationship building with local communities and attention to culture and employee attitudes; areas where public relations managers are trained to provide support. Research findings have suggested that market forces *do not* necessarily reward ethical companies and there "is no overwhelming evidence that a company's share price is affected by a lack of social responsibility, even when this results in reputational damage" (Frankental 2001: 19). Researchers have opined that a positive image/ reputation among certain stakeholder groups signifies some sort of seal of approval, social contract, or license to operate (Moon, Crane, and Matten 2005). Yet, assumptions that consumers actively support responsible organizations are not well founded in the USA or parts of the EU (Maignan and Ferrell 2003).

Those who emphasize publicity, promotion, and media relations advance a one-way asymmetrical communication model instead of embedding CSR/ Sustainability across organizations via a two-way symmetrical communication model which emphasizes dialogue by connecting internal and external stakeholders. Publicists contribute to greenwash critique by advancing business case arguments and recommend CSR as a form of *cause marketing* for boosting image. For example, a study of CSR effects warned that efforts had better be *perceived* as sincere among consumers rather than stipulating that the efforts *must be authentic* (Yoon, Gürhan-Canli, and Schwarz 2006, italics added). Convincing organizational decision makers that public relations' value is inextricably linked to profits short changes the profession and overlooks public relations' normative potential as a powerful insider-activist social change agent. A consistent theme among CSR/Sustainability research is the call to integrate it across organizations for the long-term; an arena where public relations coalition-building skills could prove useful. Scott Dille, Group Leader at Denmark-based healthcare provider, Novo Nordisk, opined that in many organizations, CSR/Sustainability still is not embedded in organizations:

> We have a Sustainability Committee and it's headed by the VP of Corporate Relations and also has the Chief Science Officer, as well. The rest are populated with other senior management from various parts of the business – product supply, marketing, etc. So, in that way, it's pretty well embedded in the governance structure of the way decisions are made and the way the CEO and the board receives and acts on information, recommendations, and so on … You can say that your first step is to make sure that your own house is in order. Then you're going to be in a lot better situation … You're going to be identified by external stakeholders if you have a very strong culture around the values that are true to your heritage, your industry, etc. I know, just talking with colleagues outside of Novo Nordisk, that internal focus of CSR is often extremely lacking – except internal news that highlights great success, donations you've made, and so on.

Hank Boerner, Chairman, Chief Strategist and Co-founder of Governance & Accountability Institute, Inc., characterized CSR/Sustainability as cyclical and flexible—which means that public relations insiders must be active and dynamic:

> It's an exciting field, still growing; fairly new as a management discipline. In some cases, it's renewed. Early in my career at American Airlines, I was the citizenship officer and we had a lot of great programs. It went away because of the shift to the right in politics. The companies felt they

didn't have to do it. Now, despite the shift to the right, they *have* to do it ... As we go down into functions, risk management, issues management, public affairs, ESH [environment, safety, health] departments, PR departments, you're going to see all kinds of variations of what those top line concerns mean to the function.

Public relations' role in advising organizations through CSR/Sustainability goals, programming and measurement is supported by training in ethics and inspiration from postmodern theory. Public relations practitioners are positioned as organizational activists (Holtzhausen 2000, 2014; Holtzhausen and Voto 2002) who anticipate, recommend, and respond to change. Public relations' liaison function and commitment to the broader society is well established across our literature, as researchers have advanced a normative role as an organizational conscience in directing what organizations should do—such as "special concern for broader societal issues and approaches to problems" (van Ruler and Verčič 2005: 264). Corredor-Ruiz (2000) argued that public relations professionals are appropriate leaders for creating organizations' social responsibility philosophy.

Defining CSR and sustainability

Attempts to define CSR expose its historical, political, and economic roots. Carroll (1979) introduced one of the most widely accepted definitions of CSR: "[T]he social responsibility of business encompasses the economic, legal, ethical, and discretionary expectations that society has of organizations at a given point in time" (p. 500). However, as Clarkson (1995) and others have pointed out, application of the Carroll (1979) definition rarely yields empirical data to prove that a company is *not* socially responsible—unless unprofitability is simultaneously linked with unethical or illegal behavior. Deciding which term will be used, internally, to characterize an organization's efforts to act responsibility toward people, planet, and profit often involves a good deal of consideration. Bhattacharya (2013) qualified CSR as "doing well by doing good." Even Elkington's (1999) triple bottom-line Venn diagram representing an overlap of organizational commitment to people, planet, and profit is not universally accepted. David Stangis, Vice President Public Affairs and Corporate Responsibility at Campbell's Soup in the USA, shared his perceptions:

> I use this when I explain what CSR *used to be* ... The reality is there's *one* circle and it's *business in the twenty-first century*. There are a number of things you look at ... I'm not a big fan of terminology – whether it's *triple bottom line, sustainable development, collective impact, shared value* – I think they're all ways people have tried to put a label on something they don't really understand. These are great tools to communicate to somebody. If somebody struck me with "What are we trying to do? What do you mean when you're talking about CSR and sustainability?" Using the

triple bottom-line framework is a way – not to just look at the economic bottom line – but to also consider social impacts or opportunities. It's a nice tool.

Dearth of one clear and universal definition for CSR/Sustainability—within companies and externally among stakeholders—remains a primary challenge of the function, field, and movement. Overall, multiplicity suggests vibrancy and saliency for academic inquiry, but can yield frustration given varied complexities, contexts, and cultural values central to defining CSR/Sustainability around the globe. Skeptics suggest that this is by design in order to avoid transparency and accountability, while others have resolved that the term must remain fluid. Sethi (1977) argued that a legitimacy gap emerges when fundamental understanding of what an organization does and what society expects of it fail to correspond. Votaw (1972) said that CSR "means something, but not always the same thing to everybody" (p. 25). An overly simplistic definition for CSR is "good risk management" (Kytle and John 2005), since responsible organizations engage in boundary spanning and anticipate potential opportunities and challenges. However, highly complex issues may loom too large for simplistic definitions. Parsons (1961) suggested terms such as *environmental adaptation* (e.g., resources and economics), *goal attainment* (e.g., politics), *social integration* (e.g., culture and values); phrases which suggest qualities and themes which also permeate most research designed to test and explain CSR. Waddock (2004) suggested that multiple terms and theory streams compete for salience among academics and practitioners, while others offered that *corporate* is too limiting and should be replaced with *business* or *organization* (Cheney, Roper, and May 2007). Roles of nonprofit organizations, NGOs, and governments also must be accommodated; relationships that are not necessarily considered when an umbrella label like *CSR* is used. Nancy Mancilla, CEO and Co-founder of ISOS Group, a CSR consulting firm in the USA, explained that corporations use the *CSR* term while nonprofits use *sustainability*. Even the *corporate citizenship* term is found wanting for conservative leanings which negate potentially radical solutions. Jeff Leinaweaver of Global Zen Sustainability, a US-based consulting group, opined:

> [I]f you go into a room, they will all have different opinions about what terms mean and some people will combine them and some will see them as completely separate. I see a lot of organizations who say, "Well, I don't even connect into *CSR* because I'm not corporate" even though they may be a big organization, "I don't even feel invited" … The future for CSR, sustainability … some people are going to say it was a fad and nothing changed, or, at some point the fad helped optimize out a bad system.

Another popularly used term—*sustainability*—has somewhat seamlessly merged with the CSR literature. Leading firms tend to give attention to *sustainability* more than other terms (Ricart, Rodríguez, and Sánchez 2005).

Critics suggest that *sustainability* offers a label for something that nearly everyone can agree upon—caring for the environment—so, it devolves into "green business discourse" (Springett 2003: 74) with a more sinister agenda for deflecting blame. The Brundtland Report defined *sustainable development* as "meet[ing] the needs of the present generation, without compromising the ability of future generations to meet their own needs" ("World Commission on Environment and Development" 1987). Also, the United Nations (2004) encouraged an understanding of sustainable development as a sum of attention to economic, social, institutional, and natural resources. Degree of importance attached to the investment community may impact choice of term that corporations use. Hank Boerner, Chairman, Chief Strategist and Co-founder of Governance & Accountability Institute, Inc., explained:

> The vocabulary is all over the enterprise and not settled down. But *sustainable investing* is capturing the top guys' attention and the supply chain practices and the demands of customers – like Wal-Mart, a consumer goods company – is driving them in the direction of at least asking in the executive suite and the board room "Are we responsible and what does that mean?" *Sustainability* has two meanings ... One is "Come invest in a company that is sustainable. We are not Lehman Brothers, we are not Bear Stearns. We're going to be around for 100 years." Then another meaning is for a discrete audience that really is looking for this narrative – "We are sustainable in our products, how we go to market, how we treat our people, our supply chain practices and so on" – and that resonates with a growing number of people ... If you're a very large company and doing well financially, chances are you're going to be put in an index like the S&P 500. People are going to buy your stock because you're in the index. So, you have to do something.

Jenny Carty, Reporting and Governance Manager at Royal Bank of Scotland (RBS), explained why RBS chose the term, *sustainability*:

> I think originally this team was called *Corporate Responsibility*, but we moved away from that ... The head of our team felt that it's more than a corporate responsibility. Because *that* implies that you're doing it because it's your responsibility to do it rather than doing it a) because it's the right thing to do, but b) some of the aspects that our work covers are wider than that in a way.

Jennifer Pontzer, Co-owner of the Albuquerque-based consulting firm in the USA, Concept Green, explained that semantics really matters:

> Everybody wants us to feel good about what their company is about and what it's doing. Tackling some sustainability challenges doesn't undermine that – it doesn't advise that a company was not [responsible], but I think

that's why a lot of companies gravitate to the terms like *corporate responsi-bility, corporate social responsibility*, because it seems to be more in alignment with the founding of the company and its core values and governance.

Carrie Christopher, Concept Green Co-owner, added:

> [I]t's a fuzzy line but I think the responsibility in the CSR piece is more around the governance and doing the right thing, "we comply with the laws" – versus sustainability is really trying to transform from the inside out … I don't think there's consensus there because of the boundaries of responsibility. Sometimes organizations review in what they have direct control over, versus the impact in their supply chain or further down with the end use of their product.

Critics have opined that *sustainability* tends to emphasize environmental issues while downplaying significance of corporations' impact on social issues (Sharma and Ruud 2003). Similarly, Zovanyi (1998) pointed out that individual company assessments of sustainability efforts do little to track cumulative *global* impacts on limited natural resources.

Collectively, there has been no shortage of private sector organizations, trade groups, government policymakers, and university think tanks organizing meetings and offering best practices for CSR/Sustainability. Perceived rights of external groups to reward organizations or to impose sanctions also have been examined (e.g., Accounting Standards Steering Committee 1975; Swift 2001). Radical critical theorists lament that power differentials between corporations and others in capitalist societies nullify democratic debate about any responsibilities corporations have beyond wealth accumulation (Lehman 2002).

Defining CSR by the numbers

To address limitations of CSR definitions, some researchers offer a numbering scheme of CSR1, CSR2, CSR3, and CSR4. Frederick (1998) classified CSR1 as a philosophical concept and CSR2 as an action-oriented managerial concept (Wartick and Cochran 1985). Carroll (1991) further refined CSR1 to distin-guish among economic, legal, ethical, and discretionary features. Miles (1987) sought to clarify CSR2 activities as involving a company's external affairs—a move which Clark (2000) hailed as incorporating communication's role in social responsibility. Frederick (1998) later added CSR3 to explain CSR's normative attention to ethics and values, as well as CSR4 to extend the con-cept to arenas of science and religion. GRI Director, North America, Eric Israel, opined that some organizations favor ambiguity and avoid defining CSR/Sustainability:

> It's also a lousy excuse for people to say, "I don't know what to do because it's all different." The concepts are all the same, but the translation – what

this means for corporations – is definitely different. Even though Coca-Cola and PepsiCo are producing the same drinks, they are completely different organizations; how they do this. That's sustainability also. Sustainability is a concept in order to differentiate a company and to make its strength even stronger and to eliminate some of its weaknesses. It's a real strategic tool. It's not a PR tool at all. It's all about surviving in this incredibly difficult environment – how to sustain your business ... It's not about definition. It's not about compliance. This is really about business strategy and to translate that concept into ways that make sense of the company so it will have so-called license to operate.

CSR/Sustainability's historic roots

Notions of CSR/Sustainability have a rich tradition. Perhaps the spirit of CSR emerged back during the French Revolution (1789–1799) when individual rights were contrasted with aristocrats' power and privilege. Robber barons of the late 1800s in the USA divided into either "public be damned!" or industrialist-philanthropy camps (Carnegie 1900). Some have attributed philanthropic impulses among business owners during the early twentieth century to meeting workers' social needs (Post, Lawrence, and Weber 2002) and a desire to produce good worker-citizens (May 1993). However, paternalistic charitable efforts have been critiqued as a means for maintaining dominant-subordinate power systems (Adeola 2001). Corporate response to social needs after World War I in the USA has been linked to the late 1800s to early 1900s populist Progressive Era response to governmental pressure to reform child labor practices and unsafe work conditions (Clark 1916). By the 1930s, the Great Depression facilitated even greater attention to corporate social performance (Kreps 1940). CSR's development as a concept and practice escalated during the second half of the twentieth century. Free enterprise growth following World War II was tied to corporations' obligation to curing social problems in the USA through worker welfare (Bowen 1953). In Europe, the state and church forced companies to consider more than profit-centric goals.

The public relations profession extends back to the turn of the twentieth century as a means to enable companies to communicate with the public. The relationship between public opinion and media (Lippmann 1922) coincided with the professionalization of public relations; social responsibility in terms of *what's good for relationships is good for business* (Golden 1968). CSR/Sustainability movements took shape globally during the 1960s–1980s and connections were made with public relations. Civil rights and feminist activism, as well as consumer awareness and environmentalism of the 1960s and beyond, inspired demands for corporate accountability. Carrie Christopher, Co-owner of the Albuquerque-based consulting firm in the USA, Concept Green, shared her perceptions of the historical development of CSR/Sustainability:

If you look at the trajectory of things that were happening, the Exxon Valdez oil spill ... this whole vibe of *global village* in the common lexicon ... late eighties, early nineties really, growth with multinationals and a lot of "We can do what we *want*" in these areas" and then a lot of tragic events. Then going back to the seventies with Union Carbide in Bhopal. There have been 20 years of multinational growth and environmental degradation ... Going back to Rachel Carson's *Silent Spring;* that was the zeitgeist or the epiphany that grew.

CSR/Sustainability's political roots

Separating CSR/Sustainability from a wider political context is ill advised. Most corporations participate in some broad political system (Moon, Crane, and Matten 2005) and it is suggested that only government taxation and strictly enforced regulation by lawmaking bodies can hold corporations truly accountable to respecting shared natural environment resources. Privatization and deregulation movements have increased globalization, re-invigorated colonization, weakened governmental power (Cheney, Roper, and May 2007), and placed too much faith in the International Monetary Fund (IMF) and the World Bank (n.d.) to keep corporations in check. It is CSR/Sustainability's voluntary-ness which has led to widespread critique that nonexistent or non-binding guidelines invite corporate resistance and local community push back. Such was the case of the International Organization for Standardization's (ISO) attempt to develop global CSR standards in South Africa (Hamann, Agbazue, Kapelus, *et al.* 2005).

Economics of CSR/Sustainability: the business case

Corporate power usually is measured in financial terms even though it is said that businesses' responsibilities must be proportionate to their social power. Davis (1960) called this the "iron law of responsibility" (p. 71). Even though corporate power often is framed in terms of stockholder investment and profit, stock prices can reflect a company's ethical dimensions since some consumer segments may be willing to reward socially responsible corporations by paying a higher price for an ethical company's products (Nelson 2004), or switching brands to support companies that help charities (Smith and Alcorn 1991). Such business case arguments have been difficult to prove, however, due to multiple intervening variables such as competition and market conditions (Bader 2014a). The profit motive or business-case view holds sway when trying to convince organizational decision makers of CSR/Sustainability's attributes. When shrouded in an argument for cost reduction (avoided litigation costs, boycotts), relationship building (donors, legislators), and activist pacification, public relations managers may find CSR to be an easier sell to top management (Grunig and Huang 2000).

Critics have argued persuasively that the quest for profit at all costs erodes morality in business when there is little incentive for ethical behavior.

Frankental (2001) opined that CSR/Sustainability is a morally corrupt concept since corporations expect a return on their investment in the form of a more compliant workforce and consumer base. Following accounting scandals at WorldCom, Enron, Adelphia, Tyco International, Qwest, Global Crossings, and other large corporations, the US Sarbanes-Oxley Act (SOX) of 2002 (Pub. L. No. 107–204, 116 Stat. 745) passed into law on July 30, 2002 following near-unanimous Congressional support. SOX has forced a re-focus on internal controls, thereby ending self-regulation, in order to restore public confidence in financial information used by investors (Pompper 2014). Conversely, some corporations expect to get something just for the *appearance* of responsibility—as promoted via corporate advertising and public relations campaigns—whether efforts are authentic or not. Such activities constitute what Ihlen (2013) characterized as "attempt[ing] to put a human face on capitalism … a form of manipulation" (p. 209).

Distancing CSR/Sustainability from philanthropy

Despite historic links to philanthropy, some have been careful to distance CSR from old-fashioned charity. CSR's staunchest critics have suggested that the concept has "moved a long way from genuine philanthropy" (Frankental 2001: 20). Yet among public relations research, *strategic philanthropy* endures (Heath and Ni 2009). Corporations that interpret CSR as philanthropy and execute it via nonprofit third parties find their efforts criticized as inauthentic (O'Connor, Shumate, and Meister 2008), fodder rife for drawing media skepticism (Tench, Bowd, and Jones 2007). Brenda Colatrella, Executive Director of Corporate Responsibility at Merck, explained: "[W]e see philanthropy as a component, but not all corporate responsibility." Scott D. Tattar, Senior Vice President, Director of Public Relations & CSR at LevLane, a Philadelphia-based advertising and public relations firm, used a marketing lens to further distinguish philanthropy from CSR:

> [C]ompanies have been doing this for a long time. How many checks does a bank write in a year for women's auxiliary, little league? Up until ten years ago it was behind the scenes and companies weren't really recognized for it. They kept it because it was gauche to say "We're a good company." McDonalds has never been quiet about it – the best example of CSR and it goes back to the late seventies. Other companies followed and people like Warren Buffett and Bill Gates said companies have an obligation to do this. I make the distinction between CSR on the marketing side, which is what I do, and CSR on the operational side, which is like sustainability, green initiatives, maternity leave, all those things.

Stakeholder communication often is characterized as cause-related marketing (Kropp, Holden, and Lavack 1999); a shift which took hold in the USA during the 1970s when "companies attempted to turn public relations problems into public relations assets" (Cheney, Roper, and May 2007: 5).

Corporations must exercise discretion in philanthropic giving so as not to appear frivolous. Ihlen (2013) warned with regard to difficult-to-prove business-case arguments that such moves could "amount to stealing from business owners," (p. 208). Ben and Jerry's learned the power of this critique when it faced accusations of favoring too many philanthropic activities over focusing on economic performance (Taylor 1997). Heath and Ryan (1989) found that CEOs still thought of little league baseball donations as acting in the public interest, but more recent findings suggested that many managers differentiate CSR from philanthropy (Pompper 2013). Doug Bannerman, Leader Social Performance at Statoil, explained how his role at this Norway-based oil and gas production company strategically navigates the term *philanthropy* while emphasizing *social performance*:

> [T]here's really no common model. I've worked in the field long enough that I've seen the center of gravity shift. At one point, sort of the HR people seemed to rule the roost, I think because they own philanthropy and then it shifted to the Ethics officer and then the position of CSR was created. Often I saw it in and continue to see it in the Public Affairs and Communications area … My job under Social Performance includes aspects of local stakeholder engagement … Then, I have other aspects that are typical social and economic pieces – dealing with community foundations, providing direction around donations and social investment, and trying to figure out what our contributions through local content are … I am separate from PR, but there's a bit of a reputation management aspect to it.

Defining CSR/Sustainability according to cultural values, tradition, and power differentials

One area where CSR/Sustainability researchers and practitioners tend to agree is that unique cultures and value systems must be accommodated in CSR/Sustainability work. Brown and Fraser (2006) argued that since groups have unique understandings of business–society relationships as "starting points" (p. 104), attempts at a universally-accepted definition for CSR may be doomed. As the public relations profession must be steeped in respect for moral values of impacted cultures, so too must CSR/Sustainability. Cultural value systems emerge in debates about business organizations' role in society; sometimes considered secondary when profits are on the line. These may be times for "the activist within" to tap into her/his intellectual domain (Dozier and Lauzen 2000: 4) by pondering consequences of business in society; a postmodernist perspective for the public relations insider-activist to ensure that viewpoints and conditions of "the Other" are respectfully and wholly represented "without asking anything in return" (Holtzhausen 2014: xv).

Shortcomings of authentic and long-term CSR are most visible among developing nations, such as those on the continent of Africa, where Frynas (2005) opined that CSR serves as a short-term calming agent to assuage local communities—but then outreach ends when commercial ventures cease operations.

CSR/Sustainability definitions and practices also vary according to European Union standards. Europe has been labeled as the best corporate social responsibility reputation (CSRR) performing continent, and the UK and Finland as the top performing countries (Soppe, Schauten, Soppe, *et al.* n.d.). The European Commission (2011) called CSR the "responsibility of enterprises for their impacts on society" (p. 6). Consumers in France and Germany respect organizations' preparedness to meet legal and ethical obligations over their economic goal achievements (Maignan and Ferrell 2003). However, in the USA, companies actually may forego social responsibilities and still maintain a positive image as a responsible organization so long as they turn a profit. Some cultures have experienced a sea change shift in how people consider environmental impact, an overall goal of many organizations' sustainability programs. For instance, a waste governance study in Sweden revealed a new narrative order—changing human behavior associated with creating waste in the first place rather than framing landfilling as a social problem (Corvellec and Hultman 2012). Cynthia Figge, COO and Co-Founder of CSRHub and Partner and Co-Founder of EKOS International, USA, explained that European corporations have been sustainability's early adopters:

> The Europeans have traditionally been ahead of us. For all the reasons of smaller land space and more people – perhaps culture that had a higher consciousness – and that might be true for Japan, as well. There are certain industries that you look to, like the automotive industry, leading car companies in Germany, Sweden and thinking about the tremendous need for reducing waste and looking at what percentage of the car is recyclable – they were way ahead of us.

David Stangis, Vice President Public Affairs and Corporate Responsibility at Campbell's Soup in the USA, similarly opined: "The US market is 20–30 years behind the expectations around sustainability than Europe. There's a lot of socio-economic factors ... [T]hey were all that much more forward thinking." Because CSR/Sustainability terms are linked with greenwashing the world over, in Switzerland, John Bee, Communication Manager, Public Affairs, Nestlé, explained why this global food manufacturer adopted the term, *creating shared value* (CSV):

> It's owned by our chairman and CEO. There is a CSV Alignment Board which brings together the CEO, two of his executive board members and other senior specialists in things like HR, environmental sustainability, nutrition health wellness, and marketing. So all of those functions are represented in the CSV Alignment Board that drives the strategy into

the organization. The CEO and chairman are advised by an external independent CSV Council of 13 external experts. They meet formally on specific trends in nutrition, rural development, the role of business in society.

Organizational culture as it extends across multinational corporate operations also shapes attention to CSR/Sustainability. Doug Bannerman, Leader Social Performance at Statoil, a Norway-based oil and gas production company, told about how being foreign-owned creates a unique dynamic in the USA:

> We just have a very different culture ... Norway punches way above its weight class. So, it supports the Extractive Industry Transparency Initiative ... voluntary principles on security human rights ... So, of course we've signed up to United Nations Global Compact ... The Norwegian government, they write white papers on CSR all the time. It's sort of an environment where on one hand, it's supportive and nurturing of that and then on the other hand it's also like, "By the way, we own 70% of you and we expect you to do these things. We want you to be a leader in this stuff. You should be best in class, etc., etc." So, it's kind of like fire under our feet. I don't mean that we don't have a choice, not negatively. But you're definitely inspired to do your best when that's who your owner is.

Businesses operating in non-capitalist economies and developing nations provide a unique context for CSR/Sustainability. Overall, Asian countries have under-developed CSR agendas (Welford 2005) and attention to CSR generally is low in developing nations—even those which host multinational corporations (Krishnamurthy, Chew, Soh, *et al.* 2007). Yet, research findings of CSR practices in China suggest many similarities with CSR as practiced in

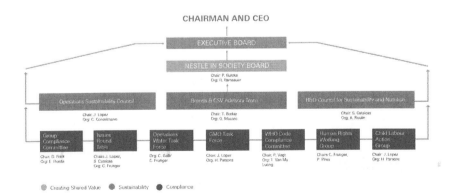

Figure 1.1 Creating shared value model at Nestlé

other economic systems. See (2009) prophesied that political considerations would continue to play a significant role in CSR among China's state-operated enterprises, but added that greater resistance to CSR could emerge among private-sector enterprises that cling to an economic-growth-at-all-costs model. Should unrestrained labor unions and an NGO sector develop in China for influencing governmental policy, more companies could be encouraged to adopt CSR programs (Doh and Guay 2006). At the time of our interview, Cynthia Figge, COO and Co-Founder of CSRHub and Partner and Co-Founder of EKOS International, USA, had just returned from a speaking engagement in China:

> I think there's a lot of pressure, but there isn't as much disclosure, so it's very hard to know how those companies are doing. For example, if you look at CSRHub, we have less than 500 companies that we rate that are based in China. The reason is that we just don't have the data. When I was at this conference in Shanghai, I literally felt that I was back a decade or more. It reminded me of the earlier days when we would see CSR more through a philanthropic lens – more about giving back and kind of a social responsibility ... Chinese really, really know that data is really critical. The government wants to collect it ... I came home from that conference just blown away by the opportunities in that country.

Tim Hui, Global Reporting Initiative (GRI) Director in China, concurred that China is warming up to CSR/Sustainability but likens it to philanthropy:

> [I]n China, the term *sustainability* still refers to sustainable human development and sustainable environment and national resources. But not to the extent of sustainability that GRI is talking about – which includes not only environment, but social – including human rights ... Sustainability is CSR in China. CSR is very straightforward. If it is translated into Chinese, literally, it's *corporate social responsibility*. But corporate social responsibility in China is very much focused on this charity, like donations, like natural disaster alleviation ... and very little time and effort was spent on areas like social impacts, like human rights.

CSR contrasts sharply among the Asian countries of India, Indonesia, Malaysia, the Philippines, South Korea, Singapore, and Thailand, due to varying relationships between business enterprise and government—and framing of the debates. Chapple and Moon (2005) found that multinational corporations are more prone to implement CSR programs than national firms—and some businesses more than others fund political causes and lobby government bodies. Crouch (2006) argued that these socio-political dynamics enable multinational corporations to exploit profits beyond market exchanges through favorable regulatory environments.

Guanxi, gao guanxi, *and* kyosei

Across East Asian cultures, key concepts have attracted researchers' attention for better understanding of CSR/Sustainability. *Guanxi* represents a significant feature of Chinese culture, characterizing relationships embedded within a hierarchically structured network of business connections (Wong and Leung 2001). This framework is relevant among public relations theorists' relationship management approach (Grunig, Grunig, and Ehling 1992). *Guanxi* is rooted in Confucianism, which advances an unequal distribution of power and wealth and hierarchical authority in China, Thailand, and Korea. Yet, Confucius' teachings also value humanity and human life over property, as when he asked after stables were burned, *Was anyone hurt?* (Rainey 2010). Tensions between Confucian attention to both power *and* humanity are central to CSR/Sustainability studies, too. Multiple applications for the *guanxi* term make it relevant to postmodern theorizing about CSR/Sustainability. In Indonesia, *bapakism* refers to relationships in business (Engholm 1991). In Korea, *gao guanxi* refers to personal connections linked to favors and obligations. In Singapore, *guan-xi* earmarks a sense of trust, obligation, and face-giving (Tan, 2000). In Japan, Pawlik (2014) called *kyosei* "more organic than perhaps CSR in some other parts of the world." *Kyosei* also is rooted in the Confucian tradition (Boardman and Kato 2003) and forms the bedrock of Canon's corporate philosophy (Katu 1997); one that employees interpret as a "Japanese expression of CSR" (Pawlik 2014), or "working together for the common good," according to this imaging and optical product manufacturer's website ("Canon's Corporate Philosophy of Kyosei" 2014):

> Truly global companies must foster good relations with customers and communities, as well as with governments, regions, and the environment as part of their fulfillment of social responsibilities. For this reason, Canon's goal is to contribute to global prosperity and the well-being of mankind as we continue our efforts to bring the world closer to achieving *kyosei.*

Public relations' stewardship role in navigating CSR/Sustainability

Public relations counselors may inspire a top-down commitment to a CSR/Sustainability organizational culture and help with embedding it across departments and geographies. Specific tasks may include writing CSR/Sustainability position statements, developing an ombuds program, assembling reports and conducting social audits, nurturing corporate governance, developing communication campaigns, and developing mutually-beneficial stakeholder relationships. Most importantly, public relations counselors should support CSR/Sustainability as a management function by serving as an insider-activist to ensure stakeholders' concerns are acted upon and that CSR/Sustainability represents authentic commitments. Clark's (2000) communication-management-in-CSR framework followed the inspiration of J. Grunig's (1992) excellence studies and Kelly's (2001) call for stewardship in the public relations process. Complementing this edifice is the introduction of postmodern theory to the public relations literature, framing public relations' normative function and urging public relations practitioners to serve as activists within organizations (Holtzhausen 2000, 2014; Holtzhausen and Voto 2002). CSR/Sustainability offers an ideal context for making the insider-activist role a reality. Overall, considering public relations' full value and range of benefits to organizations and to the public sphere could enable the field to eventually shed part of its negative reputation as frivolous or merely a publicity arm for greenwash.

Indeed, public relations counselors need not be complicit in toeing any company line that conflicts with their personal values. Explicating the *agency* concept through postmodern theory, economics, and communication management lenses, Holtzhausen (2014) defended the internal-activist role for public relations by forcefully arguing that "those little resistances in everyday life" (p. xv) both accumulate into social change and empower practitioners committed to continual learning about how organizations and the larger society inter-connect and a willingness to critique and fight for solutions. Among the public relations literature, *agency* generally is an under-examined concept; often defaulting to a *public relations agency* (firm) context (Ledingham and Bruning 2000). In Europe, *agency* is used more reflexively in public relations practice (van Ruler and Verčič 2004)—as when public relations counselors give agency to organizations' ideologies designed to reinforce and perpetuate their power (Holtzhausen 2002). As Giddens (1984) instructed, *agents* have choices and may obey or resist established rules through (in)actions. Vice President Public Affairs and Corporate Responsibility, David Stangis, at Campbell's Soup in the USA, explained that Elkington's (1999) message profoundly informed his views and shaped his approach to working with companies in making the required hard changes: "We're not just driving benefits to us, we're driving benefits to society, as well; collective impact—a lot of people working on one common goal."

Discussion

Despite at least four decades of scholarly and practical attention to CSR/Sustainability, the concept defies a common definition due to cultural and other contextual nuances among organizations and nations globally. Public relations' links to CSR/Sustainability goals, programming and measurement, however, are becoming understood—even though opportunities and challenges lie ahead. The search for universal understanding of CSR/Sustainability is ongoing because the stakes are so very high—for both organizations and the larger public sphere. This first chapter has addressed connections between public relations and CSR/Sustainability across central topics such as: CSR/Sustainability's roots and scope of the field, defining CSR and sustainability, and public relations' stewardship role in navigating CSR/Sustainability.

Corporations around the globe have grown significantly in economic and political power since the mid-twentieth century. A voluntary framework for CSR/Sustainability and a lack of universal regulations with punitive controls means that individuals and smaller organizations that make up the larger public sphere are comparatively powerless in the shadow of large multinational corporations and rely almost exclusively on their goodwill to *do the right thing*. On the whole, safeguards against potential abuses of corporate power remain minute and ineffectual and critics such as Bakan (2003) have accused corporations of pathological behavior with a negative-consequences-be-damned attitude. Consumer attitudes toward CSR/Sustainability are mixed, too. Vogel (2005) found that consumers care more about price and quality than CSR. Globally, barriers to CSR/Sustainability include nations' resistance to groups working to develop global standards, as well as business claims that imposed standards would interfere with operations (Hamann, Agbazue, Kapelus, *et al.* 2005). Time and again, research findings have suggested that when faced with doing the right thing by people (beyond stockholders) and the planet—or preserving profit margins—corporations inevitably opt to protect the latter (Reich 2008). Hence, trust in firms continues to decline. The argument which maintains that "corporations exist because the polity allows them to [and] that corporations are accountable for the use of the vast financial, human and community resources entrusted to them" (Brown and Fraser 2006: 108) increasingly rings hollow. Of course there exist trade/industry watchdog groups and unions, NGOs, and activists organized to shame bad corporate behavior through the media, by organizing resistance, and by lobbying governmental policymakers. These have achieved some degrees of successes, such as when groups organized a boycott and pressured Nike to improve labor practices (Burns 2000). Public relations researchers have recommended that CSR goals be firmly entrenched at the core of business operations (May 2009) and others have argued for legal structure changes to make CSR mandatory, transparent, and "embedded across the organization horizontally and vertically" (Frankental 2001: 23).

Throughout this book, I argue that the public relations profession has the opportunity to perform a normative function in stewarding CSR/Sustainability. Public relations counselors are uniquely positioned to manage communication and to build relationships within organizations and across stakeholder groups. At the same time, public relations practitioners manifest the opportunity to overcome a negative reputation for mere publicity and image/reputation promotion. Public relations counselors must enact the insider-activist role to flesh out "predatory capitalism" (Holtzhausen 2014: xvi) and to confront instances of injustice and immorality—negative impacts on the public sphere—in order to inspire positive social change.

2 CSR/Sustainability, public relations, and ethics

Doing no harm and doing the right thing

Public relations practitioners routinely navigate ethical dilemmas. In business, ethics is an activity and a form of social practice (Surma 2006). Knowing *the right thing to do* for organizations, stakeholders, and the environment represents no simple task. It is one fraught with difficulties and paradoxes. Jonas (1984) linked contemporary environmental challenges to an "ethics of responsibility" first formulated by sociologist Max Weber (1947). The ethics of responsibility suggests that *consequences* of an organization's decision serve as the final evaluation criterion when determining success or failure of that decision. Numerous theories developed among public relations and business management researchers seek to explain responsibility and ethics dynamics and offer perspectives on how the public relations function brings to bear in organizations globally involved with CSR/Sustainability programs. This chapter explores these contexts, and amplifies voices of professionals who engage with ethics in CSR/Sustainability across industries and settings.

To probe interplay among CSR/Sustainability, public relations, and ethics, more deeply, this chapter examines establishing a foundation for understanding ethics in public relations and CSR/Sustainability, engaging with oxymorons and paradoxes, public relations practitioners as ethics counselors, theoretical underpinnings to guide counselors with CSR/Sustainability, moving forward with public relations ethics in CSR/Sustainability.

Establishing a foundation for understanding ethics in public relations and CSR/Sustainability

Revealing some universal agreement about ethics in CSR/Sustainability and public relations' role amidst political and economic dynamics is no small feat. Undeniably, genuine commitment to ethics in CSR is sorely needed (Munshi and Kurian 2005), but since CSR is not well defined, it follows that ethics in CSR also defies definition (Banerjee 2008). Jenny Carty, Reporting and Governance Manager at Royal Bank of Scotland (RBS), quipped: "What is it they say? That 'integrity is when you do the right thing when no one else is looking'. But then, again, for companies to continue to invest in sustainability programs, then they need to be seeing some kind of return." Carroll (1979) was among the first researchers to offer a practical explanation of CSR in terms of responsibility to and impact upon society; a definition that underscores significance of ethics among the range of organizations' social obligations. Furthermore, attempts to establish international business ethics standards have failed, more or less. Carrie Christopher, Co-owner Concept Green, a firm which provides sustainability consulting and support services, explained that increase in awareness and resistance among stakeholders in the 1990s led to a greater emphasis on ethics in business:

> [T]here was a demand for transparency and responsibility. I think this is really where CSR had its beginnings of "Hey, you're a corporate citizen, you're a citizen of the world, you're part of the global village, you have to be a good citizen" … Corruption and environmental spills, civil rights issues; it was a wakeup call and it got to a certain point where people really started to become concerned.

Jeff Leinaweaver of Global Zen Sustainability in the USA warned that power structures within organizations and between insiders and external service providers add a layer of complexity to implementing ethical CSR/Sustainability policies and programs:

> People are more concerned with being clever than smart and I think that's a real danger for the future of CSR and sustainability. What's the afterlife of the stories you tell as a CSR/Sustainability PR person? What impact does it have? … [P]eople have a basic goodness, but they still have to stand up for the right things – even in organizations. How we cultivate those things early on. Stand up for the right things against the client … Understand the power structures. It's a greater call.

Codes and standards have been advanced worldwide and concepts of *social responsibility, ethics,* and *public relations ethics* often are used interchangeably across literatures. CSR and corporate codes of conduct must be integrated for triple bottom-line reporting (Painter-Morland 2006). Public relations ethics, according to Parsons (2004), is "the application of knowledge, understanding and reasoning to questions of right or wrong behavior in the professional practice of public relations" (p. 10), as she advocated that ethnics and professionalism go hand in glove. Considering social responsibility as "a kind of ethical framework," Parsons (2004: 159) suggested that corporate decision making could be greatly improved with professional public relations support. Moran (1996) pointed out that "corporations … live by habit … there are people in the company—supervisors, managers, administrators, executives—who are paid to be conscious of what the company is doing" (p. 137). The Public Relations Society of America (PRSA) promotes a Statement of Professional Values as the foundation for the Member Code of Ethics to "set the industry standard" for the profession in guiding behaviors and aiding in decision making; qualifying ethics as "advocacy, honesty, expertise, independence, loyalty, and fairness" ("PRSA Member Code" n.d.) In addition, the International Public Relations Association (IPRA) has a Code of Conduct and other public relations groups around the world have crafted their own ethics codes, principles, and missions. All are unique but tend to share a common theme of "transparency, honesty, integrity, and protection of the public interest" (Cap n.d.). Most of these groups offer ethics seminars and training for support. Researchers explore moral frameworks to "facilitate judgments about right and wrong behaviors or good or bad practice" (L'Etang, Lugo-Ocando, and Ahmad 2014: 172), and to gain insights into organizations and professions.

To help keep ethics front and center, public relations insiders write codes of ethics for corporations. Llewellyn (2007) noted that as "gestures," codes of ethics can prove helpful, but they must be extended to even those at the highest organizational levels to be effective (p. 184). Ironically, Enron had a code of ethics bearing the acronym RICE (respect, integrity, communication, and excellence) at the time of its downfall (Prentice 2003). Earning a profit and having high ethical standards with regard to CSR/Sustainability need not be diametrically opposed goals for organizations. Ray Anderson, a radical industrialist and futurist, proved it could be done at his company, Interface, Inc. a US-based carpet manufacturer that originally used 80% petroleum-based raw materials (Ray Anderson Tribute Video n.d.) Today, the company works toward a goal of zero footprint by 2020. Anderson explained:

> Sustainability is living within the care and capacity of the Earth – for an industry that's a very big challenge because we very naturally have huge environmental footprints. We truly need a new model if we're to live sustainably and operate our business in a sustainable way.
>
> ("Legacy of Interface" 2011)

A video produced to honor Anderson's enduring vision after his death in 2011, featured an Interface employee who explained the mindset shift often required to embrace a sustainability model: "You have to have some really weird thinking to do that" (Ray Anderson Tribute Video n.d.). Optimally, CSR/Sustainability should be embedded throughout the organization, both philosophically and operationally; a move that often requires new ways of doing business that may seem strange at first blush.

Perhaps any attempt to develop a universal definition for *ethics* is ill conceived given the risks of essentializing and imposing upon any definition the ideology of powerful multinational corporations. The Global Ethic Foundation, based in Tübingen, Germany, was inspired by the writings of Swiss theologian and postmodern religious scholar Hans Küng (1993), who suggested, "A global ethic means a fundamental consensus on binding values, irrevocable standards and personal attitudes which can be shared by people of all religions and also by nonbelievers." Even though some public relations researchers have supported development of an international code of ethics for business (e.g., Kruckeberg 1993), ethical relativism perspectives suggest that differences among nations and cultures around the globe mean that it may never be possible to achieve some acceptable *fundamental consensus* about basic moral values (French and Granrose 1995). Mere talk of *social responsibility* invokes "norms that express legitimate and stable expectations respecting the conduct of persons in positions of public trust or power within a social practice or institution" (Wueste 1994: 2) and calls into question, *Whose norms? Whose expectations?* Researchers' linking of *public relations ethics* with "specific moral values of each culture" begs questions of *Whose moral values? Whose culture?* There is no one way to operationalize CSR, so defining ethics in CSR/Sustainability contexts where organizations vary may be improbable. Moreover, *culture* is neither "static, clearly definable ... synonymous with territory" (Bardhan and Weaver 2011: 2), nor should any nation-state be conceptualized as a "container" of culture (Wallerstein 1996: 92).

The public relations profession has sought to engage with a gap that exists between what society expects of organizations and what organizations actually deliver. Ihlen (2013) reminded us that "it is *expected* that companies do and will behave ethically" (italics in original, p. 208). Public relations practitioners are charged with *ethical guardianship* (Gregory 2003), serving as an organizational *conscience* (Parsons 2004), and as *activist* (Holtzhausen 2014; Holtzhausen and Voto 2002). L'Etang (2003) problematized the ethical guardian concept and resolved that it is a myth. While public relations practitioners place a high value on ethical behavior (Lee and Cheng 2011), critics question just how qualified public relations practitioners are to assume an ethical guardianship role since the profession has a reputation for being "morally dubious" (L'Etang 1994: 61). Public relations' *issues management* function offers the potential to advance CSR/Sustainability's underlying principles of *doing the right thing* in order to build and strengthen relationships with stakeholders by identifying their interests and then working with them to develop policies for support. *Issues management*, coined in the 1970s following 1960s activism in the USA (Heath 2013a), evolved as activist groups pressured public policy and business agendas. See Chapter 3 for an expanded discussion of issues management. Interrogating interplay among culture, communication, context, and power is essential to understanding relationships in order to engage with issues of ethics and social responsibility in global public relations. Carrie Christopher, Co-owner Concept Green, a firm which provides sustainability consulting and support services, shared her perceptions of business ethics as they evolve according to cultural differences in organizations:

There are more state-run corporations – Italy, Scandinavian countries, Spain. I just think there's a different awareness and then going back to the precautionary principle ... This "If this thing appeared to do harm, we should pull it off the market until we know for sure." And in the US if something appears to do harm, you need to prove it first before we pull it off the market. So, it's the difference between a proactive and a reactive stance.

Nancy Mancilla, CEO and Co-founder of ISOS Group, a CSR consulting firm in the USA, agreed that approaches to risk and responsibility vary widely: "[I]t's cultural. In the USA, it's more test and evaluate before adopting something and the reverse in Europe. They're early adopters." Organizations' approaches to and perceptions about various cultures unfurl distinctly. Importantly, "alleged impacts" experienced by indigenous cultures of the Ecuadorian Amazon since petroleum companies set up business in their communities ("Human Rights Impacts" n.d.) is worthy of scrutiny for any ethical implications and avoidance of what Casmir (1993) characterized as a dominance–submission approach to communication. Frankental's (2001) case study of an oil company in Burma explored the corporate framework of perceiving operations in remote parts of the world as "invisible;" flawed logic in today's global and wired community scrutinized by NGOs and other critical stakeholders more than willing to exert public pressure on multinational corporations (Brown and Fraser 2006). Physical distance should not diminish the role of public relations insider-activists in helping organizations to live ethical responsibilities and to avoid violating stakeholder expectations. Roberts' (2001) normative conclusion recommending that corporate players anticipate consequences of their actions on others resonates with Jonas' (1984) linkage of environmental challenges with an *ethics of responsibility*; arguments which mutually endorse a public relations-in-CSR/Sustainability role.

The two-way symmetrical model of public relations helps to visualize how ethical dimensions of communication position public relations as a "process" of facilitating dialog among parties as opposed to an "outcome" (Grunig and Grunig 1992: 308). Inherent in the process, however, is a paradox—when an organization or stakeholder group benefits from a given decision, but the greater social good does not—and vice versa (Pieczka 2006). Such effects further complicate business conducted across transcultural contexts. Public relations practitioners who work for multinational corporations must be ever mindful of power differentials conducive to press agentry and manipulation which requires balance of "... joining with the publics in the process of uncovering new interpretations of the world, some of which may benefit the client, but some of which may benefit the public" (Botan 1993: 76).

The public relations function is charged with facilitating communication, including messaging about ethics. A central purpose of ethics statements is communicating about them, but too often targeted audiences are internal— while external audiences gain little insight about organizational ethics (Murphy 2005). Yet, employee volunteer programs associated with CSR programs enable employees to serve as community ambassadors and to amplify companies' moral commitment to helping others (Pompper 2013). Promoting messages about the CSR/Sustainability good that a corporation does has the potential to reap rewards such as enhanced reputation in the minds of stake-holders and as armor in the event of a crisis (Eisenegger and Schranz 2014). Ethical missteps by organizations may reap negative media attention. For example, "Cheers & Jeers," a regular column in the print and online magazine of *Friends of Animals*, a nonprofit international animal advocacy organiza-tion, critiques ethical behaviors of individuals and corporations. Sometimes the "jeers" portion is longer than the "cheers"—such as the Summer 2013 issue that lambasted the World Wildlife Fund and Greenpeace (for support-ing polar bear hunting), entertainers Jay-Z (for wearing custom sneakers made of animal skins), and Shania Twain (for using real horses in her act)—but championed Al Gore for requesting vegan catering while on a book tour and Bill Gates for acknowledging greenhouse gas effects on animal farming (Shishkoff 2013). Similarly, companies that are "too blatantly clean" (Eise-negger and Schranz 2014: 139) could become targets for ethics-lapse witch hunts in the news media. Ben & Jerry's may have experienced this effect when the company was criticized for paying too much attention to philanthropy and too little to bottom-line profits (Page and Katz 2010; Taylor 1997).

Another lens for contemplating ethics in a public relations–CSR/Sustainability context is its juxtaposition to law and the ethical investing movement. In cases of fraud or corruption, ethical violations also may constitute legal vio-lations, as the world learned throughout the Enron scandal that saw at least four executives prosecuted and jailed for wrongdoing (Partington 2011). This outcome prompted Cap (n.d.) to opine on the IPRA website: "I just wonder whether those who stand to incur the most damage, or already have (like the executives at Enron) ever bother to read the codes of ethics they put their names to and whether we're the ones in greatest need of heeding them?" The *ethical investing movement* has emerged in recent decades to reward ethical companies by linking selective investment decisions with a social conscience to do good for others and the planet (MacLeod 1996). Socially responsible investing (SRI) is animated by social shareholder activism (Guay, Doh, and Sinclair 2004). The Forum for Sustainable and Responsible Investment, a US-based association for those involved with SRI, supports corporations' atten-tion to financial needs in conjunction with social needs. Moreover, social shareholder activism has inspired organizations trading securities in large quantities to pressure corporations into socially responsible behaviors (Smith 2012). Hence, many organizations' official declarations about CSR include ethics statements (Carroll 1979)—such as among Scandinavian companies which boast a tradition for incorporating ethics and CSR into corporate strategies (Morsing, Midttun, and Palmas 2007). Hank Boerner, Chairman, Chief Strategist and Co-founder of Governance & Accountability Institute, Inc., sees these trends on the rise: "The two big drivers that we see is the move toward sustainable investing on the part of asset owners like pension funds and the managers they hire and the financial analysts that are doing profiles of companies and looking at how they are or are not more sustainable than other choices."

Engaging with oxymorons and paradoxes

Critics denounce *ethics* in a context of business management or public relations in the service of CSR/Sustainability as an oxymoron. Publicly-traded corporations are driven by self-interest to favorably impress investors, shareholders, media, and other stakeholders—and private companies and nonprofit organizations hope to do the same among donors, employees, volunteers, and others. Consequently, the urge to put only the best foot forward and to obscure or mask negative issues presents an ethical dilemma: how to balance what an organization *wants* to talk about with what it is *expected* to reveal. Susan Sabatino, Account Manager, Marketing Partnerships Team at the Nature Conservancy (TNC), explained that nonprofits' engagement with corporations presents a fine ethical line which sometimes inspires TNC to help corporations improve upon environmental practices:

> Some people have issues with us working with *any* companies. Some of our existing longer-time donors don't think we should be aligning our ground with corporations … It's a balance. We have a very rigorous process that we go through as an organization where we do a full risk assessment on the company and we have a risk assessment committee that reviews basically every deal … We don't do *corporate practices* with a lot of companies; it's a very select few that we do. .

Too many organizations have found it easier and less costly in the short term to promote an *illusion* of ethical behavior than to *actually be ethical*. An "ethics of narcissus" (appearance) is very different from "being responsible for" (Roberts 2001: 125, 123). Ethics in business should represent an end in itself, rather than simply a means for increasing earnings (Zsolnai 2002). Management strategies designed to perpetuate "talk alone" (Roberts 2001: 122) rather than to affect transformative organizational change for authentic ethical behavior may seem sufficient. Corporations engage in an "escalating game of cheating their stakeholders," but it is only a matter of time before a façade of high moral character dissipates at the hands of motivated stakeholder groups and media exposés; consequences which Aasland (2004: 4) suggested eventually perpetuate a paradox of business—resorting to actually being ethical in order to avoid being outed.

The public relations profession takes much blame for aiding and abetting superficial lip service to ethics in business, inspiring criticism that *public relations ethics* is an oxymoron, too. Public relations and its practitioners have faced serious accusations over the years for deficient standards, corruption, manipulation, and a character that is "less than spotless in the area of ethics" (e.g., Ewen 1996; Moloney 2006; Nelson 1989; Parsons 2004: 29; Roberts 2001; Stauber and Rampton 2002). Public relations practitioners' ethical lapses continue to tarnish the field—perhaps inspiring critics like Jensen (1997) to opine that practitioners "present only the bright side and leave the dark side hidden" (p. 68). Pratt (1991) found that the public image of practitioners' sense of social responsibility was poor. Mudslinging reporters consider public relations people *flacks* (DeLorme and Fedler 2003). Such negative sentiments about public relations may be rooted in the asymmetrical model of public relations, which Grunig (1993) characterized as "using communication to get members of the public to do what the organization wants them to do" (p. 128), also known as the press agentry or the publicity model (J. Grunig 1992). One research team poignantly critiqued a symbiotic public relations + CSR pairing (L'Etang, Lugo-Ocando, and Ahmad 2014: 177):

> CSR needs communication and publicity for stakeholder relations and public positioning (reputation/public opinion) and to justify expenditure on such programs internally. Public relations needs CSR to position itself as a morally desirable practice that contributes to the public interest.

Even some academics tend to emphasize public relations' technician function in CSR contexts in terms of producing a "blaze of publicity" (Micklethwait and Wooldridge 2003: 180) rather than emphasizing public relations as a management function. Overall, short-changing a broader view of what public relations can do diminishes its potential in supporting CSR/Sustainability and reduces public relations to some propaganda strategy (Brown 2008). Doug Bannerman, Leader Social Performance at Statoil, a Norway-based oil and gas production company, shared a recent encounter with a public relations practitioner which suggests that press agentry persists: "They drive me nuts. I think the worst insult I've heard, somebody said to me, 'Don't you just hand out story money?' I'm like '*What*'?" Research findings have suggested that hiring publicists to herald "good works [or] gloss over ethical problems" threatens more harm than good (Heath and Ryan 1989: 22). On the other hand, organizations that remain silent on CSR/Sustainability efforts could signal dispassion or carelessness in stakeholder relations (Ihlen 2013), inattention to issues management, or low ethical commitment to the larger public sphere. Such symptoms also remind us that the public relations roles' dichotomy of communication technician and communication manager endures (Dozier 1983). The technician role predominates in organizations that perceive public relations as a publicity machine.

Numerous case studies differentiate one-way publicity models from two-way symmetrical models—with the former's focus on image and the latter's embrace of communication, relationship building, and responsibility. Ethics in business emphasizing the *other* instead of an ego-centric image of the self (or organization) represents a struggle between reality and appearances (Roberts 2001). Postmodern philosopher Emmanuel Levinas (1966) suggested that ethics is being "the-one-for-the-other" (p. 41) and noted its strength in building personal relations. Similarly, Surma (2006) argued that public relations practice constitutes a "process of putting oneself in the place of the other" (p. 47). Critics have been especially quick to bash corporations that offer "token philanthropic aid" and inadequate response to economic and environmental crises in developing nations (Cloud 2007: 228). Public relations researchers agree that most short-term attempts to mold corporate image using symbolic gestures bear little resemblance to substantive, authentic relationships between organizations and stakeholders built upon a foundation of trust and ethical behavior. In particular, alcohol, chemical, oil, pharmaceutical, and tobacco industries are often characterized as "being out of step with social values" (O'Connor 2006: 81) and as having bad reputations (Yoon, Gürhan-Canli, and Schwarz 2006) which can be *remedied* by public relations. Arnold (2001) found that BP and Shell sought to change corporate image by stressing environmental and social initiatives, but the same strategy failed for Monsanto and Exxon. CSR campaigns which ultimately were unsuccessful may have hurt Philip Morris' reputation (Fairclough 2002). Because the business of some corporations inherently poses environmental risks this sets up a dynamic for disaster (Munshi and Kurian 2005). Use of the terms *public relations, spin,* or *PR stunt* usually signifies less-than-responsible management behaviors. Labeled *public relations failures,* events negatively impacting the environment, consumers, and other stakeholders, rarely escape media scrutiny for their dramatic visuals and widespread impacts—often labeled as a *PR problem* or *PR backlash*—as if *positive publicity* could expunge *negative publicity* or mask organizational irresponsibility. Well-traveled textbook examples of ethics lapses framed by *ir*responsibility include the 1984 pesticide gas leak in Bhopal India, the 1989 Exxon Valdez crash in the USA, and the 2010 BP Deepwater Horizon spill in the USA. Also, case studies of high profile accounting fraud at Enron, Kodak, WorldCom, and Xerox underscore ethics ruptures at corporations and an erosion of trust among stakeholders (Sagar and Singla 2004). Public opinion critical of organizations' ethical shortcomings have reached critical mass since the 1990s (Moloney 2006) and to offset demands for better and more governmental regulation, many companies have opted to create or enhance their social responsibility programs. Public relations students display inconsistencies between likelihood for engaging in questionable behavior and attitude toward that behavior (McKinnon and Fullerton 2014) and university programs have been urged to enhance attention to ethics in public relations curricula (PRSA Commission 2012).

Just as the terms of *ethics-in-business* and *public relations ethics* are negatively critiqued as oxymorons, so, too, is the concept of *ethical CSR* cast down as a contradiction. To some, CSR is "a form of public relations that enables business to continue as usual" (Roberts 2003: 249); a means for manipulating corporate image (Fineman 2001), or greenwash. Roberts (2001) resolved that "this new regime of ethical business is no ethics at all" (p. 110). Solving ethical problems in public relations means working directly with people affected by corporate actions and not masking the issues with "an extra gift to a local charity or by giving Thanksgiving turkeys to the faithful" (Olasky 1987: 151). Roberts (2003) defended corporations' senior leadership as capable of acting on ethical sensibilities even though too few seem to do so and earlier argued that ethics is not absent from corporate environments, just "obscured, deferred and marginalized" amidst business climates shaped by intense competition, deregulation and globalization challenges (Roberts 2001: 109). Multinational corporations' job outsourcing practices and development of labor markets among developing nations has fomented critical inquiry into globalization effects (Zambrana and Dill 2009), with an emphasis on abuses to people and the environment linked to greed and a dearth of ethical commitment. Because many political and economic structures in these nations are unable to stand up to large Western corporations, there is very little to hold them accountable to their activities' externalities (Crouch 2006), save the scrutiny and monitoring of NGOs (Waddock 2007) and other activists.

The ethics-business-CSR-oxymoron critique intensifies when it is discovered that organizations' ethics standards are unevenly applied. Cloud (2007) posited that corporations' treatment of their own workers offers a litmus test for CSR commitment. News media critique of Amazon, a large corporation considered "notoriously mum about how it operates" (Moss-Coane 2014–4:30) but quick to publicize an ethical standard for satisfying customers, exposed the company's decision to provide a row of ambulances and paramedics to treat warehouse employees suffering from heat-related illness—rather than to improve work environment conditions. Amazon's apparent ethical breach in its attitude toward temporary workers in a high-unemployment area received national US coverage (Streitfeld 2011; Soper 2011). The message of these stories resonated with website-published views of a "strategic advisor on CSR" (Baker 2008):

> Corporations don't really care – they're just out to screw the poor and the environment to make their obscene profits ... CSR [serves] as a business framework which enables the common solution of wealth creation as if people and the environment mattered.

Engaging with negative perceptions that profit-centric motives trump ethical behavior in companies requires a commitment to accountability and open communication. *Ethical accounting*, reporting on a wide range of issues from an ethics perspective, provides a window on organizations' internal value systems (Holland and Gibbon 2001) and may be accommodated as part of CSR/Sustainability reporting.

Public relations practitioners as ethics counselors

Considering public relations only as a means for generating positive publicity negates its maximum value for providing ethics counsel and insider-activism as part of a management team engaged with CSR/Sustainability programs. Public relations practitioners have counseled on corporate ethics for decades and counseling a boss or client represents "the crème de la crème function of the public relations profession" (Heath 2013b: 213), for herein lies the opportunity to influence key decision makers on ethics. Public relations practitioners may contribute significantly to CSR/Sustainability work by inspiring ethical behavior and building relationships, while counseling senior-level management (Moreno, Zerfass, Tench, *et al.* 2009). Understanding and advising in the public sphere is crucial to business success, and discovering stakeholders' needs and concerns enables public relations counselors to develop a sense of community standards for avoiding missteps that could inflame stakeholder activism or regulatory infractions (Heath and Ryan 1989). The ethics counselor function requires public relations practitioners to act responsibly and ethically as representatives of the organization *and* civil society (Bowen 2008)—so public relations practitioners are ideally positioned to counsel top management on "which values fit best with the interests of their markets, audiences and publics" with regard to CSR (Heath 2001: 46). The PRSA accreditation process specifically trains practitioners on counseling ability. Among best practices offered for public relations counseling on CSR issues was a recommendation to "operate with integrity and offer the best advice without being a self-interested promoter" (Spangler and Pompper 2011: 217). Public relations practitioners can help organizations to actually improve infrastructural systems by ensuring that organizations have an authentic commitment to CSR/Sustainability and high ethics standards. Public relations provides counsel, strategic insights, and facilitates proactive, transparent, and open communication in the service of CSR/Sustainability and the larger public sphere; expertise that deserves greater organizational clout than it seems to be getting. As I have argued elsewhere, propositions for CSR theory emphasize the importance of ethics in terms of "living CSR from the inside out, earning trust of the public and the media, giving back as a community citizen, and accepting that we're all in this together" (Spangler and Pompper 2011: 217).

Two-way symmetrical public relations encompasses both individualistic and communal approaches to moral responsibility; an anchor for top management counseling. Bivins (2006) qualified the first approach as responsibility for one's own behavior and the second approach as responsibility for one's self *in conjunction with* other community members—not dissimilar from Levinas' (1966) "the-one-for-the-other" (p. 41) perspective. Much of the public relations literature focuses on individualistic behaviors, while there remains a great deal more to be discovered about ethics, responsibility, and accountability inside organizations. In-house corporate public relations departments represent just one facet of a complex organization, wherein multiple levels of decision makers play significant roles in CSR/Sustainability programs. The interplay of individuals when CSR/Sustainability is *embedded throughout* the organization exposes unique views on public relations' role. For example, David Stangis serves as Vice President of Public Affairs and Corporate Responsibility at Campbell's Soup Company, where he and his diverse team work across multiple company functions to ensure that CSR/Sustainability is fully and seamlessly integrated:

> I definitely don't come from that (publicity) perspective ... I look at my job as creating the context, the proof points, and frankly a lot of the education for the rest of the company to use. When I developed the strategic plan, among the critical keys to success, one of the six sectors was communication.

Counseling by providing education in CSR/sustainability contexts serves as a portal through which public relations practitioners emphasize ethical values and influence corporate behavior. Public relations managers are well positioned to educate other organizational members on ethics codes of behavior, hosting training sessions, and communicating via traditional media and "continual conversations" embedded in meetings, speeches, and other materials (Heath and Ryan 1989: 33; Starck and Kruckeberg 2003). An ability to work communally in complex organizations where decision making is decentralized (Grunig and Hunt 1984) is a prerequisite when CSR/Sustainability programs are embedded. Employees and managers must work well together toward well-defined and measurable goals, develop trust, and operate at the highest ethical standards. Parsons (2004) identified ethical principles as "public relations pillars" (p. 21). Ethics and social responsibility is a premiere public relations responsibility in Brazil, in addition to counseling and advising (Molleda and Ferguson 2004).

As much as some public relations researchers and practitioners might wish it so, any correlation between high ethical standards associated with CSR/Sustainability programs and bottom-line profits remains elusive. Those who use business case arguments to justify CSR/Sustainability believe that there are legitimate reasons for corporations to invest in such activities (Brown and Forster 2013). Yet, consumers in many parts of the world tend to be lukewarm about social responsibility (Vogel 2005). As Ihlen (2013) pointed out, "there is a plethora of examples of highly profitable business functioning with little if any attention paid to CSR and related issues" (p. 209). At the time of this writing, General Motors' chief executive Mary Barra testified before the US House of Representatives that a business case rationale should not trump safety when a senator reminded her that GM "made the same mistake as Ford 40 years ago, when that company infamously decided not to make safety improvements to the Pinto because they cost more than the $200,000 value that Ford set for a human life" (Bader 2014a).

As individuals and as communal members, public relations counselors navigate palpable challenges when prescribing and acting on high ethical standards. Public relations counselors are responsible for counseling management toward ethical decisions and mutually-beneficial relationships with stakeholders. This work constitutes a balancing act of pondering a common good for self, organization, stakeholders, and the public sphere; constantly weighing and negotiating (Wilcox, Ault, Agee, *et al.* 2000). Parsons (2004) enumerated important steps of "recognizing, facing, and dealing with ethical dilemmas in our everyday practice of public relations and corporate communications" (p. 1). So central are ethical values to public relations practice that Kruckeberg (1993) opined that "transgressors who choose not to conform" should be banished from the professional community (p. 2). Moloney (2006) characterized *unethical public relations* as "an act of deception against colleagues who seek to communicate honestly, and against citizens and consumers who seek accuracy and truth in public messages" (p. 104).

In CSR/Sustainability, public relations counselors face obstacles involving copyright, defamation, financial disclosure, rights of others, insider trading and more. In-house public relations counselors' advice may be "diluted" and departments challenged to perform their responsibilities ethically. Multiple variables impact ethical practice in organizations, such as degrees of autonomy, status/support for the public relations function, and placement of the department head amidst organizational hierarchies (middle-level, upper-level, or executive) (Bivins 2006: 29). Even the best-intended advice about ethics may not carry through to the highest echelons of organizations when it comes from a public relations manager stashed into a lower-floor corner who is simply expected to churn out good-news stories. Banerjee (2008) opined that few managers have absolute freedom in CSR/Sustainability implementation since an organization's interests and best practices are often predefined at higher organizational levels. Conditions of "weak job tenure ... [and working] as agents for an interest or a cause" (Moloney 2006: 105) offer public relations practitioners little support or comfort. Public relations agency team members' employment is even more tenuous, since gain and loss of a client base determines job security. Roberts (2001) critiqued the organizational form itself for jeopardizing ethical possibilities when he argued that CEOs may possess genuine ethical sensibility, but (in)actions of other organizational managers and employees both near and across the globe (in the case of multinational corporations) intervene.

Theoretical underpinnings to guide counselors with ethics in CSR/Sustainability

Drawing from numerous, intermingling theory streams offers a useful approach to supporting public relations practitioners as they provide counsel about ethics and wrangle with their personal concerns about ethics. A strong theoretical groundwork for understanding the public relations function and CSR/Sustainability interplay is embedded in the *relationship management* perspective which provides generalized support for advancing organization-public relationships and a premise for encouraging attention to ethics with emphases on commitment, openness and trust (Ledingham and Bruning 1998). Also useful is the *integrative social contract theory* (ISCT), a powerful conceptual framework for normative theorizing and empirical research "at the intersection of business, management, and ethics and law" (van Oosterhout and Heugens 2009: 729), wherein societal actors determine which norms will be created and enforced within a network. Certain social actors central to a network bear great *responsibility* for the management of ethical behavior. Some public relations scholars have sought wisdom of the *classical philoso-phers* (e.g., Aristotle Kant, Mill, Rawls) when pondering moral issues and ethical dilemmas, while others have consulted *excellence theory* (Grunig 1992), *contingency theory* (Cancel, Cameron, Sallot, *et al.* 1997), *situational theory* (Grunig, Grunig, and Dozier 2002), and more. Specific theories that lend toward deeper understanding about the CSR/Sustainability–PR–ethics dynamic are discussed here: postmodern theory, ethical responsibility theory, stakeholder theory, and postcolonial theory.

Postmodern theory

As applied, postmodern theory advances the concept of *agency*, which is a state of awareness (Taylor and Winquist 2001), a useful and important tool for public relations practitioners willing to serve as an insider-activist. Post-modernism offers a relevant underpinning for critiquing effects of industry and capitalism on the public sphere, which inspired CSR/Sustainability movements in the first place. Because the postmodern scholar subscribes to "reverence for nature, respect for life, sustainability, and ecological balance" (Best and Kellner 2001: 11), the postmodern theory framework promotes resisting and exposing power imbalances which create injustice and manipulate language to wield and maintain power. As Holtzhausen (2014) argued, the public relations practitioner is uniquely positioned inside organizations to serve as an activist who points out organizations' violation of common humanity— locally, regionally, nationally, and internationally. Furthermore, postmodern scholar Jean-François Lyotard (1984) posited that information must be trans-parent and available to promote free thinking. This provides public relations insider-activists with an opportunity to build trust between organizations and stakeholders by sharing information via multiple communication vehicles and by inviting stakeholders to organizational decision-making tables for joint problem solving through dissensus *or* consensus (Holtzhausen and Voto 2002). Personally, public relations counselors must use their bio-power from within to assert themselves (Dozier and Lauzen 2000) and resist complicity in fostering managerial discourse that disrupts cultural plurality—as well as develop an ever-questioning mind with the goal of improving institutions to make them more just (Lyotard and Thébaud 1985).

Ethical responsibility theory

Borrowing from the management studies literature, *ethical responsibility theory* calls for strengthening stakeholder rights through corporate self-restraint and altruism. It is important to theorize about ethical responsibility, according to Windsor (2006), because businesses have grown "morally indifferent," while stakeholder groups have grown "morally sensitive" (p. 98). In this framework, public relations may play the communication facilitator or liaison role (Broom 1982), removing obstacles to open communication channels among organizations and stakeholders and by serving as an organization's conscience and by counseling senior management on ethics issues. Following core ethical responsibility theory tenets, some organizations are moved to embed attention to ethics within their overall mission statements and/or across CSR/Sustainability philosophies and programming. Brenda Colatrella, Executive Director of Corporate Responsibility at Merck, explained how *access to health, environmental sustainability, employees and ethics,* and *transparency* serve as the pillars for corporate responsibility efforts at this pharmaceutical company:

> [This is] where we needed to focus our efforts and report out on how we're behaving from a responsibility perspective in those four broad categories ... My group really works with the organization to better understand those issues to advise on where we think we need to do something differently ... [W]e liaise with those folks on a regular basis to better understand "What are the CR issues, for example, in Ireland or Korea or India?" We want to make sure, from a global perspective, we're doing what we need to do to better understand expectations and to ensure we're behaving responsibly in terms of what matters most in those local countries, regions, geographical areas.

Stakeholder theory

Stakeholder theory offers much utility for examining public relations–CSR/Sustainability dynamics with regard to ethics, even though the research stream features much disagreement on the degree of debt that businesses owe to the public sphere. Stakeholder theorists in public relations regard stakeholders' needs and concerns to be on par with business objectives (Starck and Kruckeberg 2003). Researchers have advocated for empirical evidence of effects (Schreck 2011), moving beyond contingency-based approaches to stakeholder roles (Moloney 2006), overcoming limited CSR commitment expectations (Brown and Forster 2013), and personalizing stakeholders beyond generic labels (McVea and Freeman 2005). A developing literature of authenticity studies offers promise for furthering stakeholder theory development (Shen and Kim 2012) in CSR/Sustainability contexts, since the authenticity concept, like a genuine commitment to ethics, requires two-way communication. Authenticity characterizes self-awareness, transparency, and inclusion (Walumbwa, Wang, Wang, *et al.* 2010), which may be hypothesized as constituting a prerequisite for ethical, genuine relationships among organizations and stakeholders. See Chapter 3 for more on stakeholder theory.

Postcolonial theory

Postcolonial theory, as applied across a range of disciplines, remains a singularly useful framework for exposing unbalanced power relations among corporations and stakeholders. Foucault (1980) suggested that it is impossible to exclude power from social relations and a number of public relations researchers have highlighted implications of this in studies of globalization trends and international public relations practice. Fundamentally, Munshi and Kurian (2005) argued that CSR/Sustainability thinking perpetuates "the old colonial strategy of reputation management" without acknowledging power differentials (also a shortcoming of the two-way symmetrical paradigm), recognizing diversity among publics, or resolving a "profits at any cost" paradox (pp. 513, 517). Banerjee (2008) also critiqued "stakeholder colonialism" undergirded by a desire to control behavior (p. 51). Beaver (2005) opined that multinational corporations symbolize "what is wrong with twenty-first century capitalism" (p. 159). One critique of postcolonial theory is generalization of culture and insufficient scrutiny of indigenous populations for "differing and sometimes even incompatible agendas" (Perera and Pugliese 1998: 69). Postcolonial theory helps public relations counselors of multinational corporations to acknowledge ethics and power differentials.

Moving forward with public relations ethics in CSR/Sustainability

For the public relations profession to maximize its potential in supporting CSR/Sustainability programs, practitioners must be fully resolved to remain loyal to self, employer, profession, and the public sphere. The charge to act as an ethics guardian in social responsibility fits with the normative, *insider-activist* perspective of public relations (Holtzhausen 2000, 2014; Holtzhausen and Voto 2002). In reality, however, a number of conflicts, challenges, and issues present barriers to fulfilling such a promise, a naïve one, some would argue. So, how *should* a practitioner process all of this in order to think and act ethically and to counsel organizations to do the same? Pratt (1993) recommended an "eclectic moral framework" (p. 219) when deciding on some ethical course of action—weighting circumstances against principles such as justice and duty, and then examining these in conjunction with potential consequences. Using a moral relativism philosophical approach—considering context and avoiding absolute rights or wrongs—can go a long way in thinking through an ethical dilemma. Moreover, public relations counselors must remain on alert; always diligent and prepared to serve organizations and stakeholders. Moran (1996) reminded us that organizations are considered "responsible for [an] effect if it did know of the effect or could have known" (p. 137). The following offers four generalized entry points as stimulation for ethical decision making in public relations–CSR/Sustainability contexts.

Patience on a mission

First, building authentic, lasting, and ethical relationships between organizations and stakeholders takes trust and time. Employing some cost–benefit analysis or risk-avoidance metrics for comparing alternatives may help. However, at the bare minimum, public relations counselors should consider industry ethical standards and take a leadership position in helping organizations to develop and update standards for behavior which genuinely embrace sensitivity to stakeholder issues. This mindset should help corporations operate ethically by shifting from self-interest—with all eyes on the profit-centric bottom line—to being a global community member that is mindful of *all* stakeholders and not just stockholders (Munshi and Kurian 2005). Generating profits to benefit shareholders, employees, and others is important, but processes must be ethical and socially responsible. Because Heath and Ryan (1989) found that public relations practitioners rarely are allowed to participate in ethical decision making in organizations, the campaign to gain respect for public relations within organizations continues.

Change is inevitable

Second, public relations counselors must take advantage of all manner of formal and informal research methods for active public relations. Tasks central to CSR/Sustainability for the practitioner include boundary spanning, regularly reporting on findings and using them to change internal systems and to improve decision making, and continuing to build stakeholder trust. These activities should help to reduce perceptions of public relations as greenwash; a side effect when public relations is used to manipulate. The communications audit research method may help to keep pace with and to accommodate change—ultimately improving stakeholder relations. Furthermore, public relations counselors must convince top management that external stakeholders (not only stockholders) are equal in importance to internal stakeholders. Ethical analysis is an "indispensable and unavoidable" task for corporate affairs practitioners (Frederick 1986). Roberts (2001) challenged corporations to invest resources in learning about and planning for the consequences of their actions on others.

Make room at the table

Third, public relations practitioners must bring their insider-activism expertise to senior management decision making. Public relations practitioners are highly capable of designing CSR/Sustainability policy (Freitag 2007). However, research findings have suggested that public relations counselors are routinely shut out of high-level meetings (Fitzpatrick 1996a) where management course plotting and correction takes place, diminishing public relations' ability to ensure that their ethical guardianship and organizational conscience roles are maximized. Understanding how public relations counselors negotiate sometimes conflicting ethical challenges in shaping and/or promoting CSR/Sustainability is important because public relations practice influences society and the ways society perceives the profession. For example, advocacy tasks for the practitioner may easily shift into unethical territory when they are urged to lie, deceive, or distort. Consultant Jeff Leinaweaver of Global Zen Sustainability, headquartered in the USA, perceives this dynamic as the cutting edge space for public relations to mature and advance beyond the negative stereotypes and to support authentic CSR/Sustainability in organizations:

> [It's] not just giving-campaigns and throwing money at people. How's *that* authentic? Not just throwing happy talk ... [T]he biggest elephant in the room when it comes to PR in companies ... Part of the ethics is continuing to *challenge themselves* as persons; separating that organizational bubble ... It means some really brave conversations that need to be driven by the people who are in PR who are going to go out there and say it – not just kowtow to it ... There's an American marketplace and then there's a global marketplace. How PR can play a role in that depends on the quality of the people who are doing the work – the ethical stuff, smart not clever; to question. I look at it – they should be like an activist journalist internally ... They should know the organization deep down – understand and get ahead of the question, Does this organization know its full supply chain? Have they gone on a social audit? ... For a lot of people who are into CSR because it's cool to care, or they got there and they think they know it, [but] once they have the title, they stop learning and then they get drunk on the power and status.

Be prepared to blow the whistle

Finally, public relations practitioners are ethically bound to report wrongdoing; and to become a whistleblower. In the USA, some whistleblowers have been heralded as heroes for bringing to light significant ethical violations at Enron, Worldcom, the FBI (Lacayo and Ripley 2002), and CIGNA (Potter 2009a, 2009b). Whistleblowing is an insider-activist strategy for public relations practitioners (Holtzhausen 2014) even though it once was not considered a public relations role (Berger and Reber 2006). Two-thirds of public relations executives employed by Fortune 1000 corporations did not view reporting of wrongdoing about illegal or unethical activities (i.e. whistleblowing) as part of their jobs—with nearly one-third fearing retaliation if they did (Greenwood 2012). Perhaps public relations practitioners have grown comfortable with *golden handcuffs*—satisfactory salary, benefits, and power (Goldfarb 2009)—and choose to stay bound to a job despite knowledge of ethical wrongdoing. Passage of the Sarbanes-Oxley Act of 2002 in the wake of high-profile corporate ethics breaches in the USA has significant internal impact on financial reporting procedures in corporations for communication managers and others—and provides anonymous channels and protection for whistleblowers (Pompper 2014). So, even though whistleblowing is a communication act and probably no corporate affairs manager readily seeks to admit that their employer is not socially responsible (Frankental 2001), negative tactics used to influence organizations, such as whistleblowing, should not be overlooked as a means to keep management informed and to influence organizations. As Curtin and Boynton (2001) noted, "ethical actions are those that result in the greatest good ... some acts must be done regardless of their consequences" (p. 412).

Discussion

Stakeholder pressures and changes in management, political landscape, policy, and legislation significantly impact the public relations–CSR/Sustainability dynamic and could even impact public relations counselors' motivation to advocate for ethical decisions. This may be especially true if the client or boss fails to consider public relations as an important senior management team member or outright eschews insider-activism. Any benefits derived from short-term solutions to thorny ethical dilemmas must be weighed against long-term implications of organizational behavior on the triple bottom-line model of people, planet, and profit. In other words, public relations counselors must be allowed to play an instrumental part in organizational transformations; infusing and embedding organizations with a new ideology of respect for context, engaging in dialog with stakeholders, and using communicative interaction to rebuild organizational culture into something which equally esteems people, planet, and profits.

Many years ago now, Small (1991) wrote a case study about how the Exxon Valdez oil spill disaster cost the company a billion and still earned it a black eye—in disbelief that spending of such magnitude failed to render the company clean in the wake of so much damage. Exxon's "industrial accident" involved a debacle by the CEO and blunders by the public relations team for failing to consider ethical implications on a wider scale among multiple stakeholders beyond stockholders. Exxon's stock price rebounded by the end of 1989 to 7% above where it was before the accident in March of that year (Morningstar 2010), so the company's reputation in investor circles was repaired. Yet, while Small (1991) resolved, "If public relations was an objective, it was a failed one" (p. 11), another takeaway is that large companies that have experienced adverse effects brought about by their own people are especially in need of infrastructural and systemic change guided by high ethical standards to help prevent death and destruction that impacts more than a corporate bottom line.

This chapter has pondered the rhetorical charge of *doing no harm and doing the right thing* by blending together CSR/Sustainability professionals' viewpoints on ethics, sifting through multidisciplinary literatures about ethics and morality, and offering normative recommendations for moving forward. Without doubt, doing ethics in organizations is hard. Furthermore, public relations counselors are challenged to support organizations due to barriers presented by others' lack of admiration for the public relations profession. Perhaps most salient among these are misperceptions about the full scope of public relations' potential.

3 Spanning boundaries and building CSR/Sustainability stakeholder relationships

Public relations and CSR/Sustainability significantly overlap among cultural, economic, political amidst social dimensions, offering perspectives which span boundaries and reveal importance of stakeholder relationships. Public relations researchers interchangeably use certain words and phrases, such as *audiences, target audiences, publics, public sphere, society,* and *stakeholders.* It is important to draw from among theoretical underpinnings and applied circumstances to shed light on the complexity of these terms, as well as public relations' boundary spanning and stakeholder relationship building roles in CSR/Sustainability contexts. Overall, this chapter features discussion of stakeholder theory's normative approach and moral undercurrents for encouraging and supporting stakeholder interests and needs. Power inequities among organizations and members of the public sphere are interrogated via the insider-activist role for public relations, with suggestions for redressing imbalances. Collectively, this chapter addresses themes of: public relations, CSR/Sustainability and intersecting boundaries and relationships; affecting the insider-activist role to engage with stakeholders; integrating stakeholder theory with issues management for CSR/Sustainability; nonprofit groups as stakeholders and their CSR/Sustainability functions; and differentiation and dialog among stakeholder groups.

Public relations, CSR/Sustainability, and intersecting boundaries and relationships

Sustainability and CSR paradigms dovetail with *public relations'* normative function of managing relationships among stakeholder groups and positively impacting the public sphere wherein groups and individuals constitute society. *CSR* has an underlying *raison d'être* of positively contributing to a better society (Frederick 1994) and commonly is described as "aligning a company's activities with the social, economic and environmental expectations of its stakeholders" (Heath and Ni 2009). *Sustainability* creates value along social, environmental, and economic issues (Wheeler, Colbert, and Freeman 2003). Capriotti (2007) qualified *sustainability* as essential to an organization's contract with society to do no harm and to provide information and other resources in the event of risks. Hence, organizations that assume social responsibility and communicate about this with key stakeholders maximize opportunities which may benefit all (Moreno and Capriotti 2009). Ways that public relations and CSR/Sustainability intersect and overlap are examined next, according to the general public and public sphere concepts, corporate ethics, environmental scanning/mapping, language used in CSR/Sustainability, and supplier roles in CSR/Sustainability.

Exploring the general public and public sphere concepts

Even though management researchers long have considered a *general public* when developing business strategies, public relations researchers have warned against essentializing some en masse *general public*. Instead, public relations theorists emphasize the importance of thoroughly researching groups to discover their unique needs and qualities in order to build strong relationships among organizations and stakeholders (e.g., Grunig 1992; Grunig and Hunt 1984). The two-way symmetrical public relations model offers (e.g., Grunig, Grunig, and Dozier 2002) a proven means for achieving organizational excellence through dialog and real relationship building *with* individuals and groups, a superior approach to one-way techniques used to talk *at* them. Companies engaging in conversations with stakeholders to discover their concerns are considered to be socially responsible as opposed to merely focusing on profit motives (Crane and Matten 2004). Most public relations theorists rebuff the one-way asymmetrical press agentry model, but it endures among most public relations publicists. Identifying key publics from among some larger *general public* population constitutes a key step in public relations' four-stage management process (Broom and Sha 2013). Grunig and Repper (1992) introduced activity/passivity categories to discern among stakeholders: 1) those defined by ways they are affected by an organization's decisions; and 2) those who are/ become active and coalesce as *publics*. Promoting a professional responsibility theory of public relations ethics, Fitzpatrick and Gauthier (2001) recommended that *public conscience* replace terms such as *social conscience* and *social responsibility* in the public relations literature. They recommended thinking of the *public* as a series of relationships connected by common interests; a move which "narrows the overwhelming and unrealistic focus of a communitarian model on the community or society as a whole" (Fitzpatrick and Gauthier 2001: 210). These findings remain highly valuable for public relations counselors associated with CSR/Sustainability programs as they consider coalition building, research strategies, and strategic programming.

In Europe, some public relations scholars have borrowed Habermas' (1989) concept of the *public sphere* to facilitate theory building about boundary-spanning and normatively fostering relationships beyond publicity, promotion, and profit motives. The public sphere is a space in social life where people bond over discussion, debate, and deliberation about social problems and work together to influence improvement and change. Hence, the public sphere also serves as a check on state authority. Habermas (1989) operationalized *public sphere* as:

> ... consist[ing] of an intermediary structure between the political system, on the one hand, and the private sectors of the life world and functional systems, on the other. It represents a highly complex network that branches out into a multitude of overlapping international, national, regional, local and sub cultural arenas.
>
> (pp. 373–374)

This public sphere concept proves quite useful in CSR/Sustainability contexts since public relations scholars have considered corporate power as something that must be kept in check. Many have urged resistance to models and practices which focus only on transmitting corporate messages to publics in order to sell them or persuade them to do something which benefits the corporation—rather than to engage in authentic relationships (e.g., Ihlen 2008; Munshi and Kurian 2005; van Ruler and Verčič 2004). Among CSR/Sustainability researchers, Crouch (2006) opined that little holds corporations accountable for their global and local impacts and this reality underscores a significant power imbalance between transnational enterprises—and everything else: "There is no such thing as a global society; almost no such thing as global polity; there *is* considerable global economy" (italics added) (p. 1533).

Corporate ethics

Public relations theorists have posited that authentic relationship building based on in-depth knowledge about and respect for stakeholder groups also leads to stronger corporate ethics, a key component of CSR/Sustainability programs. As noted in Chapter 2, however, critics worry that an uneasy fit between ethics and profits in CSR/Sustainability contexts creates a paradox for public relations practitioners. People around the globe are affected when organizations behave unethically, such as when wages are unfair, work conditions are unsafe, and natural resources are abused. Globalization effects and proliferation of communication technologies, including social media, means that people may become aware of any event, activity, or decision within seconds. Jenny Carty, Reporting and Governance Manager at Royal Bank of Scotland (RBS), explained that an ethics awakening following a 2008 UK government bailout included greater attention to UK taxpayers as a highly vocal stakeholder group now that RBS is owned by the UK government:

> We, as a 23-people-strong team, have come a long way from being a team of one or two people back a decade ago. Now, as sustainability has grown in importance and so has society's recognition and stakeholders demanding that companies be more responsible... [There's a] realization

that you need to behave in a responsible manner because it's just not acceptable to stakeholders when you don't. We had not behaved in an acceptable manner and we weren't even financially sustainable, never mind anything else. So the Executive Committee and the Board decided that sustainability was an area they wanted to invest in; invest in bringing sustainable thinking to the rest of the organization ... [W]e're starting from zero in terms of perception and reputation.

Stakeholder theory and the concept of defining groups based on their interests, issues, and concerns is fully exploited in business circles and has been widely incorporated into the public relations' body of knowledge. Since the 1970s, CSR's central concepts of *society* and *the social* have been narrowed to simply *stakeholders* so it may be presumed that the term *stakeholders* inherently involves larger social interests. However, this abbreviation has caused problems such as masking "misallocation of resources" (Banerjee 2008: 23) and precedence of stockholders over all other stakeholders. Clarkson (1995) astutely observed differences between someone who owns stock in a publicly-traded company and *stakeholders*—people who have some vested interest in an organization's function. Stakeholder theory is underpinned by moral, normative overtones regarding what organizations *should do* to fulfill responsibilities to all stakeholders (Banerjee 2008).

Environmental scanning/mapping

Public relations practitioners seek to build relationships with stakeholders by learning about them through *environmental scanning* (or *mapping*). Ihlen (2008) characterized the public sphere concept itself as a "mapping tool" (p. 136). Techniques are used for systematic collection of insights about people, groups, and their perceptions of organizations, operations, and issues (Okura, Dozier, Sha, *et al.* 2008). Developing sensitivity to threats and trends and "scouting the terrain" to reveal potential trouble also constitutes environmental scanning (Heath 2013a: 495). Deep listening during face-to-face interviews and focus groups with stakeholders and assessing public opinion via Facebook, Twitter, and other social media vehicles enables public relations practitioners to collect intelligence so that they effectively may manage issues on behalf of organizations. John Bee, Communication Manager, Public Affairs at Nestlé, headquartered in Switzerland, said that a significant portion of his role in CSR/Sustainability is scanning stakeholder environments by mapping concerns for action:

My specific work [is] to represent the views and concerns of the outside world towards our organization so we can keep best informed on how to drive our strategy forward to respond to those stakeholders ... Mine is a classic communication function. Within, the majority of resources are spent on listening to the concerns and views of outside opinion formers, stakeholders – and representing those internally, as much as it is communicating about what we do.

Face-to-face contact with less-powerful *others*, such as people of developing nations, is particularly important (Roberts 2003). To support this work, McVea and Freeman (2005) advocated for an approach wherein individual relationships with stakeholders begin by respecting them "as people with names and faces" (p. 57). Jenny Carty, Reporting and Governance Manager at Royal Bank of Scotland, told how RBS' Sustainability Programs team supports women, youth, and social enterprise. For example, a Money Sense community program for UK schools, teaches young people "how to be more financially literate" and another program supports "under-represented groups in UK society to become more involved in enterprise." Stakeholder relations means considering human beings with authentic concerns occupying environments with constantly shifting boundaries and circumstances conducive to public relations–CSR/Sustainability overlap.

Language used in CSR/Sustainability

Ways that language is used to characterize stakeholders can prove quite revealing when examining corporations-in-society effects on relationship-building potential. Multinational corporations' websites and CSR/Sustainability links reveal that *society, community*, and *the marketplace* are consistently used interchangeably as objects among corporations' expressions of desire to do good. Earlier, Ihlen (2008) also discovered that *stakeholders* and *society* are enjoined in CSR contexts and Kjær (2007) made similar observations about *society* and *the market*. For example, Coca-Cola Corporation's 2012–2013 Sustainability Report declared: "We help strengthen communities and provide for *community* well-being by empowering women, by providing aid and relief during a disaster, by investing in education and by respecting human rights" (italics added) ("We: Building stronger communities" n.d.). Also, Monsanto addressed improving agriculture on its website: "It is our purpose to work alongside farmers, academics and *society* and find solutions to make agriculture more sustainable" (italics added) ("What Is Monsanto doing to help?" n.d.) Such generic and abstract descriptors of those impacted by corporations tends to keep stakeholder interests at arm's length.

Hence, too infrequently do corporations amplify actual stakeholder voices in their CSR/Sustainability reports; possibly an indicator that they lack sophisticated stakeholder awareness. Institutions construct social narratives selectively (van Leeuwen 2005). Often ignored is a need for stakeholders to feel involved in advancing their own agendas and recommending solutions (Cornelissen 2004), as well as opportunities for CSR/Sustainability messaging and programming to be co-constructed by stakeholders *and* organizations (Morsing and Schultz 2006: 324). Moreover, multinational corporations' discourse about *survival* (Bakan 2003) exposes power differentials—in terms of profitability from a business perspective and in terms of living a healthful life from a person's perspective. *CSR* joins sustainable development and environmental justice among phrase strings appropriated to put a face on corporations—as revealed via content analyses of corporate websites across multiple industries. Postcolonial scholars acknowledge diversity among stakeholders, resistance at the margins, and recommend dismantling of hierarchies and putting an end to publics being co-opted into multinational corporations' neocolonial (negative) treatment of people and the planet in pursuit of profit (Munshi and Kurian 2005). Even at the boardroom level, an out-of-sight-out-of-mind outlook constrains genuine attempts to ethically relate with stakeholders, as Roberts (2003), explained: "Physical distance also has the effect of rendering faceless the objects of our actions" (p. 259).

Supplier roles in CSR/Sustainability

Suppliers are important stakeholders, businesses that exponentially extend company borders along the CSR/Sustainability chain. In 2010, an intense news media spotlight focused on Apple's relationships with suppliers who manufacture iPods and other Apple products when charges emerged of inhumane treatment of workers (e.g., poor pay, forced overtime, not being permitted to sit during 12-hour shifts) and employee suicides at the Apple supplier Foxconn factory in Shenzhen, China (Baijia 2013). Apple has established a suppliers' code of conduct consistent with the Electronics Industry Citizenship Coalition (EICC) in order to conform to a voluntary framework of "social, environmental and economic responsibility" ("Responsibility in the Electronics Industry" n.d.) The *Apple Supplier Responsibility Progress Report* explained on its corporate website: "[S]uppliers must be committed, as we are, to ensuring the highest standards of social responsibility ... We take our social and environmental responsibilities seriously ... Please note that all purchases are made in the competitive *marketplace*" (italics added) ("Apple and Procurement" n.d.) Hence, organizations' borders extend far beyond headquarter nations—through supplier operations.

Affecting the insider-activist role to engage with stakeholders

In public relations practice, the insider-activist role combined with a stakeholder approach promotes authentic, respectful, and mutually-beneficial exchanges between organizations and others for solid relationship building essential to CSR/Sustainability. Public relations managers acting the insider-activist prove instrumental in supporting organizational reform to becoming less-hierarchical and more accommodating of less-powerful people impacted by organizations. Stakeholder groups generally constitute "those people and groups that affect, or can be affected by, an organization's decisions, policies, and operations" (Post, Lawrence, and Weber 2002: 8). Scott Dille, Group Leader at Novo Nordisk in Denmark, explained that this healthcare company's corporate sustainability function is called Corporate Stakeholder Engagement:

> So, it is kind of a PR, public affairs function. It's an odd place to put corporate sustainability, because on the one hand corporate responsibility drives a lot of concrete initiatives whether they be energy reducing, emissions reducing initiatives with the human rights reviews, etc., etc. But it also plays a role in identifying and engaging with stakeholders, NGOs, governmental bodies on the global level. You can take the new SDGs [sustainable development goals] as an example where colleagues have been working very closely with various stakeholders trying to make the case that health and non-communicable diseases be an important part of sustainable goals that will be coming out in 2015 … [W]e see that as a very important role in sustainability – hence why it's in the Corporate Stakeholder Engagement area.

Due to low trust levels, some stakeholders maintain a critical eye on policies and corporate actors with regard to economic, environmental and social issues (Bowmann-Larsen and Wiggen 2004). Public relations' two-way symmetrical model is supported by a stakeholder approach, but it must be acknowledged that a corporation's boundaries are limited by awareness of its effects beyond profit making (Roberts 2003). To fully do justice to triple bottom-line accountability (people, planet, profit), organizations must engage with regular and in-depth stakeholder dialogues to reveal *all* individuals and groups who are impacted by the organization. Public relations insider-activists must participate in bringing issues and concerns to the attention of senior management on behalf of the public sphere. Jeff Leinaweaver of Global Zen Sustainability, a US-based consulting group, advocated for an aspirational role for public relations practitioners to educate people so that they understand the full scope and purpose of sustainability programs:

> … coalition build, build the data, talk to people so they're not freaked out that their job's going to immediately disappear due to the sustainability thing. If you're the person holding the vat of chemicals that will soon be illegal, you're still worried about losing your job, so you're going to fight it. All that stuff that goes on that could actually get a big organization on the escalator of change and being transparent.

Yet, instead of providing this degree of service, Leinaweaver lamented that he too often sees public relations practitioners concentrating on publicity: "They bring PR people in to do the story piece and make it look pretty and then those people take way too much credit."

The insider-activist role for public relations with regard to CSR/Sustainability work also responds to critics who debate shortcomings of the two-way symmetrical model. A net effect of enacting the insider-activist role may include eradicating the *general public* concept with its almost-exclusive attention to publicity designed to appeal to stockholders, investors, and those perceived as trouble-makers. For example, it has been suggested that trust and empowerment as byproducts of public relations' two-way symmetrical model may be impossible to achieve so long as organizations retain a dominant core position while publics occupy some neutral interactive space or even margins. Overall, multinational corporations' significant economic and political power trumps voices of the people (Pieczka 2006), especially those disenfranchised among developing nations (Munshi and Kurian 2005). Use of the stakeholder approach may risk inattention to some widely held perceptions across society simply because awareness of those perceptions may be low (Ihlen 2008)—not unlike the spiral of silence concept's premise. Noelle-Neumann (1974) argued that in public opinion formation, a vocal opinion may dominate a majority's silent opinions. Some people fear social censure if they perceive their opinion to be in the minority. Because a silent majority may be the "most vulnerable to the effects of corporate conduct" (Roberts 2003: 261), public relations' insider-activists can encourage in-depth, face-to-face dialogue across boundaries and into people's lives; an essential foundation for CSR/Sustainability. As I have argued elsewhere, organizations lacking in stakeholder sensibility frequently overlook opportunities to account for past grievances involving culture, ethnicity, and "race" among employees, communities, and others—and then seem wholly surprised when old wounds open afresh (Liu and Pompper 2012). Examples are abundant among incidences of multinational corporations' impact in developing nations and quite often exposés are exceptionally negative—such as in the documentary film, *Crude*, about Chevron's court battles and Ecuadorean peoples' claims of illness linked to petroleum extraction (DeLeon, Bonfiglio, Stratton, *et al.* 2009), as well as the *Bananas!* documentary film accusing Dole Food and Dow Chemical of providing unsafe work conditions at Nicaraguan fruit plantations (Gertten 2009). Critics doubt stakeholder theory's validity in the face of organizations' self-interest worldviews (Hendry 2001; L'Etang 1995). To sidestep promoting commercially-driven and self-serving organizational motives, some researchers have posited that CSR/Sustainability must empower public sphere members. For example, Whetten, Rands, and Godfrey (2001) re-defined CSR as "societal expectations of corporate behavior; a behavior that is alleged by a stakeholder to be expected by society or morally required and is therefore justifiably demanded of business" (p. 374). In this way, stakeholders act as agents and conduits on behalf of the public sphere when expectations of organizations become articulated and demands are made. *Systems theory* promotes environments wherein organizations (as systems) seek to establish and maintain symmetrical, mutually beneficial public relations (Broom and Sha 2013); striking a mid-point win-win zone on the *contingency model continuum* between *pure asymmetry* (where public relations benefits only the organization) and *pure cooperation* at the other (where public relations benefits only its publics). Simply adopting an accommodation worldview does more than stave off events that threaten organizational image when CSR/Sustainability is embedded throughout organizations. Public relations insider-activists must operate without a compass-point distinction so that Western stakeholders hold no hierarchical economic or political sway over other parts of the world. Hence, the public relations insider-activist may propel organizations away from inauthentic outcomes that fail to acknowledge issues of power and its inequitable distribution.

Developing and matching organizations' CSR/Sustainability goals and programs with stakeholder expectations and societal needs is no small feat; a challenge worthy of the public relations insider-activist. This represents one of the defining tensions between critics who eschew CSR/Sustainability as greenwash and those who embrace its transformational potential. To Crouch (2006), the dynamic constitutes a "central puzzle" (p. 1534). From a business ethics perspective, one research team reached back to Adam Smith's (1759) philosophies to develop guidelines for helping organizations decide with whom they should partner on CSR/Sustainability initiatives. Such foresight can help in avoiding conflict among stakeholder groups (Brown and Forster 2013) and negation of less powerful shareholders' needs (Henderson 2001). Corporations' pure philanthropic efforts are differentiated from activities strategically aligned with CSR/Sustainability goals (Siegel and Vitaliano 2007). In recent decades, business management and public relations researchers have found organizations abandoning simple check writing, or "pure philanthropy," in favor of CSR activities which are strategically aligned with organizational objectives (Pompper 2013: 275). See Figure 3.1.

Vice President Public Affairs and Corporate Responsibility, David Stangis, at Campbell's Soup in the USA, spoke of transitioning out of pure philanthropy and relating with stakeholders:

> Somebody on my team comes from the philanthropic world and that's where she's comfortable and I keep trying to remind her that her version of the company's philanthropy is money our shareholders could have access to; their right to have. It's our job to make the case that investing that money in the community is a better long-term payoff than just giving it to them. It's hard when you come out of the philanthropy world to think like that. I don't know that it sinks in yet – it's a long conversation. The business people get it. They understand that concept. It's not like we're spending philanthropy. We're spending *other* people's money. We're stewards of the Campbell's Soup Company. Not like, "Oh this is my pool of money that I get to give away." That's not how it works.

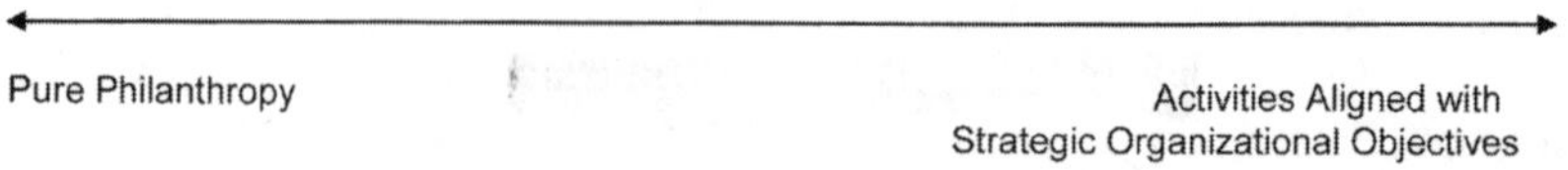

Pure Philanthropy   Activities Aligned with
                                                 Strategic Organizational Objectives

Figure 3.1 Corporate giving continuum

Increasingly, organizations develop strategic approaches to CSR/Sustainability and carefully consider stakeholders in conjunction with overall business goals. For example, technology companies target education when making donations; a tactic with an inherent benefit for helping to train future employees (LeClair and Gordon 2000).

Integrating stakeholder theory with issues management for CSR/Sustainability

Some have recommended infusing stakeholder theory with an issues management approach to more fully support CSR/Sustainability thinking. At the core of CSR are relationships between business and society (Wood 1991a)—with stakeholder theory helping to define, explain, and predict those relationships. Issues management emerged in conjunction with CSR/Sustainability in the USA and the UK in the 1970s in conjunction with activist groups pressuring media, government officials, and businesses to change discriminatory and harmful policies and practices. It was part of a management philosophy "used to reduce friction and increase harmony between organizations and their stakeholders" (Heath 2013a: 495). *Issues management* describes "corporate planning and communication response to critics of business activities" (Heath 2013a: 496). Chase (1982) coined the *issues management* term and inspired new techniques for corporations to communicate with stakeholders:

> Issues management is the capacity to understand, mobilize, coordinate, and direct all strategic and policy planning functions, and all public affairs/public relations skills, toward achievement of one objective: meaningful participation in creation of public policy that affects personal and institutional destiny.
>
> (p. 1)

Thus, as a sub-discipline of public relations, issues management provides a systematic and active means for gathering insights and nurturing mutually-beneficial relationships among organizations and stakeholders. Sethi (1977) called for use of communication to mend the *legitimacy gap* which exists between what organizations believe and do—with what stakeholders think organizations *should* believe and do. Maignan and Ferrell (2003) found that consumers in the USA, France, and Germany are determined to pass judgment on businesses that they consider to be economically, legally, philanthropically, or socially *ir*responsible by voting with their purse. In China, the role of consumer as a stakeholder group is still developing. Timothy Hui, Director Global Reporting Initiative (GRI) China, explained that consumers amplify their voices once each year during Consumer Day on March 15 and the preceding night: "Consumers' role in China is the least strong of the community. The consumers really live on the mercy of producers in China. When you understand this reality, you would not be surprised by the toxic food or poison... all these sad stories."

Blending of issues management approaches with stakeholder theory may help to overcome the latter's shortcomings as a stand-alone tool in public relations and help practitioners to advocate for a more prominent role in CSR/Sustainability work. Stakeholder theory possesses inherent shortcomings when applied to voluntary CSR/Sustainability contexts (Orts and Strudler 2002). One research team suggested that stakeholder theory presumes a static environment and persuasively argued that the stakeholder concept grows less salient with proliferation of social media when *issue arenas* themselves gain prominence over groups who champion them (Luoma-aho and Vos 2010: 315). Moreover, CSR debates often feature stakeholder theorists and CSR researchers at opposite ends of a continuum. Some researchers have distilled the debates into justification level (organization or society), justification logic (economic, ethical, political, social), and justification grounds (positivist, anti-positivist, and pragmatist) (Kurucz, Colbert, and Wheeler 2008).

Nonprofit groups as stakeholders and their CSR/Sustainability functions

An important trend to emerge in conjunction with stakeholder relationship building in CSR/Sustainability contexts is partnerships built between for-profit businesses and nonprofit organizations, such as nongovernmental organizations (NGOs). Numbers of nonprofit organization-corporation partnerships are increasing (Jamali and Keshishian 2009) and the twenty-first century has been characterized as "the age of alliances" (Austin 2000: 1). Corporate-nonprofit relationships in CSR/Sustainability contexts are considered a "win-win situation" in terms of shared public relations principles (Taylor 2013: 615). An example of for-profit enterprises coming together for pre-competitive collaboration is the dairy industry's development of the nonprofit trade association, Innovation Center for US Dairy. Laura Mandell, Vice President, Sustainability Communications at Innovation Center for US Dairy, explained that: "with sustainability—how do you get farmers, cooperatives, retailers, NGOs, government all sitting at the table solving for issues? We had to create the Innovation Center ... [O]ur primary argument and education for them is that sustainability is good for business."

Inherent power differentials exist between corporations and nonprofits, yet researchers have discovered risk factors on both sides of the equation with regard to CSR/Sustainability programs. There are ethical slippery slopes to navigate when nonprofits accept corporate funding, given their lower risk threshold with regard to reputation (Seitanidi and Crane 2009). Jenny Carty, Reporting and Governance Manager at Royal Bank of Scotland, spoke of how RBS is satisfied to work with nonprofit sustainability program partners willing to track and evaluate partnership outcomes:

[We're] pushing the onus to report back onto the groups that we support. Are you tracking where the money is going? If you are, then how are you tracking it and what are you measuring? ... That hasn't been the case in the past, but it's much more the case now. [W]e look at indicators such as how many students reached. We do surveys to show how many kids knew what APR was in year one versus how many knew what it was in year three. So, we have different ways to measure financial education. With the Inspiring Enterprise Program, we measure things like number of organizations established, number of people supported now that these businesses are up and running.

There are numerous considerations when designing and evaluating such for-profit/nonprofit partnerships. Some academic study findings offer how-to advice for these endeavors—particularly a need for agreeing on engagement levels and maximized synergies embedded in goals and expectations (Samii, Van Wassenhove, and Bhattacharya 2002).

Nongovernmental organizations (NGOs) are a special kind of nonprofit group, consisting of individuals who serve as change agents and organize around social issues to influence public opinion and to impact decision leaders in government, corporations, and the media. Taylor (2013) posited that they emerged in the USA in conjunction with eighteenth-century colonial-British conflict. Other researchers track the emergence of NGOs more closely with contemporary social issues which transcend geo-political boundaries, such as environmental issues and instances of far-reaching corporate misconduct (Jamali and Keshishian 2009). Smith (2003) posited that NGOs seek to fill gaps left by governments that prove unsuccessful or too weak to solve a nation's social problems. Hence, NGOs tend to have the most influence in countries where larger degrees of press freedom exist (See 2009). Examples of large, global-reach NGOs include Amnesty International, Ashoka, CARE International, Doctors Without Borders, and Greenpeace ("Top 100 NGOs" n.d.). NGOs see themselves as playing a watchdog role on free market economies, an important role in CSR/Sustainability contexts. Because part of NGOs' mission may be to hold corporations accountable to high ethical standards and good citizenship in the public sphere (Guay, Doh, and Sinclair 2004), they may assume an adversarial stance. Hence, NGOs may be considered controversial with contested legitimacy since some consider them a now-institutionalized corporate component (Arenas, Lozano, and Albareda 2009). Yet, other NGOs have found opportunities to collaborate with corporations on CSR programs that advance both parties' goals (Conley and Williams 2005) and NGOs may work harder than their corporate partners to ensure that relationships work (Jamali and Keshishian 2009). Still, these sometimes-uneasy liaisons between corporations and NGOs consistently undergo scrutiny. As part of relationships with businesses, some NGOs sell their survey research and desktop publishing services to earn funds (Taylor 2013); "double role" liaisons that may not always appear free of potential conflict of interest (Arenas, Lozano, and Albareda 2009: 190).

Communication lines must be mutually open between both parties and corporate leaders must have an open mind to partnering with nonprofits; a significant shift from earlier paternal relationships associated with philanthropy's charitable giving of the past. Because one research team suggested that these partnerships should become institutionalized "to address any possible skill gaps" (Seitanidi and Crane 2009: 413), the role of discovery before a final commitment cannot be over-emphasized. Similarly, Jamali and Keshishian's (2009) survey findings attributed failed alliances to lack of research at the outset of a partnership, as well as uneven motivation levels, incompatible objectives, and differing competencies and strengths. Hence, partnership selection should rise above *trial and error* to involve a significant amount of research and development of partner selection criteria before making a formal commitment—to avoid future challenges and to ensure strategic fit. Selecting the perfect partner and trying to maintain some degree of control over messaging has its challenges. Susan Sabatino, Account Manager, Marketing Partnerships Team at the Nature Conservancy, anticipates an increase in for-profit/nonprofit partnerships over time:

> I think companies are going to be wanting more and more from these types of partnerships and nonprofits are really going to have to figure out based on those tax aspects and that "selling your soul" perspective. I don't have the numbers to back this up, but I think there's a slight trend away from companies giving revenue in a philanthropic way and just giving it to support conservation work and expecting no return benefits. I think it's more moving in the direction of a marketing partnership. But I get the sense that expectations from the company will grow. I hope I'm wrong.

Motives of corporations aligning with nonprofits for credible CSR/Sustainability commitments are multiple and complex. Rationales include acting to prevent government interventions and reinforcing brand identity (Bhattacharya and Sen 2004), reducing conflicts with NGOs (Joutsenvirta and Uusitalo 2010), creating opportunities for cross sector alliance learning (Arya and Salk 2006), sharing knowledge based on NGOs' on-the-ground experiences with globalization effects in developing nations (Jamali and Keshishian 2009), increasing legitimacy for programs (Inkpen 2002), and enhancing reputation and recognition (Stuart 2000). Corporations can relinquish degrees of control over project management when they partner with a nonprofit (Jamali and Keshishian (2009). On the other hand, nonprofits seek to benefit from corporations' larger repositories of monetary support; a useful resource in economic climates marked by decreasing funding and increasing social need. Some NGOs even hope to gain a seat on corporate boards to promote CSR concerns (Arenas, Lozano, and Albareda 2009).

Differentiation and dialog among stakeholder groups

In addition to NGOs, other stakeholder groups considered central to CSR/Sustainability programs from a corporation's perspective include employees, competitors, consumers, investors, governments, media, and suppliers. Stakeholder groups may be differentiated according to normative (e.g., employees and others that organizations have a moral obligation toward) and derivative (e.g., media, competitors, and others who have the potential to affect an organization) criteria (Phillips 2003). Researchers widely have considered stakeholder groups according to their roles, attributes, power and influence, and interactivity with one another. CSR/Sustainability managers face a striking paradox: how to avoid zero-sum valuing of any one stakeholder group over another through use of ethical judgment and moral principles, while creating "sufficient wealth, value, or satisfaction for those who belong to each stakeholder group, so that each group continues as a part of the corporation's stakeholder system" (Clarkson 1995: 107). Collectively, Bhattacharya (2013) opined that stakeholders interpret CSR in terms of understanding (e.g., awareness, attributions, effectiveness), usefulness (functionality), and unity (value). Hank Boerner, Chairman, Chief Strategist and Co-Founder of Governance & Accountability Institute, Inc., explained that while it may be tempting for corporations to emphasize investors as the supreme stakeholder group, all stakeholders are essential:

> [W]e have a client who is a relatively small part of the supply chain in dollar volume, but because their customers are so attuned to corporate responsibility and sustainability and putting reports out and pushing down into the supply chain, this little company that is relatively unknown now finds itself having to define itself in terms of its responsibility and what it's doing to be more sustainable for the long term in the environmental area, how they govern the company, how they deal with employee issues and so on ... I think the dialog, internally and externally with stakeholders, about the acronyms and what it means ... Yes, *ESG* is important – environmental, social governance. Yes, *sustainability* is important, *corporate ethics, CSR*, they're all important. Here's how you're going to organize the discussion about this to help people understand if they're in a company helping to manage it or they're a stakeholder looking at companies through different lenses.

David Stangis, Vice President of Public Affairs and Corporate Responsibility at Campbell's Soup Company, shared anecdotes about his experiences developing CSR programs with his staff:

> When I worked to create the CSR function at Intel between 1998 and 2000, it took me two years and I had to build the business case and go person by person, department by department to build alignment. Communications was the last group – and they really never did come along until we had to prove it to them. I made the case to governmental affairs "Yeah, I get it, we need somebody to focus on CSR and the public affairs, the operational functions." Communications people were then, at the

time anyway – completely different today – were like, "When my phone is ringing about it, then I'll come and talk to you and maybe we need it." CSR is a forward-looking, proactive, it's a trend-spotting function ... So whatever I'm trying to do, whoever I'm talking to, I say, what are you trying to drive? Let's see how we can use what I call sustainability or CSR to lower your cost structure. Almost anything you do in a manufacturing company that'll lower cost, it's a sustainability metric. Almost anything you do inside of a company to drive engagement, productivity, and retention.

Sometimes an organization's stakeholders' concerns may conflict, such as when interests of activist stakeholders clash with those of investors and other stakeholders. Such was the case when Rainforest Action Network protested exploitation of the world's forests by companies like General Mills, which uses palm oil in food product manufacturing ("Our Work: Forests Program" n.d.) Erin Fitzgerald, Senior Vice President, Sustainability at Innovation Center for US Dairy, stressed that beyond immediate potential impacts on stock price, attending to investors when communicating about CSR/Sustainability programs has the potential for rewarding companies:

> [W]hen the investment downturn happened, we saw the Dow Jones Sustainability Index trend up as opposed to the Dow Jones, which trended down. So all the investment institutions now are saying "Hey, maybe companies that are working on sustainability are actually good bets. Or, they're more of a long-term investment" ... It's a conversation we hear all the time. Each company and corporate culture is different. I do think you're starting to see that the companies that are publicly disclosing with GRI are getting rewarded for it.

Studies featuring attempts to rank order stakeholder groups have been roundly criticized. O'Riordan and Fairbrass (2008) called it "a fragmented patchwork of ideas and concepts" with underdeveloped theoretical models (p. 748). Broadly, researchers have divided stakeholder groups according to *primary* (critical to a company's existence) and *secondary* distinctions (affected by a company's decisions) (Werther and Chandler 2006). According to Grunig and Repper's (1992) "stakeholder stage" in strategic public relations planning, messages and practices are discerned in order to reduce uncertainty as *stakeholders* become active. Identification and categorization of stakeholders according to each group's perceptions of appropriate business behavior and opinions about an organization are often linked to economic, environmental, and social issues and each may be ranked according to traits such as legitimacy, power, and urgency. *PR News* survey findings suggested that public relations professionals perceived that the most important CSR stakeholders are: customers (21%); communities where we operate (20%); employees (18%); influentials (15%); consumers (9%); governments (8%);

nonprofits/activists (4%); and investment community (4%) (Anonymous 2006). In the UK, the most important CSR "opinion leaders" are legislators, business press, investors, and NGOs (Dawkins 2004). Strategies must be formulated for each stakeholder group, multiple stakeholder concerns must be integrated, and issues must be considered from each stakeholder group's perspective. Surprisingly, *PR News* survey findings suggested that less than a quarter (23%) of public relations practitioner respondents assessed "relationships with influential stakeholders" as a means for measuring CSR communication activities and only 5% of respondents even used "stakeholder engagement sessions" as part of communication activities (Anonymous 2006). This is a significant shortcoming in CSR/Sustainability stakeholder dialogue strategy and it runs counter to best practices in public relations. Streamlining and oversimplifying complex CSR/Sustainability issues and processes by creating stakeholder hierarchies means that groups at the top of a pecking order will be prioritized over those at the bottom. Munshi and Kurian (2005) have argued that these dynamics ultimately support existing power differentials and negate developing nations; a breach of ethics. Furthermore, wildlife and the planet also represent stakeholders, particularly when they are jeopardized by human conditions (Small 1991). The public relations insider-activist can help to assure that an imbalance does not endure since stakeholder hierarchies expose organizations' underlying infrastructural biases and further promote inequities that disregard ethical obligations to the public sphere.

Discussion

This chapter has examined public relations' boundary spanning and CSR/Sustainability relationship management roles. Central to both interrelated issues is an overarching responsibility for fostering successful communication in the public sphere, where culture, economics, and politics intermingle and bring to bear on outcomes. Investigations of how CSR/Sustainability partnerships between organizations and stakeholders, which often include nonprofits and NGOs, develop and mature, provide greater insight into CSR/Sustainability possibilities and promote better practices and theory with greater parsimony. Numerous theories have been advanced in the business management, CSR/Sustainability, and public relations bodies of scholarship—and prove useful for the task. However, many gaps have been exposed and opportunities remain. Importantly, degrees to which two-way symmetry is possible without accounting for power differentials between multinational corporations and even smaller organizations and their stakeholders requires focused and sustained attention by CSR/Sustainability managers and researchers. Perhaps nowhere has this shortcoming been exposed with greater success than when the context involves developing nations already facing their own obstacles of weak government infrastructures, corruption, or general lack of resources to support any common good (Jamali and Keshishian 2009).

Yet, there is much reason to maintain an optimistic attitude toward CSR/ Sustainability insofar as public relations plays an insider-activist role in embedding respect for people, planet, and profit as mutually-dependent goals which cannot be disaggregated. Stakeholder theory and a "names-and-faces approach" (McVea and Freeman 2005: 57) offer a normative framework. Moreover, applying and committing to ethical/moral virtues can navigate organizations toward conditions that support the public sphere and the greater good where genuine relationship building and mutual understanding are possible.

Understanding how public relations supports CSR/Sustainability stakeholder partnership development, implementation, and measurement benefits the public sphere and theory building. Ongoing scrutiny of roles played by nonprofits, NGOs, and pressure and cause groups in moving organizations closer to *the right thing to do* is warranted. Furthermore, CSR/Sustainability programs may lead to even more public relations—possibly a double-edged sword if public relations practitioners continue to focus on self-serving publicity and philanthropy for identity purposes rather than remembering the discipline's relationship-building *raison d'être*. Clarkson (1995) opined that corporations manage relationships with stakeholder groups instead of society on the whole and recommended distinction between social issues and stakeholder issues. A broader perspective suggests that the two are inseparable: the planet Earth and the people who live here. Surely, public relations practitioners charged to manage CSR/Sustainability cannot ignore corporations' track records for ethical and legal lapses and must respond to charges that public relations serves as an enabler for bad behaviors undergirded by self-interest and burgeoning corporate profits. All stakeholders—the entire public sphere—must be able to trust organizations to respect diversity among these groups and to move to the center any who exist in the margins so that their concerns and needs become equal in importance to those of the largest stockholders. Public relations can help with this; encouraging top-management organizational leaders toward organization reform and substantive action—not just while cameras are operating or when annual financial reports or CSR/Sustainability reports are due.

4 Communicating CSR/Sustainability and managing information flows

CSR/Sustainability requires good communication—and public relations practitioners can play an indispensable role when applying their skills in this area for relationship management among organizations and stakeholders. Moreover, the public relations function's potential for insider-activism in CSR/Sustainability contexts complements communication processes. By providing counsel and maximizing organizations' communicative potential, public relations offers a significant contribution to CSR/Sustainability management—and not just when navigating publicity. Ethics is a fundamentally communicative function in service of organization-employers, as well as a public sphere of stakeholder groups and individuals who rely on information and open communication channels for voicing their concerns and participating in problem solving. Yet, communication represents what the Associate Director of Market and Opinion Research International Ltd (MORI) characterized as "the missing link in the practice of corporate responsibility" (Dawkins 2004: 108) and perhaps one reason why organizations' CSR/Sustainability activities may go unacknowledged or underappreciated among both internal and external stakeholders. These points are explored across this chapter's themes of communication management as central to CSR/Sustainability; the public relations–CSR/Sustainability pairing nemesis—Greenwash; language of public texts used in CSR/Sustainability communication; implications of the new media landscape for CSR/Sustainability communication; and communicating through CSR/Sustainability partnerships.

Communication management as central to CSR/Sustainability

Communication management is synonymous with public relations. While Wood (1991b) once opined that few common models or theories explain or predict CSR, we know that today it is the communication function which serves as the tie, binding studies of corporate social responsibility management, sustainability, corporate citizenship, and sustainable development, often with overlapping approaches. Communication is central to all variations on the CSR theme (Clark 2000), perhaps because communication is central to human understanding and performance measurement (Birch 2001). In public relations work, dialog consists of "negotiated exchange of ideas and opinions" (Kent and Taylor 1998: 325) and the Internet and social media increase possibilities for dialog among organizations and the public sphere with regard to CSR/Sustainability, in particular.

Public relations counselors manage CSR/Sustainability communication by using their expertise in writing and speaking in the service of organizations and the public sphere through relationship building. Humans are inter-dependent and public relations practitioners use communication to achieve consensus among organizations and their publics, as well as to harmonize organization–public interests; work that enables public relations to reveal its true potential as a social change agent. Surma (2006) underscored the importance of writing and language as "a crucial dimension of responsible and effective public relations theory and practice" (p. 43). Fostering open communication for the purpose of developing trust and nurturing commitment inside organizations and when supporting two-way symmetrical communication is a task central to effective CSR/Sustainability. The public relations counselor as insider-activist can perform an essential service when advancing open dialog with stakeholders as a member of the CSR/Sustainability team.

The public relations function also manages communication flows to support integration and embeddedness of CSR/Sustainability within organizations and across their geo-political boundaries. Internal communication processes tend to improve with full integration and membership. At Johnson Controls, Inc., Karen Sommer, Director of Global Public Affairs and coordinator of CSR/ Sustainability reporting, detailed how communication supports deep integration of sustainability initiatives:

> [W]e have a global energy and sustainability committee that consists of global representation across our supplier, procurement, communication folks; cross functional representation. As things come up and need action, they're brought to the committee. We meet every other month – sometimes more, sometimes less, depending what's on the agenda. I think that has really brought to light what's going on across the organization to the point that I don't think we're finding challenges from one another on what we should or shouldn't do. It's more we need to do that, how much is it going to cost, where are the funds coming from, how should we prioritize it? … It's led to great corporate initiatives around our operations, procurements. Policies that we have in place are a result of that.

Good communication is required for embedding CSR/Sustainability. Cynthia Figge, COO and Co-Founder of CSRHub and Partner and Co-Founder of EKOS International, US, explained that communication is not just about publicizing profits and goals:

> You can't engage people – stakeholders – because you have efficiently told a story about your *number*. I remember many conversations with professionals

in the field, saying: "We almost have now two different needs – to be very clearly disclosing on goals, how we're doing against goal measurements." Then we also have a need to tell a story about the *company's values*, what we stand for, who we're partnering with, what we're doing in the community, how we're changing the world, essentially. That's been traditionally much more the role of PR. I think now, I see all those functions really working together. When you look at a really sophisticated company like Coca-Cola, for example, it's the reporting itself is still driven out of their communication department. But the *interplay*, where they're drawing all of the information is really complicated. It crosses a lot of boundaries in the company.

Likewise, Consultant Jeff Leinaweaver of Global Zen Sustainability, encouraged public relations managers to use communication to integrate sustainability thinking throughout organizations:

This is where you start seeing overlap between true organizational communication – organizational development and PR that really needs to happen. For the longest time, PR would sit separate from organizational work, per se, maybe be the mouthpiece for it or crafting this perfect story. The problem is that can't go on anymore. The exterior story needs to really start meshing. The tumblers need to all fall into place and what's going on with regard to the true internal organizational work and the metrics – beyond just the carbon metrics, but understanding where's all their waste go? How are they responsible for any chemical effluents? How are they responsible for the community footprint around where their buildings are?

Multiple elements come together and contribute to organizations' communicative activities, globally. Tasks often are managed by public relations in the form of media relations, investor relations, community relations, employee relations, issues management, philanthropy, and sponsorship. At the Norway-owned petroleum company, Statoil, Doug Bannerman currently serves as Leader Social Performance in the North America office and shared an anecdote about the significance of communication for good community relations in the wake of a well pad fire in the USA:

[L]ast week, we had a community meeting ... and a reporter from a local newspaper was speaking with me and I said, "Why *wouldn't* we do this?" It's actually the second one we'd done in two weeks. We had an incident, you know, we want to *work with* this community. We want them to feel like they're our hosts. [At first], we went into lock-down mode. Not exactly the way to build trust. What are you going to do? You're going to have the meeting and we had probably 20 people there to answer questions and we were like, "Ask away. What do you want to know?" We had a presentation and then answered questions. I guess it looked funny because there's still the image in this industry that we're super-secretive and don't want people to know anything and then when we tell people, "The federal and state governments are both doing investigation into the incident. We're doing an investigation also and we'll share the results of that." People are like, "Really?"' and I'm like, "Yeah, that's what we do."

Yet, even though academics and key stakeholders such as governments and activist/pressure groups encourage corporations to enact policies supporting transparency and regular communication with stakeholders as a means of demonstrating responsible behavior (Capriotti and Moreno 2007), organizations are not *required* to communicate about CSR/Sustainability or to maintain any sort of social conscience. However, forward-thinking organizations have discovered that maintaining open and transparent communication with stakeholders pays off in degrees of trust (Ledingham and Bruning 1998).

Including stakeholders as part of CSR/Sustainability programs and fostering communication among them is paramount to CSR/Sustainability success. Research findings suggest that organizations cannot reap the benefits of CSR/ Sustainability practices without effective communication (Maignan and Ferrell 2004) and that even skeptics can become better informed through "intelligent communication of CSR motives" (Kim 2013: 20).

One-way vs. two-way communication is critical to CSR/Sustainability work

Communication's direction—being *talked at* versus being *talked with*—has intrigued public relations scholars for decades and the challenge emerges afresh as public relations interplays with CSR/Sustainability. Debates about one-way versus two-way communication in public relations (J. Grunig 1992, 1993) and public relations practitioners' roles as communication facilitator or technician (Broom 1982; Broom and Dozier 1986) have helped to clarify and elevate public relations' status.

One-way communication occurs when an organization disseminates messages or information. The process is illustrated by the asymmetrical press agentry model (J. Grunig 1992), and characterized as publicity (Surma 2006) or media relations used to influence public opinion (Ewen 1996). By the 1960s, public relations practice often involved using communication to talk about an organization's social responsibility because doing so is good for business (Golden 1968). This framework is consistent with the early Shannon–Weaver sender-receiver communication model (1949). Ultimately, recommendations to amend the Shannon–Weaver communication model's uni-directional platform to one that can be multi-directional while accounting for encoding, decoding, feedback, noise, and context lead to the Wilbur Schramm (1964) communication model. The development supported emergence of the public relations *excellence* paradigm a few decades later (J. Grunig, 1992)—with symmetrical two-way communication designed to inspire organizational behavior change (Mishra 2006: 358). Public relations counselors who embrace the two-way symmetrical communication model can prove themselves valuable assets at organizations' internal CSR/Sustainability-related planning sessions when they are enabled to extend skills beyond publicity in order to affect power de-centralization and to foster open communication lines for ethical dialogic relationships with stakeholders in conjunction with environmental scanning and issues management (Black and Härtel 2004). At Humana, a US-based health-care company, Jim Turner, Director Corporate Communications, explained how he has used communication for coalition building to establish a network of employees committed to CSR:

> [O]ne of our ongoing goals is doing more to make sure everyone feels connected to what's happening with CSR ... [W]hen I discussed our new management team or executive level sponsors, we're hoping, among other things, having those folks in place to be our liaisons to the entire leader-ship team of the company will help us promote the growth of what we're trying to do with CSR throughout the company, including throughout all the acquired companies.

Facing communication management barriers as a public relations counselor

Challenges associated with public relations managers' communication for CSR/Sustainability may be inevitable. Overall, multinational corporations are hard pressed to roll out universal CSR/Sustainability communication programs across geo-political borders unless they are tailored according to cultural expectations among consumers and other stakeholders. In some parts of the world, economic structures thwart CSR/Sustainability impulses. See (2009) found that the 2005 rollout of a "Harmonious Society" policy in China may have been designed with an eye toward private-enterprise-development-with-a-conscience, yet "constraints" and "political considerations" further complicate a measure that appears to have much in common with CSR (p. 1).

Public relations' hierarchical status and physical location in organizations presents a significant internal communication challenge for CSR/Sustainability programs. Public relations counselors may fail to garner CEO support (Kim and Reber 2008); a particularly disappointing dilemma given that CEOs consider public relations to be a uni-directional publicity arm (Benn, Todd, and Pendleton 2010). Within corporations, the public relations function often is housed within and reports to marketing, human resources, corporate affairs, or corporate communication departments. Even though a handful of corporations are developing CSR or Sustainability departments, recent studies suggest that public relations is rarely the "source of CSR direction" (Benn, Todd, and Pendleton 2010: 419). Nancy Mancilla, CEO and Co-founder of ISOS Group, a CSR consulting firm in the USA, opined that negative per-ceptions of public relations' internal role in the CSR/Sustainability mix could dissipate over time. She added that practitioners always may encounter internal resistance when working to produce consumer-friendly messages about highly complex issues:

> As PR becomes more aware and educated about how different departments work together, as CSR becomes more "institutionalized" the critique will fade. It's complex and PR people are required to simplify. What PR writes has to go through many channels for approval, the lawyers, and what comes out is diluted and then media change it more. They have to write in a certain way and it is perceived as insubstantial to the media. PR people write in terms of stories – and while that can be useful for the media, the media do not have a positive reaction to that sometimes. There's a learning curve for PR.

The public relations–CSR/Sustainability pairing nemesis – Greenwash

Perhaps the steepest barrier for public relations in managing CSR/Sustainability communication is battling skeptics among media, activist groups, and others, who consider public relations to be disingenuous, deception, spin, puffery, publicity, window dressing, and greenwash. Overlap of the public relations and CSR/Sustainability literatures reveals two related varieties of cynicism toward corporations' "good works" and public relations' role in communicating about CSR/Sustainability: 1) negative public perceptions associated with *paid* communication services, and 2) self-promotion and one-way communication. Public relations managers shoulder negative perceptions of their profession akin to those in marketing, sales, and advertising (e.g., Ewen 1996). When attempting to create and promote a "socially responsible image," marketing ranks with accounting and finance among consumers' most distrusted departments within a corporation (Jahdi and Acikdilli 2009: 103). Image advertising used for CSR/Sustainability purposes stands out as particularly "embarrassing self-congratulatory rhetoric" (Ihlen 2013: 209). On the other hand, strategic organizational responses used to manage potential risk issues are among communication materials developed as part of CSR/Sustainability programs, public relations campaigns, and issues advocacy advertising. For example, Mobil Corporation's CEO during the 1970s and 1980s took to advertorials placed in *Time* magazine to put across the petroleum company's perspectives on issues such as domestic versus foreign oil supplies and oil industry taxes; a move that predated social media and strategically enabled the company to control the message (Gerow 2013). Even corporate websites' mission/vision statements' profit-centric motives undergird claims of quality, value, and moral goodness and can contribute to low credibility among distrusting stakeholders (Jung and Pompper 2014).

The public relations profession was borne of using communication to support organizations that want to have a voice, even when what they represent or have to say may prove unpopular. The "father of modern public relations"— Ivy Ledbetter Lee—suffered reputational damage after working with the

Soviet Union in the 1920s and Germany's Nazi Party in the 1930s (Hiebert, 2013: 512). Today, public relations trade organizations the world over seek to protect the profession by offering codes of ethics, guidelines, seminars, and training so that practitioners may avoid ethics breaches—including the Public Relations Society of America (PRSA) in the USA, the International Public Relations Association (IPRA), and the European Public Relations Education and Research Association (EUPRERA). "Green attempts" fall flat in the wake of negative environmental impact (Jahdi and Acikdilli 2009: 107), particularly among industries of coal mining, steel manufacturing, chemical manufacturing (Cox 2013), as well as lead-acid recycling and smelting, ore processing, tannery operations, industrial/municipal dumping, gold mining, product manufacturing, and the dye industry ("Top Ten Polluting" n.d.).

In the service of these and other industries, public relations has earned a reputation for using communication merely to boost organizational reputation and/or image rather than to affect positive organizational change. Growing skepticism among stakeholder groups turns even the most informative of CSR/ Sustainability stories into greenwash believed to be motivated by corporations' profit-centric worldview and unwillingness to offer transparency, or to build real relationships with stakeholders. However, public relations insider-activists' use of communication to directly involve stakeholders in CSR/Sustainability planning, activities and measurement could affect real, infrastructural change in such industries. Jenny Carty, Reporting and Governance Manager at Royal Bank of Scotland (RBS), explained that being responsible includes careful and strategic thinking before communicating. She shared a particular challenge inherent to the UK finance industry—generating sustainability program publicity in the wake of a UK government's 2008 bailout:

> As a team, we receive feedback from colleagues that questions why do we not do more PR for the programs that we run at the moment – investments in the community that we make. We feel as a team, I suppose, the guy who heads up the Corporate Affairs team feels that because our standing and the protection of the brand is so low and so damaged that it wouldn't be appropriate to go out with positive stories on where we're investing money because: a) we're still owned by the taxpayer and b) stakeholders aren't ready for those kind of stories just yet.

Public relations counselors would do well to avoid extensive reliance on one-way communication activities—by diversifying talents in the service of CSR/ Sustainability programs. Management of *"communicative aspects"* of an organization's activities (as opposed to crafting *"activities for external communication purposes"*) should constitute public relations' role in CSR (Benn, Todd, and Pendleton 2010: 417) (italics in original).

Corporations carefully deliberate about whether or not to respond to negative news media coverage which accuses them of acting *ir*responsibly or *un*sustainably—especially when the context is a widely distributed documentary film featuring interviews with activist groups that paint an unflattering portrait. Businesses generally seek to avoid negative publicity and appearing as acquiescing to pressure groups, but also may want to tell *their side* of a story without appearing too defensive. Here is where public relations counselors have proven invaluable as crisis communication management experts. Larissa Grunig's (1986, 1992) early case studies about public relations crises and activism found that news media coverage was minimal and balanced. However, documentary filmmakers have popularized corporation bashing at least since the late 1980s with *Roger and Me* (Moore 1989), *Food Inc.* (Kenner 2008), *Super Size Me* (Morley and Spurlock 2004), *Wal-Mart: The High Price of Low Cost* (Levit and Greenwald 2005), *Blackfish* (Cowperthwaite 2013) and more. Elsewhere, I argued that grassroots activism plus news media coverage which frames debates and shapes public opinion about corporations has grown too significant to ignore. So, corporations usually choose among corporate response typologies of *corrective action* or *defiance/attacking-the-accuser* (Pompper and Higgins 2007). Erin Fitzgerald, Senior Vice President, Sustainability at Innovation Center for US Dairy, opined about public relations as liaison between organizations and the news media; an indispensable tool for CSR/Sustainability communication and crisis events:

> We always joke that it would be easy to just quit and do an exposé documentary about everything that's wrong with the food industry. I think that people who are in this space – such as sustainability reporting – are trying to quantify the good and the bad and actually work on solving the issues, which is ten times harder. I think that's where the license of how does PR fit into the sustainability reporting of actually telling the story ... We just need to get people behind them and start focusing on the solutions as opposed to all the negative stuff. There's so much science behind the data that proves we can solve this today. But everyone's still into that fear mongering ...

Also at Innovation Center for US Dairy, Erin Coffield, Vice President, Health and Wellness Communications, explained that two-way communication benefits consumers:

> From the standpoint of the *Food Inc.*s and *Fed Up*s and various books that are out there, because of what we're doing, it helps us to provide the facts versus the sensation and scare mongering. Interestingly enough, a lot of these books and films are taking things from 15 and 20 years ago without reaching out to us to find out what innovations and troubleshooting and solutions we've been working on. Flavored milk is a perfect example. They always bash the industry as a whole for flavored milk in schools – but the industry joined together almost six years ago to address added sugars in flavored milk. Now, it's just a minimal amount that's in flavored milk. It's only about 25 calories more than white milk.

Discovering why cynicism and mistrust about public relations persists and is exacerbated when linked with CSR/Sustainability efforts demands introspection about its free-market enterprise underpinnings. Corporations' emphases on short-term planning and quarter-by-quarter earnings undergirds public relations thinking, too—in terms of generating publicity as a reputation building strategy to favorably appeal to investors and stockholders. CSR/ Sustainability's roots as a business strategy for maximizing long-term profits, public relations professions' notorious publicity function, and its media relations focus—combined with the enormity of decades' worth of corporate wrongdoing and recent accounting scandals with global implications perpetrated at WorldCom, Enron, Adelphia, Tyco International, Qwest, Global Crossings, and other large corporations—explains much low regard for public relations in CSR/Sustainability. The more frequently organizations promote their CSR/Sustainability activities, the greater amounts of public criticism they gather (Morsing and Schultz 2006). Grunig (1993) argued a little over 20 years ago about a "paradigm struggle" in the field, opining that public relations practitioners had grown preoccupied with images and symbolism and had forgotten that public relations is in the business of building "substantive behavioral relationships between organizations and publics" (p. 121). Publicity may work when consumers believe an organization's motives are sincere, but not when they are perceived as ambiguous or hypocritical (Yoon, Gürhan-Canli, and Schwarz 2006). Ihlen (2013) warned that "[a]ttempting to hide the profit motive does not help improve a corporation's reputation" (p. 209) and Kim (2013) suggested that one means to combat CSR skepticism is for organizations to be fully transparent about self-serving motives while simultaneously touting society-serving motives. Some public relations researchers have found that companies with established, positive reputations among stakeholders find it easier to deflect CSR/Sustainability skepticism than their poor-reputation counterparts (Kim 2013). Other findings suggest that people are actually inspired to dig deeper to reveal CSR program motives when a company's reputation is poor (Szykman, Bloom, and Blazing, 2004). Moreover, Ihlen (2013) opined that CSR programs can help some organizations to build a "halo effect" and positive media attention.

Language of public texts used in CSR/Sustainability communication

Public relations practitioners use their persuasive writing and speech skills on behalf of organizations; co-creators of narratives used to communicate with stakeholders. As addressed in Chapter 3, language used to describe stakeholders reveals much about relationships among organizations and the public sphere. Also, narratives are powerful tools used by organizations to affect public opinion (Crowson 2009; Elkington 1999). Some researchers find these processes inherently flawed. Moloney (2000) drew upon the capitalist roots of big business, media, and political institutions to characterize public relations as supporting powerful voices while silencing those less powerful—and Surma (2006) opined that social practices of writing and speaking-for-hire introduces inauthenticity to communication processes since "preferred rhetorical discourses" are severed from their sponsor (p. 58). Examining ways organizations' narratives are constructed and perceived can reveal much about how to affect change and to create successful CSR/ Sustainability programs. For example, asking employees to share stories about acceptance of and resistance to sustainability projects they had worked on, Stoughton and Ludema (2012) posited that change and commitment occurs at three levels—organizational (senior leadership) by aligning sustainability with business priorities, functional (managers) by developing tools and programs, and individual (employees) by interpreting tasks through personal lenses shaped by cultural influences. Across organizations, leaders and managers prioritize and construct narratives about sustainability in their own way (Cherrier, Russell, and Fielding 2012).

Companies have found that telling their side of a CSR/Sustainability story often is best shared in reports they produce themselves—and Dawkins (2004) posited that over time, companies are producing more and longer reports. As detailed in Chapter 7, some organizations blend CSR/Sustainability reporting with their regular annual report, while others post online pdfs and devote microsites to CSR/Sustainability. Readers include employees, activists, investors and analysts, consultants, NGOs, news media, think-tanks, and more. Publishing reports on a company's CSR/Sustainability activities is essential to gaining credibility among stakeholders and for demonstrating compliance with Global Reporting Initiative (GRI) and other standards. Only 50 organizations published reports when GRI guidelines were first published in 2000 (Epstein-Reeves 2011). According to GRI Director, North America, Eric Israel, nearly 6000 companies now produce sustainability reports and 80% or more use GRI guidelines. CSR/Sustainability ranks among corporate webpages' most accessed links—especially among job-hunting college graduates (Dawkins 2004). The website, glassdoor.com, regularly features employee reviews of companies, often expressing opinions about CSR/Sustainability-related topics. CSR/Sustainability reports have been characterized as strategic messaging via "slick" publications (Surma 2006: 52) and "glossy corporate" images (Jahdi and Acikdilli 2009: 110).

Content analyses of CSR/Sustainability reports' words and visuals reveal a number of universal themes that bring to bear on perceptions about authenticity. Rämö's (2011) content analysis findings of CSR/Sustainability reports suggested that companies tend to focus on some *future* point in time by talking about what they anticipate doing rather than offering here-and-now assessments. Another research team found that CSR/Sustainability reports are heavy on visuals and photographic images (Breitbarth, Harris, and Insch 2010). Talking about the future and emphasizing photographic imagery could mean that organizations put up a smokescreen. Invoking Bourdieu (1990), Halverson (2004) warned that use of beautiful imagery in this way obfuscates and fails to make "practical wisdom" accessible (p. 90). Use of a "journey metaphor" in the reports strategically precludes communication of any concrete details, a move that masks real problems (Milne, Kearins, and Walton 2006).

Implications of the new media landscape for CSR/Sustainability communication

The number of messaging media available to public relations practitioners for communicating with internal and external stakeholders has exploded in recent decades. Two-way communication, as promoted with interactive tools, is possible on Web 2.0 for high levels of stakeholder engagement and feedback to help ensure understanding gained by examining counter-narratives and stakeholder needs; dynamics which may lead to CSR/Sustainability initiatives (Fieseler, Fleck, and Meckel 2010). The World Wide Web is used to "push" an unlimited amount of information to stakeholders, but it also serves as a "pull" medium by active information seekers (Pollach 2005). Online exchanges among stakeholders and organizations support CSR/Sustainability work as mutually engaging communication contact points which can lead to raising awareness of issues, establishing priorities, and sharing ideas for solving problems and creating opportunities. New technologies help organizations to satisfy stakeholders' demands for accountability and transparency (Capriotti and Moreno 2007). Information diffusion about CSR/Sustainability programs via online channels has high utility for organizations (Godes and Mayzlin 2004). Also, stakeholders increasingly rely on Internet sources for company and product information (Dellarocas 2006). David Stangis, Vice President of Public Affairs and Corporate Responsibility at Campbell's Soup Company, said: "People most of the time now just reach out to us via social media. We do use email; it's there and we monitor it. People know they can get a pretty quick answer. We keep a separate page on the website just for Campbell's CSR." With so many choices as to where to place messages, the urge to use this messaging landscape simply to disseminate symbolic communication in the form of publicity must be great. So, public relations communicators must discern between *symbolic communication* (what an organization says about itself) and *behavioral communication* (reflections of an organization's actions) (Grunig 1993) and avoid a preponderance of one-way asymmetrical messaging. Organizations that engage in behavioral communication stand a better chance of maximizing new and social media as a foundation for two-way symmetrical, mutually-beneficial and long-term stakeholder relationships.

Much CSR/Sustainability reporting and information-seeking takes place online, and public relations managers sometimes use these communication tools to circumnavigate traditional media gatekeepers—and to set their own agenda to engage one-on-one with stakeholders. Where once mass mediated messages were filtered by editors, assignment editors, and others, now individuals and groups may send messages themselves via Internet message vehicles, such as producing websites, blogs, Facebook pages, Twitter feeds, and more. However, the social media landscape so fills corporate communicators and attorneys with trepidation that they confessed late adoption of online communication vehicles due to risks associated with organization/brand preservation, offensive/defensive monitoring, and litigation avoidance (Pompper and Crider 2012). Stohl (2013) opined that CSR increasingly forms part of the global institutional landscape, featuring a "simultaneous loosening of boundaries and tightening of the connectedness associated with new media." Brenda Colatrella, Executive Director, Corporate Responsibility at Merck & Co., Inc., spoke of online chats as a useful tool for collecting stakeholder feedback at this pharmaceutical company:

> We've engaged 10–12 stakeholders in a one-hour long online chat room to get their perspectives. We've used a variety of mechanisms. At the end of the day, if you're not providing information that's meaningful to the people who care about this, then you're not really doing the job. From a stakeholder standpoint, it's really important. Then on a regular basis as part of our corporate responsibility function, we engage with social responsibility investors – planned meetings with set agendas. We'll engage with policymakers, advocacy groups to better understand what they're interested in, what are their expectations of a company. And for us to gauge how we're responding to that … [It] allows people to be very open about they're thinking, saying, and feeling. That information, we go through it with a fine tooth comb. Where are we doing well? Where could we perhaps report more robustly on something? Is there an issue that we haven't addressed as a company that came out through this stakeholder engagement? It's more of an internal tool for us to better understand … [I]t's educational and informative … We're actually trying to understand from them what they feel that we're doing well, what we're not doing as well. From a reporting perspective, are we reporting to the level that they feel is useful to them?

In recent years, significant space has been awarded social media and public relations in academic journals, textbooks, and conference papers. Both definitions of *public relations* and *new/social media* emphasize engagement, participation, and two-way communication (Kelleher 2010). Interactivity may be the Internet's primary attribute and this continues to intrigue researchers (e.g., Schultz 2000). We know that online communication platforms and social media tools such as blogs, wikis, and social networking sites such as Twitter and Facebook are conducive to participation and involvement of stakeholders with corporate decision-makers. CEOs see value in the Internet with regard to communication about/for CSR, but are highly cautious about it (Lee, Hwang, and Lee 2006). Karen Sommer, Director of Global Public Affairs and coordinator of CSR/Sustainability reporting at Johnson Controls, Inc., explained that social media, as a communication tool, plays only a small role in the company's mix:

We're just starting to dabble our feet into the social media space as a company. What we're finding out is that companies are a lot more susceptible to bad PR, just as much as good PR via social media. People having cameras and videos capturing it instantaneously – good or bad – and being able to respond appropriately.

Hence, much formal CSR/Sustainability reporting remains unidirectional—one-way communication of information launched at stakeholders (Young and Benamati 2000); quickly devolving into a marketing tactic for promoting a positive image/reputation which misses the mark of fostering open and transparent communication with stakeholders (Kent, Taylor, and White 2003).

CSR/Sustainability issues appeal to stakeholders beyond customers, employees (including prospective ones), competitors, and investors who use their websites. Watchdog groups, such as the Center for Media Democracy's SourceWatch (a sister site to PRWatch.org), are concerned about economic and political issues associated with CSR/Sustainability and frequent corporate websites to monitor degrees of corporations' authenticity in CSR/Sustainability commitments and to campaign against those perceived to be engaging in greenwash: "CMD strengthens participatory democracy by investigating and exposing public relations spin and propaganda such as corporate greenwashing, and by promoting media literacy and citizen journalism" (Center for Media and Democracy n.d.) Specific CSR/Sustainability communication vehicles are examined next.

Websites

The Internet and information platforms collectively referred to as Web 2.0, which create the World Wide Web, has become an essential organizational communication medium. Public relations communicators have maximized the trend in the USA (Kent, Taylor, and White 2003), Europe (Maignan and Ralston 2002), India (Sagar and Singla 2004), and around the globe. Websites have become a ubiquitous communication tool (Stuart and Jones 2004); important for corporate communicators (Esrock and Leichty 2000), employees, customers, and shareholders (Connolly-Ahern and Broadway 2007), as well as journalists (Kent and Taylor 2003).

Interactivity is a complex theoretical concept, but researchers have found practical ways to interrogate behaviors associated with *liking* and general *involvement* online. Guillory and Sundar (2014) examined mediated relationships between websites and users and discovered that much more is going on in terms of perception-shaping than meets the eye. About 70% of IBEX-35 organizations (Spanish Exchange Index) devoted part of their websites to CSR/Sustainability (Capriotti and Moreno 2007). Specifically, public relations practitioners have advocated for effective Web design to boost stakeholder interaction (Springston 2001) since research findings suggest that greater perceptions of company website interactivity among users may lead to more positive attitudes toward the company (McMillan, Hwang, and Lee 2003). Corporations began creating home pages in the late 1990s and principles for online relationship building include dialogic feedback loop, usefulness of information, generation of return visits, intuitiveness/ease of interface, and conversation rules (Kent and Taylor 2002). Brenda Colatrella, Executive Director, Corporate Responsibility at Merck & Co., Inc., shared the merits of creating a corporate responsibility website that is distinct from the main corporate site, but is accessible from the landing page:

> It's its own site, but very much aligned with other websites, including merck.com. It is the one place where you can really see exactly what we're doing, what our progress, our performance has been in the area of corporate responsibility ... affords us the opportunity to report out more robustly about what we're doing from a corporate responsibility perspective ... having a separate site actually gives us the opportunity to speak more fully to corporate responsibility. The feedback we've gotten from our internal and external stakeholders has been very positive. Folks feel like they can go to that site and get a good feel for what our priorities are in corporate responsibility, what some of our programs are, our activities, the progress we're making on performance.

Corporate websites serve as a key channel for managing organization–public relationships with regard to CSR/Sustainability, but there is room for improvement. Elsewhere, I found that more than half of managers who head a department or division devoted exclusively to CSR, characterized their websites as moving cautiously and slowly; stuck in an infrastructure-crafting phase (Pompper 2013). Jeff Leinaweaver of Global Zen Sustainability, a US-based consulting firm, describes himself on the firm's website as a "sustainability strategist" and a "positive deviant," counseling clients on avoiding greenwash on websites: "Are we telling authentic stories? Is there a courageousness in the stories you tell or not? I look at Intel or HP—who've courageously taken on conflict minerals and they're doing a lot to try to educate people about what's going on. Apple, as well." Among business media, analysts and investors, Dawkins (2004) found that companies' information about environmental and social issues was poor. Moreover, corporate websites tend to promote unidirectional graphic imagery rather than offering interactive two-way communication mechanisms dialoging (Capriotti and Moreno 2007); two-way message boards are rare (Robbins and Stylianou 2003). Hence, feedback loops are limited or nonexistent on many corporate websites. According to Webb (2005), a website is truly interactive when it enables users to "directly contribute permanently archived and linked content to a site ... The gold standard is that users can change the navigation of a website and/or the order and visibility of content on a site." This advice has been echoed among public relations researchers who have suggested that website interactivity can be boosted with even minimal resources (Guillory and Sundar 2014).

Blogs

Weblogs (shortened to *blogs*) have captured the imagination of corporations as a means for publishing and managing content to promote its strategic goals. A network called the blogosphere has emerged from comments and links in blogs on the Internet (Schmidt 2007). In the process, corporations also promote the appearance of interactivity with stakeholders about CSR/Sustainability on websites—what one research team characterized as a "valuable new practice ... new horizon" for nurturing micro-dialogues (Fieseler, Fleck and Meckl 2010: 599). Blogs look like short diary entries based on the personal opinions of their authors, which appear in reverse chronological order with space at the bottom for readers to post comments. Smudde (2005) described the act: "To blog is to continually post one's own ideas, opinions, Internet links ..." (p. 34). Much of blog content is dialog based and Lenhart (2006) found that readers are often more attracted to comments accompanying posts than the blogs themselves. Generally, CSR/Sustainability-related blogs provide a forum for ongoing discussions and a font of data for audience and issue research used to inform policy and campaigns.

The weblog medium suggests the possibility of full democratic self expression among sponsors and visitors; a potentially useful medium for organizations. Corporate blogs feature top-down strategies based on "thought leadership or promotional content strategy" (Lee, Hwang, and Lee 2006: 316). Often, public relations managers write blogs or ghost write them for CEOs (Gallicano, Brett, and Hopp 2013). Interviews conducted with CSR/Sustainability and public relations professionals for this book revealed high degrees of concern about bottom-up blogging strategies (posts originating among employees and unfiltered through managers), as suggested a public relations manager at a US-based health organization: "Blogs, unlike traditional media can be very difficult to control or even provide responses to ... It's made the PR world a much more difficult place to work in." One means for controlling blog content is eliminating autonomy by assigning a moderator and by featuring rules and terms for participation. Disney Post, an official Disney website blog, explains that visitors' posts must pass approval by official Disney gatekeepers before appearing on its website ("Comment Policy" n.d.):

> Thanks for visiting Disney Post, an official Disney blog. We welcome your comments. Please understand that this is a moderated blog. Blog comments will be reviewed prior to posting. As a result, there will be a delay in the posting of comments. Not all comments will be posted. Comments may also be removed after they are posted. Please see our **Terms of Use** for more information [bold in original].

Jones (2005) called blog-comments a "Wild West" environment featuring multiple high-profile and very public disputes between employees and employers playing out publicly on the Internet. On the other hand, some employee blogs on corporate websites exemplify good will. For example, Southwest Airlines' *Nuts about Southwest* blog features posts by employees who encourage co-workers to support CSR/Sustainability efforts by going green and halting junk mail (Allen 2013). Such blogs tap into online behavioral research findings which suggest that net-generation employees offer organizations a competitive advantage due to their strong brand loyalty (Hannegan 2004). Five types of corporate blogs have been identified among the Fortune 500 firms that sponsor blogs and use a top-down blogging strategy: employee, group (several focusing on a specific topic), executive, promotional, and newsletter (Lee, Hwang, and Lee 2006).

Facebook and Twitter

Facebook is a dialogic website featuring simple opportunities for sponsors and visitors to post wall comments and to discuss issues of mutual interest and significance in real time. So popular is the social media phenomenon that 15 million brands use the social network (Koetsier 2013). As a branding medium, Facebook is useful for generating product publicity and communicating about brand personality qualities of *excitement* and *sincerity* (De Moya and Jain 2013). Even among nonprofit organizations such as the American Red Cross and environmental advocacy groups, the two-way dialogic platform and its potential for relationship building on Facebook is not maximized (Bortree and Seltzer 2009). Swiss-based Nestlé Corporation uses Facebook to counter a 1970s boycott over a controversy that occurred when developing world babies died after mothers mixed its infant formula powder with contaminated local water. Today, with its Creating Shared Value organizational structure and Facebook page, Nestlé champions combined issues of nutrition, clean water, rural development, environment, sourcing, and human rights ("Nestlé" n.d.) In this way, Nestlé is managing an issue that never will go away by taking it head on, working to eradicate its former reputation as "the Baby Killer," so dubbed by War on Want, a London activist group (Muller 1974; Solomon 1981: 92). Thus, public relations practitioners in charge of issues management frequently work in a CSR/Sustainability context when they help companies to find and avoid threats. Another social media vehicle launched in 2006 and increasingly gaining in popularity among public relations practitioners is Twitter, an online social networking and microblogging service. Twitter boasts 271 million monthly active users, with 500 million Tweets sent per day ("Our Mission" n.d.) Twitter's 140-character limit for instant messages (Tweets) offers a primary benefit for public relations' use due to its real-time simplicity and portability in mobile, wireless, and instant messaging applications. However, as with blogging, both Facebook and Twitter suffer *authenticity* concerns among stakeholders because one never really knows the true identity of social media communicators (Ali 2013) and this has ethical implications for the public relations profession and CSR/Sustainability applications. Both Facebook and Twitter may be underused as dialogic communication tools for stakeholder relationship building (Rybalko and Seltzer 2010), yet many organizations create distinct Facebook pages to promote their CSR/Sustainability initiatives.

Communicating through CSR/Sustainability partnerships

Open and mutual communication about CSR/Sustainability is required for partnerships to work among for-profit firms as well as between for-profit and nonprofit organizations—including NGOs. Both remain popular business approaches (Austin 2000) and strategic alliances are well acknowledged in policy areas of environmentalism and public health. The popularity of public–private partnerships has grown out of organizations' creative approaches to "looking across sector boundaries for new ways to meet their own needs" (Sagawa and Segal 2000: 106). CSR/Sustainability program partnerships among corporations and between corporations and nonprofits exceed philanthropic giving, which proved so popular in cause marketing campaigns during the twentieth century's latter decades. Today, potential partners perform risk assessment investigations for compatibility before sitting down to sign contracts. So, from inception to final evaluation, strong communication remains an essential component of partnerships. Susan Sabatino, Account Manager, Marketing Partnerships Team at the Nature Conservancy, explained that communication between a for-profit corporation and its nonprofit partner may be the most important ingredient of the relationship:

> [W]e're trying to do a good job of staying connected, so nothing comes out and hits us in the face. We have found out about companies doing charitable self-promotions to benefit the Nature Conservancy without us even knowing about it and that's a big no-no. Companies should never do that. Obviously, they should engage with the nonprofit before ever using our logo or name before promoting their products. So, a couple of times we've had to work through that with a company.

These partnerships feature unique communication issues in CSR/Sustainability programming. Jamali and Keshishian's (2009) examination of five partnerships between for-profits and NGOs featured a lack of collaboration and strategic communication in terms of aligning goals, expectations, and commitment; outcomes which contributed to an inability to move beyond minimal expectations. Royal Bank of Scotland partnered with the NGO, Prince's Trust, and put together a virtual team for a CSR effort which included Prince's Trust's communications manager and RBS's media relations manager. Upon close inspection, however, power differentials between the two organizations manifested when RBS expected the Prince's Trust to perform a reporting function comparable to that of a counseling firm on retainer (Seitanidi and Crane 2009). Partnering among for-profit businesses and nonprofits is not without its critics. Munshi and Kurian (2005) warned of potential ethical complications when for-profit corporations sponsor environmental groups such as the Nature Conservancy and the World Wildlife Fund as a means to boost their "green image" (p. 516). Moreover, Moloney (2006) advanced the concept of "CSR subsidy" (p. 110) as a resource made available to nonprofits by for-profit corporations to support the nonprofit's causes.

Discussion

There has been no dearth of academic researchers in public relations, communication management, and strategic communication who offer advice on ways to use communication to boost corporate image and reputation. However, communication processes as they affect CSR/Sustainability represents an under-researched arena (Aguinis and Glavas 2012). Also less travelled are investigations of the broader view on actively involving the public sphere and respecting stakeholder groups as partners in CSR/Sustainability; a foundation for open communication and transparency. Here is where public relations may draw inspiration from the postmodern impulse as an insider-activist to lead and guide corporations toward ethical behavior as it plays out in policy making, infrastructural change, authentic partnerships or collective action with activist groups and other stakeholders beyond simply stockholders and investors.

Public relations practitioners have a duty to both employers and the public sphere—to sift through, interpret, and communicate about issues integral to CSR/Sustainability. Precisely here is where public relations counselors may stand apart from other managers in their communication expertise and guardianship of relationship-building among the organization and its collective stakeholders; a perspective comparable to those shared by Van Ruler and Verčič (2005) and articulated as "a capability development role" (Benn, Todd, and Pendleton 2010: 419). Perhaps, also, this is what Steyn and Bütschi (2004) may have intended when they recommended that public relations take a more significant leadership role in organizations. Transparency paired with open communication is a critical component of ethical CSR/Sustainability programs— for organizations and for the public sphere of groups and individuals impacted. Unfortunately, these two standpoints often are at odds and expose a legitimacy gap (Sethi 1977); a divide between organizations' behaviors and what members of the public sphere think the organization *should* believe and do. Minimizing conflict and maximizing understanding among organizations and stakeholders in issues management contexts also holds true for CSR/Sustainability communication, which Heath (2013a) considers a "subdiscipline of public relations" (p. 496).

Overall, public relations counselors engaged with CSR/Sustainability activities must discern between simply *creating and getting stories out there* and providing *information of substance*. Enabling public relations to serve as the insider-activist and to use communication as a means to support organizations in authentically embracing CSR/Sustainability shifts the focus from simply performing one-way asymmetrical, symbolic reputation/image work to a two-way symmetrical communication-driven mindset for keeping organizations ethical and mutually linked to stakeholders and the larger public sphere. For some organizations, this could represent a seachange. However, making it a reality would directly respond to critics' charges that organizations come up far short in any real commitment to ethical CSR/Sustainability and resort to using communication for greenwash. Hence, public relations must have access to policy making and gain the respect of senior management. Bonyton (2002) framed CSR as an important heuristic for balancing organizational with stakeholder interests, while others also consider CSR as a platform for expanding the "repertoire of communication activities available to achieve organizational goals" (Benn, Todd, and Pendleton 2010: 406). This stance separates public relations from cause marketing campaigns and point of purchase product/labeling strategies. Also, public relations insider-activists should work closely with industry leaders to help them demonstrate that they *walk the talk*.

Perhaps no communication vehicle is more potent for engaging with the public sphere and individual stakeholder groups *interactively* and in real time than social media and the Internet and the communication tools available there. Researchers continue to probe techniques for using them to assess CSR/ Sustainability effectiveness and to maximize opportunities to connect with stakeholder groups. Stewart (2003) recommended that corporations form liaisons with NGOs, governmental regulatory departments, universities, and nonprofits by providing links on their websites to these groups. Also, I worry that a preponderance of attention to social media in academic journals and trade publications for its utility as a publicity tool could threaten a throwback to one-way asymmetrical practice which public relations scholars have fought against since the 1980s. Instead, these new communication channels' value for stakeholder relationship building and CSR/Sustainability program research await widespread use.

5 Engaging employees with CSR/Sustainability

Public relations makes a substantive contribution when directly involving employees in CSR/Sustainability programs within organizations and enabling them to connect externally as volunteers providing community services in support of organizational CSR/Sustainability goals. As a key stakeholder group, researchers often overlook employees even though they increasingly play a central role in linking CSR/Sustainability across organizations' departments and geographic locations. Cynthia Figge, COO and Co-Founder of CSRHub and Partner and Co-Founder of EKOS International, US, explained: "[O]ver time, companies came to realize that one of the most important stakeholders is internal: the employees." Indeed, May (2009) warned against aiming CSR/Sustainability projects exclusively at external publics because doing so may lend an appearance of inauthenticity and raise concerns about organizations' ability to involve diverse sets of stakeholders—starting with their own employees. Brenda Colatrella, Executive Director of Corporate Responsibility at Merck, explained integration of corporate responsibility goals and programs throughout this pharmaceutical company:

> So it's not only a top-down approach ... [O]ne of the things we like to say around here is that corporate responsibility is not just the responsibility of the Office of Corporate Responsibility. It's the responsibility of every employee at Merck. So, it's really important that we do what we have to do to embed this into the organization to get not only our senior management and CEO aware of these issues and buying into this approach, but also people at every level of Merck.

Social exchange theory helps to explain a variety of techniques used to connect internal and external organizational stakeholders through CSR/Sustainability efforts. In addition to disseminating information about CSR/Sustainability and collecting feedback, organizations may directly involve employees as community volunteers, or provide matching gifts, loan executives, install employees on nonprofit boards to interact with government and community leaders, and deliver community-based nonprofit information on corporate websites. Providing free services to people and donating one's own time and energy as a community volunteer may take place either formally (employer-sponsored) or informally (employees find their own). Social exchange theory explains and predicts psychological or social resource transfer processes. For example, employees who volunteer as part of employer-sponsored community activities may anticipate being rewarded by their employer in some way. Moreover, organizations have found that by offering up their employees' time and energy in support of community efforts further cements perceptions that the organization has an authentic community commitment (Flynn 2005). These dynamics have proved particularly effective when a company caused negative impact in the first place, such as by cleaning up waterways it may have polluted (Young-Ybarra and Wiersema 1999). This chapter addresses employee engagement in CSR/Sustainability from a number of vantage points according to themes of making the business case for strategic CSR/Sustainability through employee participation, employee stakeholders and public relations, and employee volunteerism's dark side.

Making the business case for strategic CSR/Sustainability through employee participation

In recent decades, corporations have shifted from simply giving away money through donations—pure philanthropy—to proving their social commitment by strategically linking altruistic motives with CSR/Sustainability goals. One successful means for accomplishing this transition has been for corporations to make a business case argument: a rationale for charitable giving so long as it contributes to (or does not drain from) profits. Acting on CSR/Sustainability goals enables corporations to react to perceptions that a business should prove itself and earn society's license to operate (Van Luijk 2000). For example, developing employee volunteerism programs for *giving back to the community* while building and maintaining stakeholder relationships has enabled corporations to enhance their reputation which, inadvertently, creates shareholder value. Providing employees as part of community outreach programs enables organizations to move away from old-fashioned philanthropy, widely considered to constitute greenwashing due to inauthentic motivations, as discussed in Chapter 3. Employee volunteerism also enhances community-government relationships (Steel 1995) and fosters trust and cooperation at work (Ledingham and Bruning 1998); important considerations for gaining support of CSR/Sustainability programs and when battling for favorable public opinion in conjunction with downsizing, scandal, and mergers/acquisitions. Investors favor corporations that demonstrate strong community involvement in this manner (Stone 2001). Volunteerism has been qualified as "the typical US corporation's historical response to the need to establish its corporate citizenship" (Waddock 2007: 74). Using employees to support external non-profits and more loosely-defined community groups is considered an "inside-out approach" in Denmark (Morsing, Schultz, and Nielsen 2008: 97). In Canada, researchers have found that growth in corporate employee volunteerism programs corresponds to decreasing government support traditionally given to nonprofit service organizations and initiatives (Foster and Meinhard 2002). Canada, the Netherlands, and Nordic countries feature higher volunteerism rates than the USA (Curtis, Baer, and Grabb 2001), with about 25% of all formal volunteer activities in Canada sponsored by employers (Luffman 2003). Many of the USA's largest companies strategically link employee volunteer programs with important business issues because doing so enhances a corporation's public image (Wild 1993). US volunteers spent an average of 50 hours annually and about 64.5 million people (1.3%) performed at least one kind of volunteer service either "through or for" an organization (US Department of Labor 2012).

Globally, organizations' CSR/Sustainability service projects tend to cluster into specific areas. Organizations receiving the most volunteer support in the USA include religious (33.1%), educational or youth services (25.5%), and social/community service organizations (14.2%) (US Department of Labor 2012). Organization managers have discovered that managing volunteer projects on behalf of employees promotes strategic selection of issues/causes and avoids disorganized programs that would occur if employees were to orchestrate them on their own (Weaver, Treviño, and Cochran 1999). On the other hand, corporations may experience difficulty in identifying social issues to support (May 2009); an area where public relations managers could prove instrumental by ensuring CSR/Sustainability connections. A public relations vice president for a US-based military defense contractor explained the importance of strategic CSR/Sustainability efforts:

> We want CSR to be very purposeful in what we do. So, we've taken the initial stages… defining where we want to focus our efforts. Right now we have three buckets defined. One of those buckets is our customers, and an education bucket, and a diversity bucket. Under the customer umbrella, we're going to focus on our veterans, wounded warriors, military families – what happens to them when they're left behind and their loved ones are deployed. And, how can we take some of the burden off service members when they're deployed? In the education bucket, because we're a technology company, the focus is on early childhood development – how can we help children to be better prepared as they enter the school system? Once they're in the school system, how can we get them engaged and excited in activities? As they go into college and the graduate degrees, can we then make them part of the [state] system's work force? For diversity, we're focusing on honoring heritage and making our workforce diverse.

Employee volunteer activities linked with CSR/Sustainability programs can enhance corporate reputation among stakeholders. Moreover, a community-service-and-environmental-campaign dynamic provides content for news and social media.

As depicted in Figure 5.1, synergies may enable organizations to advance their reputations. One entry point for monitoring impacts on employees as human capital in this CSR/Sustainability→employees→nonprofits→media→ reputation cycle is to ascertain whether or not employee volunteers are "on the clock" or otherwise paid for volunteering with release time or paid leaves—as opposed to performing volunteer duties after work hours, such as on weekends. Some researchers have suggested that enabling employees to volunteer on company time demonstrates a company's genuine commitment to social responsibility (de Gilder, Schuyt, and Breedijk 2005). A survey of Canadian companies revealed that passive support is more widespread than active support—71% of employees are allowed to take time off for volunteering without pay or adjusting their work schedules—and 29% of companies allow employees to have time off with pay for volunteering (Basil, Runte, Easwaramoorthy, *et al.* 2008). For example, Timberland, a US-based manufacturer of outdoor footwear and clothing, permits employees to volunteer for community service while on the clock at work ("Timberland Responsibility" n.d.). Munemitsu and Knowlton (2004) reported on formal employee volunteer programs of Bank of America, Citigroup, Home Depot, Merck, Starbucks, and Xerox, summarizing that "a handful ... about 5%" of companies offer paid leave and promise of a job to return to for certain employees so that they may pursue altruistic impulses; a trend that may correlate with downsizing trends (p. 12). Research findings are mixed as to correlations between employee volunteer hours and companies that pay employees to volunteer while on the company clock (McPhail and Bowles 2009). Jenny Carty, Reporting and Governance Manager at Royal Bank of Scotland (RBS), explained how employee volunteerism is linked to sustainability:

> We also support our employees to participate and volunteer and donate to charitable causes through giving them time off. Or, if you're an employee and you volunteer a certain number of hours or raise a certain

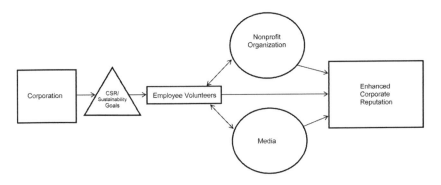

Figure 5.1 Employees as CSR/Sustainability human capital for enhanced corporate reputation

amount of money, then the bank will match that. Those kind of employee engagement – charitable giving elements – are looked after by the Sustainability Programs Team.

Several theories are used to explain and predict the employee volunteerism phenomenon. Management scholars often use human capital and social capital theories to make business case arguments in support of CSR/Sustainability as it relates to rewards for good deeds via external stakeholders and internally in terms of employee attraction/retention. Coleman (1988) explained that *human capital* "is created by changes in persons that bring about skills and capabilities that make them able to act in new ways just as physical capital is created by changes in materials to form tools that facilitate production" and *social capital* happens when there are "changes in the relations among persons that facilitate action" (p. S100). Human capital is undergirded by the belief that "you cannot separate a person from his or her knowledge, skills, health, or values" (Becker 1993: 16). Both theory streams help explain how employee participation in CSR/Sustainability programs constitutes a win–win for organizations and stakeholders. Informal volunteering is more closely related to individuals' interactions with one another (social capital) and can reveal their motivations for volunteering. High levels of human capital are required for successful formal volunteer programs (Freeman 1997) and employees provide organizations' value externally by supporting CSR/Sustainability goals. Employees may volunteer more when expected to do so by their employer (Houghton, Gabel, and Williams 2008). Employees also provide a wellspring of ideas for organizations' engagement with external communities and are most likely to offer them when they feel supported by supervisors (Muller and Kolk 2010; Ramus and Steger 2000). Overall, outcomes of employee engagement with employer-sponsored CSR/Sustainability programs may lead to firm attractiveness among prospective employees (Turban and Greening 1997). Organizations with well-established CSR/Sustainability reputations tend to appeal to certain kinds of employees who cite company-sponsored volunteer programs as playing a significant role in their decision to work there (Backhaus, Stone, and Heiner 2002). At Campbell's Soup in the USA, Vice President Public Affairs and Corporate Responsibility, David Stangis, spoke of engaging new employees with messages about the importance of CSR/Sustainability to this global food manufacturer:

We put in employee orientation a little module about CSR and sustainability ... [W]e can talk to the new employees about what our goals, what do we stand for, where do you get more information, we can go around the room. "What group are you in?" Finance. OK, here's how we're going to work with you. "You're in marketing – OK, here's how we work with you." They walk out of the room on Day 1 knowing what's up instead of six months later. It's taking a look at the entire business from top to bottom and installing all of these little acclimation points that then stick… It's like planting a computer virus. Some of these groups are very tuned in, very adaptive and want the information.

Corporations, in particular, increasingly recognize the value of establishing *branded* volunteer programs. This could be as simple as Campbell's Soup employees wearing red T-shirts and baseball caps featuring the Campbell's logo while painting an inner-city recreation center—or as complex as making charitable giving synonymous with a product/service, such as Ronald McDonald House Charities. Pfizer is widely publicized for compensating employees so that they may take a sabbatical from work for 3–12 months in order to perform community service, such as providing HIV/AIDS support in developing countries. An estimated "over two-thirds" of US-based companies provide time off for employees to perform community service (Wild 1993), such as Home Depot in partnership with Habitat for Humanity, a widely publicized program which Home Depot links to its CSR program ("Home Depot" n.d.) with a *Path of Service* program of "up to 40 paid hours." For decades, business and marketing researchers have advocated for increasing brand awareness through altruism (Hess, Rogovsky, and Dunfree 2002), arguing that leveraging stakeholder reactions is the route to building corporate responsibility value (Bhattacharya 2013). The payout often comes with enhanced customer loyalty and improved community relations and government relations (McAlister, Ferrell, and Ferrell 2010). Moreover, US businesses may declare up to 10% of pretax profits as tax-deductible charitable contributions; an amount that represents a very small percentage of overall profits (McAlister, Ferrell, and Ferrell 2010). Some organizations further inspire employee volunteer engagement through matching grant inducements to support employees' charity-of-choice when they volunteer. Among the most popular is the *Dollar for Doer* program (Weinger n.d.); a widespread effort wherein about 40% of Fortune 500 companies like Chevron and Capital One match employee contributions ("Dollar for Doer Statistics" 2013). Also, companies may designate specific days during which employees come together to support charities and nonprofits focused on social causes.

Research findings suggest that employee volunteers report reaping multiple benefits of doing volunteer work on behalf of their company. Religion, politics, and economics, generally, are factors used to explain for volunteering (Houghton, Gabel, and Williams 2008), in addition to motivation categories of: altruistic—to help others and to contribute to society; social relations—to interact with others; ideological—to support a cause one believes in; status reward—to gain publicity or recognition; material reward—to win prizes; and to fill spare time. Volunteers are motivated by social pressure and inducement of family and friends (Ben-Porath 1980), expectation of support from the nonprofit when they need it for themselves (Smith 1980), and enhanced profile career advancement when supporting initiatives promoted by supervisors (Bruce 1994). Employee volunteers associated with CSR/Sustainability projects express increased employee loyalty, pride, and organizational attachment

(Peloza and Hassay 2006). Many are motivated by expectations associated with acknowledgements in the form of job performance evaluations (Peterson 2004a) and a positive work environment (Gebler 2006). As ambassadors, many employee volunteers provide publicity when they offer interviews to the news media, use social media to Tweet and post photos of their co-workers knee deep in mud cleaning waterways or helping those less fortunate in the community by serving warm meals in soup kitchens, or performing in fundraising stunts such as a tug of war with a Boeing 757. Often employee volunteers proudly identify with their employer's efforts because it makes them stand out in public (Peloza and Hassay 2006). For example, a Southwest Airlines employee blogged on the corporate website and posted photos of co-workers volunteering to support Clean the World by collecting mini-soaps and other hygiene products left behind in hotel bathrooms and packaging them off to developing nations (Allen 2013). Using blogs this way to show embeddedness of CSR/Sustainability programs and employee involvement helps to illustrate authenticity (Fieseler, Fleck, and Meckel 2010). Moreover, CSR programs linked to nonprofit organizations supporting children often yield highly positive outcomes in the form of "warm glow" feelings (Andreoni 1990). A health insurance employee told about how his company's support of cancer patients, through monetary donations and a steady supply of employee volunteers, provides him with an opportunity that money cannot buy:

> I went up there one day and they explained to me what the Beads of Courage was ... Each treatment you go through you get a different bead. So if you go through a radiation treatment, you get a glow-in-the-dark bead, if you get a blood transfusion, you get a bead that's red. I never thought it was really important until I heard a little girl's story. She was 18 years old, just graduated from high school. She said she was sitting there going through treatment and it was so painful and she lost her full scholarship for lacrosse to college. She was terribly upset, medically and physically. She was contemplating suicide. She said a little girl handed her a bead and said it would give her courage to get through it. The two of them had the same kind of cancer. There was not a dry eye in the house. She thought that little girl was going through the same thing she was and "How selfish am I to be thinking about hurting myself?" So she started collecting her Beads of Courage.

Benefits of serving one's organization through community volunteer activities in order to refine or to acquire new skills is documented in formal research. For example, employee volunteers may engage with such activities in order to learn about budgeting, project management, communication, negotiation, people management, time management, networking, and teamwork (McAlister, Ferrell, and Ferrell 2010). Because volunteer activities sometimes offer a training ground for grooming managers, it is suggested that employee volunteer programs can replace expensive training programs when employees learn certain skills through company-sanctioned volunteer work. At Timberland in the USA, Austin (2000) explained that leadership and team-building skills learned through volunteerism save the company thousands in employee training costs.

Employee engagement linked to CSR/Sustainability also aids with employee recruitment and retention. Eighty-five percent of surveyed Canadian employers who offer employee volunteer programs experienced enhanced reputation (McPhail and Bowles 2009). Employees prefer to stay with organizations they feel proud of and committed to (Maignan, Ferrell, and Hult 1999), which makes them more productive (Daugherty 2001), more engaged (Glavas and Piderit 2009), and better organizational citizens (Jones 2010). Employees' level of commitment to CSR/Sustainability programs is moderated by importance of issues to them (Bansal and Roth 2000) and supervisors' sensitivity toward equity and ethics (Muller and Kolk 2010). Johnson Controls, a global provider of energy-optimizing products and services, enables employees to maintain onus of volunteerism programs while still keeping projects organized and strategically linked to CSR/Sustainability goals. Karen Sommer, Director of Global Public Affairs at Johnson Controls, Inc., explained:

> We provide grants of $1000 to employee groups who submit applications for a local organization and it's all based around a volunteer project they plan to do. There are criteria around our focus areas – social service in education, conservation. The groups today, they now have to compete for the grants, because the budget is only so large. Back in the day when we didn't have as many requests for funds, it was really easy. We're just finishing up for the 2014 program year. The other one is around conservation leadership corps. We've got specific programs across the globe that are focused on hands-on conservation work.

Employee stakeholders and public relations

Public relations practitioners working inside organizations perform a liaison role in managing CSR/Sustainability programs—or serving on the team—by linking employees and external nonprofit groups. An organization's people are its "greatest resource" (Broom and Sha 2013: 189) and they represent a significant target audience for public relations work of communicating with internal stakeholders for relationship building and maintenance. With regard to CSR/Sustainability goals, public relations departments may organize employee volunteer campaigns designed to strategically support nonprofit groups and social issues. Orchestrating formal employee volunteer programs serves as a visual reminder that companies are committed neighbors that demonstrate social responsibility and enable employees to demonstrate a personal commitment to issues/causes they hold dear—such as building houses for the homeless, spending time with children battling cancer, landscaping impoverished neighborhoods, assembling back-to-school kits for children and personal care kits for military members, and launching neighborhood recycling campaigns (Pompper 2013).

Public relations managers also may be expected to coordinate contemporary versions of foundations that provide grant money to nonprofits, but now are strategically connected to CSR/Sustainability goals. Public relations scholarship has differentiated "generous charity" (philanthropy) from "obligation and duty" (social responsibility) (L'Etang 2006: 408). A passive philanthropy approach complete with staged photo-ops has given way to a social responsibility approach that involves actively soliciting for and harnessing employee volunteer energy and matching it with community activities designed to advance an organization's CSR/Sustainability goals. Consumers have responded favorably to the shift since people tend to consider monetary donations as mere tax write-offs anyway, while contribution of corporate resources (e.g., employee volunteers' time) is considered less self-serving of corporations (Hess, Rogovsky, and Dunfree 2002). Employee volunteers have responded favorably, as well, reporting that service makes them feel greater degrees of self-satisfaction (Pompper 2013) and organizational commitment (Brammer, Millington, and Rayton 2007). Thus, public relations practitioners navigating organizations' CSR/Sustainability programs concur that organizations donating employee time is more genuine than simply cutting checks for charity.

Public relations counselors may make CSR/Sustainability more strategic *and* more moral but must do so without resorting to greenwash or "wooly thinking" (Easterly 2014). Even though Bhattacharya (2013) argued that "companies need not shy away from market motive," normatively-operating public relations professionals are trained to remind organizations that they must promote respect for *all* people and ensure that benefits and burdens are equitably distributed so that no one group gains advantage over another. This mantra is embedded in the activist model for public relations (Holtzhausen, Peterson, and Tindall 2009); worth repeating frequently so that employee volunteer programs linked to CSR/Sustainability business case motives do not become merely a "public relations strategy" (Luo and Bhattacharya 2006: 15). Employee empowerment constitutes a significant part of corporate citizenship (Birch 2001) and relates to research findings which suggest that internal communication is necessary for effective and successful organizations (Hargie and Tourish 2009). Researchers have afforded more attention to consumers, stockholders, customers, and other stakeholders than they have employees with regard to CSR/Sustainability messaging. Employees consider more than profit when evaluating employers' policies (Blazovich and Smith 2011). Some research findings suggest that CSR/Sustainability programs could enhance employees' commitment to organizations, satisfaction, and identification with their employer (Rupp, Shao, Thornton, *et al.* 2013). Public relations researchers long have emphasized the importance of internal communication and two-way symmetrical communication with employees (Grunig, Grunig, and Dozier 2002). A substantial collection of inter-disciplinary literature bears findings which suggest that internal communication facilitates employee attitudes of commitment (Jo and Shim 2005), organizational identification (Smidts, Pruyn, and van Riel 2001), and job satisfaction (Gray and Laidlaw 2004); all of which may contribute to organizational learning and higher productivity (Berger 2008), as well as improved external relations (Kim and Rhee 2011). Importantly, good internal communication has the potential for engaging employees in organizational goals and priorities and for enhancing transparency among management and employees—work that expands public relations' role in fostering employee engagement (Mishra, Boynton, and Mishra 2014).

Employee volunteers take a leap of faith that their employers' CSR/ Sustainability motives are authentic. Attempting to cover unethical and socially irresponsible behaviors through CSR/Sustainability programs and reports constitutes greenwashing (Frynas 2005). For instance, by providing employee volunteers to pick up litter and engage with other green projects, a company with a track record for polluting the environment can twist altruism and social objectives to its advantage at very little cost because the human capital used consists of employees who are salaried and/or are dispatched for volunteer activities after close of business or on weekends. Such feel-good stories resonate with news media because these make better visuals than grip-and-grin photos, where a company representative hands an over-sized check to a nonprofit organization's representative. Authentic and well-organized internal communication efforts also can personify an organization's ethical commitment to employees. Carroll (2006) posited that acting with integrity and respect for employees through communication promotes trust. Hence, organizations must not presume carte blanche employee compliance to any CSR/Sustainability agenda or positive word of mouth outcomes, but gauge any employee skepticism through ongoing research to improve communication message content and delivery vehicles (Theofilou and Watson 2014) at both ends of the two-way symmetrical continuum. Brenda Colatrella, Executive Director of Corporate Responsibility at Merck, explained how corporate responsibility is not enveloped within public relations/communication, but that the two areas work toward common goals:

> I actually don't see us as a PR function. I think it's much more about behavior and responsible practices … I won't say I don't think it's important to talk about what we're doing – to put information into the public domain both internally – because I do think it motivates employees, especially the younger employees. They want to work for an organization that demonstrates its responsibility. Also, from an external standpoint, I think it's important that we make folks aware of what we do, why we do it, and how we do it. And that's why transparency is one of our four focus areas in corporate responsibility.

Optimally, inclusion of employees in CSR/Sustainability program planning, implementation, and measurement offers a normative and authentic means to address employee concerns, discover their valuable perspectives, and ultimately to win their support as CSR/Sustainability ambassadors who share good works with external stakeholders. Research findings suggest that employees seek organizations that help people and support the natural environment (Du, Bhattacharya, and Sen 2010).

Public relations counselors also facilitate communication with external shareholders about CSR/Sustainability goals and accomplishments when employees are involved. Central to the spirit of using employee labor outside the workplace to advance CSR/Sustainability goals is James Grunig's (1992) description of public relations' purpose in "building relationships with publics that constrain or enhance the ability of the organization to meet its mission" (p. 20). Kelly's (2001) concept of *stewardship* in a context of development/fundraising helps to explain the importance of managing relationships among "donors, investors, community residents, government officials, members of the media, consumers, or others" (p. 280). Dhanesh (2012) characterized CSR as a relationship-strengthening and maintenance strategy for employee relations. For example, when a US-based insurance giant inspires employees to donate their free time to visit terminally ill children or when a food company recruits employees to load backpacks with supplies for the homeless, employee labor enables a corporation to position itself as intrinsically linked to and committed to the community. Outcomes associated with these processes further underscore the public relations profession's function of navigating moral obligations and responsibilities—and fulfilling public relations' normative potential. A North American-based paper manufacturer's employee explained why she and co-workers volunteer for community activities:

> I volunteer extra because I want to. I think it's important ... [W]e're very active in the community where we're located. This facility is in a community of about 4700 people ... We have 1000 employees, so we're the largest industry in this area. You know everybody and everybody's connected in some way. We're involved in everything from Clean-up Days in the community to Jr. Achievement where we work directly in the schools ... For Clean-up Day, we do that twice a year and I try to recruit our employees to get involved and get out and help the community ... It was like 80–90 degrees and mosquitos everywhere. It was not fun – but it's all for the cause, right? ... This is a dry county, so we go out afterward for Dr Peppers.

Nonprofit organizations also have discovered how to advance their own goals in conjunction with corporations' CSR/Sustainability programs. Because competition for volunteers among nonprofits is stiff (Bussell and Forbes 2002), teaming up with companies willing to furnish free labor seems a mutually-beneficial opportunity for both nonprofits and corporations. CSR/Sustainability managers have discovered advantages of carefully considering talents among an employee pool for their social capital value. Loaned executives with technical, accounting, legal, and medical skills are in high demand among nonprofits (Carson 1999). For example, a US-based global financial services company executive attributed success of CSR/Sustainability volunteer activities to her company's careful match of employees' talents with nonprofit organization goals. She shared a story about serving as an employee volunteer who conducted mock job interviews for immigrant women served by a nonprofit organization:

> I did a one-on-one interview with her so she could look at what a Fortune 500 company might have to say about her interviewing abilities. She said it was very humbling because she was a big shot in her country. I noticed she was very nervous. I helped calm her down and tell me her story. This helped with her confidence – in how she shook hands, how she sat down. It was 45 minutes and … she wanted to cry and hug me and didn't know whether she could do it because it was a mock interview.

Yet, the public relations manager for a US facility of a British multinational defense, security, and aerospace company explained that nonprofits are eager for companies to provide volunteers, but still are developing an appreciation for CSR/Sustainability partnerships:

> I came from a nonprofit background … I don't think their mindset has shifted much to knowing that they actually have to provide something to the sponsors. It's more along the line of gimme-gimme mentality. I think there might be a little bit – shift in the focus, knowing they have to do something, but not knowing *how* to do it. I still don't think nonprofits are where they need to be. They're thinking the pure philanthropy model and it's not like that anymore. Businesses are really being a lot more – they have to for the stakeholders – more smart with how they're spending their dollars and there's a responsibility there and stewardship that nonprofits don't realize.

So, establishing sustained communication between corporations and nonprofits and demonstrating gratitude toward one another through recognition events and via traditional and social media attention enables partners to extend the relationship over time.

Undoubtedly, corporations recognize the value of engaging with CSR/Sustainability via employee volunteer programs. Thus far, too few guidelines have been developed for forming employee volunteer programs that focus on firms' core competencies, monitoring effects once initiatives are realized, or formal evaluation measures (Pompper 2013). Here is where public relations expertise could make all the difference given that CSR/Sustainability-related employee volunteer programs seem consistent with public relations' *raison d'être* of relationship building. Austin (2000) succinctly summarized that embedded strategies boost multinational corporations' social capital as their business decision-making model shifts from "nice to do" to "need to do" (p. 12).

Employee volunteerism's dark side

Few researchers have examined potentially negative outcomes associated with CSR/Sustainability–employee-volunteerism links—such as when employees feel obligated or coerced into serving. Public relations practitioners have an ethical responsibility to intervene and change the course and conditions of employee volunteerism associated with CSR/Sustainability programs should employee volunteers feel pressured or otherwise ill-treated. Organization–stakeholder relationships involve a delicate balance and must be carefully managed (Ledingham 2006). Stewardship implies that public relations plays an ongoing role in stakeholder relationship management "as agents of accountability and the organization's conscience" (Kelly 2001: 284)—and this extends to CSR/Sustainability activities. Among public relations practitioners interviewed for this book, very few were willing to share any stories about negative outcomes associated with employee volunteer programs. Furthermore, most acknowledged a general failure to regularly evaluate programs according to employee perspectives or to monitor employee satisfaction with the volunteer experience. A pharmaceutical public relations vice president summed it up: "Hey, employees vote with their feet. If they don't want to volunteer or they have other commitments, they won't show up for the Saturday morning bus." On the other hand, a food manufacturer employee who had participated in inner-city community rehab projects opined:

> I was never asked. It was assumed. I never told anyone that I was feeling taken advantage of because I was afraid of how it would look. Everybody else in my department there in the company newsletter photo except me? You know, the company wants people who are happy with their job and support the cause.

What goes on in organizations when assembling employee volunteer teams before they carry paint brushes, rakes, and energy into external communities is relatively unknown. Employees who do not embrace their employer's pet cause on ideological, moral, or other grounds might prefer to opt out of an employee activity but acquiesce out of fear of reprisal if a boss/manager perceives the employee as someone who is not a team player and negatively evaluates her/him on a performance review or overlooks her/him for a job promotion. Internal public relations counselors contribute to organizations' control and punishment by "objectifying management's scripts as rational and reasonable" (Holtzhausen 2014: 221). These metascripts (Boje, Adler, and Black 2005) represent unwritten rules about how to behave according to an organization's standards. Employees who volunteer on behalf of their company often are rewarded by supervisors (van Scotter and Motowidlo 2000), so it seems reasonable to suggest that employees who feel forced to volunteer could experience lower levels of commitment to the corporation, trust in its leaders, job satisfaction, and even perception of the nonprofit associated with the volunteer project. Ethical treatment of employees should override organizational philanthropy programs (May 2011). Organizations generally do not publish employee lists, and public relations or human resources personnel are reluctant to share names of employees who may be dissatisfied with a work environment. Even employees interviewed for this book who say they are fully satisfied with employee volunteerism programs suggest that potential for a downside exists. For example, some employees consider community service to be an individual's personal choice and regard company-wide efforts to support a particular nonprofit or charitable sector to be inconsistent with their personal values. Furthermore, some employees may go along with the program primarily because they consider it a smart move that could result in a positive performance review, transfer to a more desirable department, or a promotion to a higher position with greater rewards. In the event that such results fail to materialize, expectancies are violated and employees are left to ponder whether their time investment really was worth it.

Political ideology also can prove a source of conflict when CSR/Sustainability is linked to employee volunteerism and community service. A public relations executive for a public utility explained: "Sometimes employees feel like they have to go along with whatever charitable program the company sponsors because it supports a certain political candidate—even though they may belong to a different political party." Another employee for a paper products company explained that while she would have chosen to perform volunteer work at a women's shelter and health facility where family planning services are rendered, instead she was persuaded by her supervisor to join other department employees who were working on a neighborhood housing rehab project supported by the company's foundation: "He told me that the Center had gotten so much negative press due to demonstrations by Pro-Lifers and it would be too risky for me to be seen there. I'd be better off joining with co-workers to serve the nearby community."

Corporations that support employee volunteer service by enabling employees to do so during traditional work hours recognize that such human capital expenditures can come at a cost. Even though companies' productivity may dwindle when employees perform volunteer work with nonprofits during work hours, companies may recoup the loss in more positive attitudes and behavior among employees toward employer organizations (de Gilder, Schuyt, and Breedijk 2005)—in addition to enhanced reputation as promoted by nonprofits and media coverage of employees wearing company-logoed gear (e.g., caps, T-shirts, sweatshirts, water bottles, backpacks) and rolling up their sleeves to support communities and nonprofit goals. An employee working at an aerospace products manufacturer said that even though she supports the company's causes "in theory," the work still must be completed. She explained:

There are the usual suspects who volunteer every time and want to be called on again. They understand the importance of it. But that doesn't mean that they come back and finish their work. It's just understood that the rest of us have to chip in and stay until it's done, even though we have other things to do, too.

Consequences may arise in the workplace for both employees who volunteer and those who are left to hold down the fort while co-workers perform community service. Some companies with union contracts seem to find ways to enable employees to volunteer and to offer charitable support on company grounds, such as providing employees to mentor at-risk children through reading after school in the company cafeteria or to pack food into boxes for homeless shelters. Perhaps employees who feel coerced into volunteering on behalf of their company—or perceive that they are discriminated against at work because they do not participate in volunteering—may find an ally in their labor union when an intervention is needed.

The employee volunteerism in the service of CSR/Sustainability goals dynamic blurs lines dividing public and private spheres. Predictors of an employee's commitment to CSR activities include healthy skepticism and self-confidence (Theofilou and Watson 2014). Often, potential is high for ethical challenges to emerge when organizations expect employees to serve as ambassadors and to perform volunteer work in support of CSR/Sustainability goals that they may not believe in or that foment conflict with co-workers. This is an especially salient concern among employees who believe that volunteering is a private matter and not one that should be micro-managed in the work environment. Indeed, the potential that women may feel marginalized by the employee volunteerism process is relevant since many already work two shifts—in organizations and at home. One study's findings among Canadian employee-volunteers suggested that women were less likely to receive employer support for volunteer work in the form of flexible work hours and time-off, than men (McPhail and Bowles 2009). The question of when women might find time to volunteer in the community should the corporate sponsor not offer on-the-clock time for these activities may determine female employees' ability to support CSR/Sustainability goals and possibly diminish their standing within the organization should they opt not to participate. A healthcare provider explained that she has found ways to navigate a complicated work/personal life schedule: "What you get back far outweighs what you give out—one Saturday a month. The grocery store is open every day of the week. I can go there whenever. Hairdresser works six days a week. People think you're giving up your entire Saturday and stuff like that."

Over-emphasizing corporate-sponsored volunteer activities and recruiting too hard among employees can make them feel pressured to participate. When this happens, volunteerism comes across as something that is mandatory for employees who seek to keep their job and/or advance through promotion (Clary and Snyder 2002). Jarvis (2011) opined that employees grow irritated by constant pleas to participate in Dollar for Doer programs. The CSR manager for a producer of lumber and engineered wood products opined that employee volunteerism projects are not necessarily positioned as ladder-climbing steps: "We make note of it in the personnel file, but anybody who relies on chalking up points by volunteering probably isn't the kind of leader we want in our company anyway. There's much more to it than that."

Discussion

The global phenomenon of employee volunteerism in a context of supporting an organization's CSR/Sustainability goals offers public relations managers a highly complex dynamic deserving of ongoing scrutiny. On the one hand, involving employees in CSR/Sustainability community outreach activities underscores a new strategy for further embedding CSR/Sustainability internally across organizations and outward into external stakeholder groups. Employees bonding and networking in support of CSR/Sustainability-related activities promotes greater company loyalty and cross-training opportunities to enhance the work environment and individual advancement opportunities. This blending of human and social capital in a context of volunteerism sustains community linkages for enhanced corporate reputation as an ideal workplace which supports employee advancement and promotes a caring company neighbor which gives back to the community: a solid business case argument for CSR/Sustainability. Furthermore, corporations stand to gain many returns when news and social media are used to promote CSR/Sustainability goals and highly visual community service performed by employees wearing color coordinated, company-logoed T-shirts and caps.

On the other hand, an ethical slippery slope awaits multinational corporations and risk of employee abuse is apparent. A work environment where volunteering bears a taint of obligation, requirement and mandate—especially if the projects are scheduled beyond traditional work hours when employees must take the time from private sphere commitments such as childcare and home maintenance—contradicts the social responsibility spirit. Public relations managers in organizations may serve as guardians and insider-activists monitoring CSR/Sustainability programs. Furthermore, Holtzhausen (2014) argued that internal public relations managers—as a conscience of the organization—ultimately must side with employees in resisting management power that operates contrary to employees' best interest. Arguing for organizational transformation toward sustainability, Doppelt (2003) opined that only through inclusion of employees and other stockholders can effective information sharing and decision making prove fruitful. Transforming business to make it more sustainable requires informed leaders with vision and skill required to impact employees and other stakeholders across the public sphere (Millar, Hind, and Magala 2012)—responsibly and ethically. Berkley and Watson (2009) reminded us that opportunities for ethics breeches mount as globalization trends escalate—and many "have not performed especially well in applied ethics" (p. 275).

A well-trained public relations professional has a role at virtually every step of CSR/Sustainability processes as they impact employees. Maximizing value that public relations brings to CSR/Sustainability efforts benefits organizations, employees, nonprofits, and the larger social sphere. Indeed, using public relations as a one-way asymmetrical publicity function to communicate CSR/Sustainability-related good works may benefit employees who feel more satisfied and loyal toward their employer, as well as organizations' bottom line. However, public relations must be allowed to be more. Public relations' role in a CSR/Sustainability context also must take into account ethical considerations of volunteer programs that potentially could make employees feel coerced. Furthermore, recognizing the negative potential of forcing employees to do something that they may not really want to do—and possibly not meeting their expectations (e.g., promotion, opportunity to learn new skills)—could result in social media backlash by employees using uncontrolled media to speak out against employers in real-time.

Overall, CSR/Sustainability means going beyond what organizations are required to do according to a home country's environmental, legal, and economic compliance safeguards. Public relations' primary responsibility is to ethically develop and nurture relationships among organizations and shareholders. That some corporations have branded their altruism efforts—such as Home Depot with Kaboom in building playgrounds in under-served communities and Avon with breast cancer awareness—is a highly promotable opportunity. Such high visibility also carries risk when the story turns negative. One example of this is US-based Wal-Mart's well-publicized ongoing charitable foundation support for local communities in need—an issue that soured when employees used Facebook during Thanksgiving to urge support for co-workers living on federal assistance, claiming that the company fails to pay employees "a living wage" (Axelson 2013; Sprinkle 2013). Formal volunteer programs emerge when an individual employee's human capital and social capital come together—and it is well established that employees can be quite positive about community volunteer work on behalf of their corporate employers. Public relations makes a substantial contribution to organizational life and broader social goals when human capital is not abused in the process of creating social capital.

On being prepared to navigate ethics and CSR/Sustainability

An important means for interrogating connections between public relations and CSR/Sustainability is to explore public relations practitioners' foundational ethics training. Being accountable for CSR/Sustainability as an organizational management member means commitment to the highest ethical standards. It is the public relations insider's responsibility to ensure that prevailing ethical standards are understood and followed by top management (Heath and Ryan 1989); a responsibility even more relevant for public relations' insider-activist role. This chapter offers insight into formal classroom education and formative hands-on training to prepare for CSR/Sustainability work, and linkages with central themes in the public relations body of knowledge, particularly boundary spanning, ethics, and issues management. If public relations managers function as "collective moral actors" (Surma 2005: 5), normatively serve as a "conscience of the organization" (Holtzhausen 2000: 105), and maintain "special concern for broader societal issues and approaches to problems" (van Ruler and Verčič 2005: 264), how do they prepare for a career of counseling on ethical CSR/Sustainability?

Broadly examining public relations as it relates to CSR/Sustainability promotes greater understanding of ways that the public relations discipline contributes to public communication and its ties to culture, economics, and politics. Postmodern and postcolonial theory frameworks provide especially useful theoretical underpinnings for facilitating this inquiry. Public relations instructors around the world undoubtedly face significant obstacles in teaching students about liaisons between public relations and CSR/Sustainability if they subscribe to an understanding of public relations as primarily a tool for enhancing an organization's reputation and public image, what excellence researchers classify as the press agentry or public information one-way asymmetrical models (Grunig 1993). Sending information without accounting for feedback or circumstances and viewpoints of stakeholders is not conducive to the practice of authentic CSR/Sustainability and represents a source for the most widely articulated criticism of public relations as a greenwashing tool. On the other hand, public relations instructors who emphasize utility of the two-way symmetrical model offer a more straightforward means for helping students to understand the role that public relations managers play in navigating corporations toward ethical CSR/Sustainability triple-bottom-line outcomes based on respect among the organization, people, and the planet. Moreover, even researchers who acknowledge public relations' role in building relationships and mutual trust between organizations and stakeholders do not necessarily share a common framework for differentiating between ethics, as in: "When is ethics about the right thing to do and when is it about making an organization look good?" (Parsons 2004: 157). This chapter examines these key themes: integrating public relations ethics and CSR/Sustainability, learning leadership for public relations in CSR/Sustainability, ethical CSR/Sustainability training in the public relations classroom, acquiring ethical CSR/Sustainability training on the job and beyond.

Integrating public relations ethics and CSR/Sustainability

Because public relations serves as a conscience and ethics touchstone in organizations, CSR/Sustainability and public relations are inherently inter-twined. CSR's guiding principle is business–society inter-dependency (Wood 1991a)—to the degree that organizations must go above and beyond what is *legally* required locally, nationally, and globally. It could be hypothesized that ethical organizations which highly esteem public relations to the degree that it is considered a management function with a seat at the policy-making table have the wherewithal to hire a professional who practices public relations excellence and adheres to the highest ethical standards without using public relations as window dressing. Unfortunately, research findings suggest that public relations managers rarely play a central role in the institutionalization of ethics (Fitzpatrick 1996b)—inspiring Holtzhausen (2000) to warn that practice of *ethical* public relations represents the twenty-first century's greatest challenge for practitioners. By extension, public relations educators must use the classroom to prepare students to meet the challenge.

Ethics constitutes a check on connections among organizations and the public sphere. Organizations may act on *social* pressures to "do the right thing" as encouraged by individuals, nongovernmental organizations (NGOs), and nonprofits. Ethics also represents a central component of Carroll's (1979) classic CSR definition: "The social responsibility of business encompasses the economic, legal, *ethical*, and discretionary expectations that society has of organizations at a given point in time" (italics added for emphasis) (p. 500). Surma (2006) emphasized that organizations take on community responsi-bilities when they enter into the larger social milieu and that public relations has the potential to help organizations perform ethically in relationships despite power differentials. This characterizes a central balancing act of public relations practice—persuasion and advocacy on the part of the employer–organization (Kruckeberg and Starck 1988), while enabling organizations and their publics to accommodate one another for mutual benefit (J. Grunig 1992). The public sphere holds multinational corporations accountable and has expectations which, when violated, inspires attempts to have a corporation's *license to operate* revoked through boycotts and negative publicity. Perhaps nowhere has this played out more visibly in the USA than with Wall Street ethics ruptures and, in particular, the Enron scandal involving top managers who were convicted of accounting fraud, poor corporate governance, and abuse of public trust; outcomes which saw employees and shareholders robbed of substantial financial assets and, ultimately, the energy giant's demise. Incorporating such case studies in public relations classes provides demonstrable evidence of how insider-activism is necessary.

Integrating ethical standards with CSR/Sustainability marks an important step in expanding our understanding of public relations' internal-activist function. Public relations practitioners are bound to ethical behavior on behalf of both clients/employers and stakeholders as part of core values promoted by trade organizations such as the Public Relations Society of America (PRSA), or they could have their Accredited Public Relations (APR) credential revoked. Incorporating postmodern values that call for "immediate and just action" of a public relations insider-activist (Holtzhausen 2000: 110, 2014) offers public relations managers broad justification for counseling on ethical considerations of business decisions with regard to CSR/Sustainability. One way to affect this outcome is to consider the corporate financial bottom line *in conjunction with* interests of employees, activist groups, other stakeholders, and the natural environment. Exposing the postmodern condition reveals ethical considerations inherent in power dynamics associated with CSR/Sustainability policies—and enables the public relations manager to present multiple facets of issues for enriched policy decision making. Public relations normatively embodies cooperation and collaboration among stakeholders and supports valuing perceptions of those both inside and outside the organization (Grunig, Toth, and Hon 2000), as advanced by the two-way symmetrical model (Grunig 2000a) and collaborative advocacy for social change.

Boundary-spanning work in public relations facilitates some degrees of objectivity when simultaneously serving both organizations and stakeholders. This position could be likened to the public relations liaison function (Toth, Serini, Wright, *et al.* 1998). A boundary-spanning role means investing resources in researching multiple stakeholders' needs and well-being rather than subjectively considering *only* a corporation's interests. Bowen (2013) used systems theory to explain how it is incumbent upon public relations managers, as boundary spanners, to collect important insights of stakeholders and bring them back to share among organizations' policy makers. Among organizations where managements tend to emphasize internal publics at the expense of external publics—and, subsequently, focus too much on profit and status quo maintenance—public relations can fill a significant void (Heath and Ryan 1989). Work in an organizational environment shaped by change supports reconceptualization of the boundary-spanning role (Holtzhausen 2000)—such that public relations managers have many masters; not just those who sign their paychecks. We must teach students that as boundary spanners shaped by high ethical standards and an authentic commitment to CSR/ Sustainability, public relations managers can affect coalition building among organizations and stakeholders by opening communication lines and facilitating mutually beneficial relationship building.

It seems that multinational corporations' *un*ethical treatment of people and the planet keeps public relations managers most busy on the CSR/Sustainability front. Critics, activists, and postcolonial theorists accuse public relations of bolstering hegemonic, status quo practices that perpetuate global inequality (Dutta and Pal 2011) through spin which blows a smokescreen and fails to hold multinational corporations accountable to stakeholders for CSR/ Sustainability-related promises. Instructors should consider fusing historical context in public relations classes, such as the environmental justice movement launched in the USA in the 1980s to protect lower socio-economic communities from having waste products dumped in their neighborhoods. According to the Environmental Protection Agency (EPA), environmental justice is "the fair treatment and meaningful involvement of all people regardless of race, color, sex, national origin, or income with respect to the development, implementation, and enforcement of environmental laws, regulations, and policies" (EPA n.d.). As I have argued elsewhere, environmental justice goals are thwarted when elite government and industry sources serve as primary environmental risk framers in mainstream newspapers, far outnumbering non-elite public and interest group sources (Pompper 2004). Ongoing claims of environmental racism persist in several US states, such as Dixon County in Tennessee, where toxic waste from landfills leeched into drinking water supplies (National Black Environmental Justice Network n.d.). Students need look no further than multinational corporations' websites to discover how companies nurture and sustain their values, identity, and moral relationships; also known as a "discourse of ethics" (Surma 2006: 55). For example, petrochemical industry corporations such as Chevron include a Corporate Responsibility link on their website home page. Because viewers are greeted by large colorful photographs of smiling indigenous peoples ("Chevron" n.d.), marine life swimming in crystal clear water, men and women wearing hardhats and clean white lab coats, and charts featuring large headlines quantitatively promoting corporate investment in sustainability, quantities of trees planted, and numbers of babies nurtured ("Corporate Responsibility" n.d.), such treatment suggests that branding discourses rule.

As future relationship managers and counselors, public relations students must be taught how to employ communication to help organizations establish and maintain ethical business practices—and not just for generating publicity. Communication tools are used to inform publics of ethical business practices and to research external stakeholders' points of view in face-to-face and mediated (traditional and social media) contexts, as addressed in Chapter 4. Even though a public relations manager may work for a multinational corporation, her/his responsibility to the larger social sphere trumps self-interest or advocacy on behalf of the corporation (Bowen 2013). In reality, however, public relations' commitment to the public sphere fails to ring true amidst extant critique that public relations merely uses media to provide window dressing for showboating CEOs who claim to support CSR altruism (Banerjee 2008) and for greenwashing multinational corporations' environmental pollution track records (Benn, Todd, and Pendleton 2010). Similarly, one-way messaging in the form of image advertising that promotes CSR/Sustainability activities is "embarrassing self-congratulatory rhetoric" and failure to point out any CSR-related profit motive is disingenuous and potentially damaging to a multinational corporation's reputation (Ihlen 2013: 209).

Some other researchers have resolved that power differentials are so great between multinational corporations and community members that public relations devolves into a tool for deflecting unethical behaviors away from the corporations. This constitutes a paradox, since public relations is *supposed* to make organizations *more* ethical (Munshi and Kurian 2005, italics added). These tensions offer a plethora of contexts for classroom discussions and student research papers that involve interviews with organization representatives. Perhaps at the heart of challenges associated with affecting ethical behavior relative to CSR/Sustainability is confusion about how to operationalize *ethics*. Here is where PRSA and other trade organizations' case studies and in situ examples illuminate ethics for practical application. Parsons (2004) argued that *organizational ethics* ("broadly related to overall business practices and focuses on the ethical implications of the operational policies and practices of the business itself") differs from *public relations ethics* ("ethical implications of the strategies and tactics that are applied to solve the public relations and communications problems of organizations") in a CSR/Sustainability context; resolving that these are related, but different (p. 158). Parsons (2004) also argued that *social responsibility* is an overused term. Some public relations practitioners and business journalists prefer *integrity* over *ethics* as a euphemism (Nash 1990), while public relations scholars offer *guardian* (L'Etang 2006), *watchdog* (Heath and Ryan 1989), and *corporate citizenship* (Matten and Moon 2004).

Learning leadership for public relations in CSR/Sustainability

Beyond playing a key part in keeping organizations true to ethical standards, public relations may take a leadership role in organizations' CSR/Sustainability programs. Public relations theory and applied practice both support and provide direction for CSR/Sustainability in organizations. Ethical action in corporate responsibility means "respecting the rights of others" (Curtin and Boynton 2001: 416), advocating for them with organizational management, and working to ensure that no one group gains advantage over another; according to an insider-activist model for public relations (Holtzhausen, Peterson, and Tindall 2009). As addressed in Chapter 3, issues management work that involves systematically monitoring environments and responding to them enables practitioners to demonstrably respect stakeholder rights and respond to calls for ethical behavior (Heath 1997). Also, according to stakeholder theory, CSR/Sustainability means going beyond compliance by attending to the widest range of stakeholders (Freeman, Wicks, & Parmar 2004). Furthermore, public relations practitioners' expertise in relationship building, reputation management, communication with publics (Bowen 2013), strategic conflict management (Cameron, Wilcox, Reber and Shin 2007), and leadership in navigating CSR/Sustainability programs is invaluable because they are uniquely prepared for work that requires flexibility and a contingency approach dependent upon culture and situation (Shin, Heath, and Lee 2011). These lessons suggest role playing opportunities for students as part of public relations coursework.

Unfortunately, public relations has earned a damning and damaged reputation in conjunction with CSR/Sustainability and students must enter the field with eyes wide open. Banerjee (2008) has criticized public relations as a reputation repair and brand value construction tool rather than an authentic and ethical leadership function for organizations' CSR/Sustainability programs aimed at improving society and protecting the planet. L'Etang (2003) suggested that public relations could escape the bounds of superficiality by engaging with the more complex ethical challenges of CSR/Sustainability. Rather than enabling public relations as an instrument for integrating management processes or for facilitating change in organizations or social systems that improve people's lives (Aldoory and Toth 2004), however, CEOs in Australia still view public relations through a publicity lens (Benn, Todd, and Pendleton 2010). Scott D. Tattar, Senior Vice President, Director of Public Relations & CSR at LevLane, a Philadelphia-based advertising and public relations firm, unapologetically explained that public relations can and does take a leadership role in CSR/Sustainability:

> Way before spending money on PR and advertising in order to get the word out, you've got to spend money on the actual program. It's got to stand up. It has to be a legitimate community-focused, successful, community-driven program. It's not about the PR. That's the business proposition and maybe academics will never believe that but companies who choose on their own free will to do positive things in the community should be able to benefit themselves from that.

Regardless of degree of acceptance of CSR's business case arguments, because public relations must become embedded in organizations and be permitted a seat at the strategic-planning table, faculty must help students to prepare for the challenge. Several public relations researchers have suggested that public relations professionals use communication to influence the management agenda (Steyn 2007) and organizational culture (Stark and Kruckeberg 2003).

Ethical CSR/Sustainability training in the public relations classroom

Perhaps at the heart of challenges associated with affecting ethical CSR/ Sustainability policies and practices in organizations is insufficient college classroom training. A proposed theory of the public relations professional's dual obligations to serve client organizations and the public interest—or, *responsible advocacy* (Fitzpatrick and Bronstein 2006)—should serve as a foundation in public relations classroom attention to ethics. Sockell (2013) responded to recent Wall Street scandals by inviting business school colleagues to "take some responsibility for developing students' ability to discover and apply values. There's no longer any question that critical thinking about obligations to society must be as much a part of business success as finance and other traditional skills." Carol Adams, a senior researcher and professor of CSR/Sustainability on faculty at Monash University and Director of Integrated Horizons consultancy in Australia, also lamented the string of ethics lapses among executives at corporations, globally: "[I]t's the way people are educated. Certainly, people who are leaders now have been educated often from a fairly narrow discipline perspective without attention being paid to those broader skills and the leadership skills that might be needed." Even though ethics is recommended as a top priority for public relations study by professors and practitioners (Commission on Public Relations Education 2012), as well as by students (Jain and Winner 2013–2014), there appears to be no solid consensus as to how or where in the public relations curriculum that ethical CSR/Sustainability should be taught.

Findings of some of the earliest studies of ethics in the public relations classroom suggested how woefully inadequate pedagogical materials of the day were—and begs questions about how adequately equipped faculty are *today*. Preparing tomorrow's public relations professionals to navigate moral issues which will play an important role in their professional and personal lives is of paramount importance. Harrison (1990) reported that while 93 percent of public relations faculty reported including ethics in their course content and advised for integrating ethics across the curriculum, textbooks' attention to ethical systems was lacking. More recently, public relations textbooks rarely have more than one chapter devoted to ethics and routinely subjects of ethics and law are paired (Austin and Toth 2011). Overall, a commitment to teaching ethics across and throughout the public relations curriculum is lacking and inconsistent (Hutchison 2002). Beyond textbooks, support is available from professional trade organizations and in the USA the accreditation in public relations (APR) exam, which is designed to promote and reinforce ethics, may offer classroom discussion points. On the other hand, Harrison (1990) suggested that because faculty may be uncomfortable talking about moral values with students, for fear of imposing their own beliefs on them, it is essential that textbooks adequately address the issues. Research on the teaching of ethics–CSR/Sustainability has reached critical mass, and aging content analyses of public relations textbooks now are joined by contemporary examinations of graduate and undergraduate public relations curricula as revealed by content analyses and interviews. For example, among the most recent findings is a recommendation that instructors consider cultural approaches and contexts in CSR/Sustainability education (Austin and Toth 2011). Another positive research outcome is that ethics–CSR/Sustainability may be one of the few areas where academics and practitioners continue to agree; it is supremely important that students learn about ethics-CSR/Sustainability so that they are prepared for their first *and* last jobs counseling clients and organizations about doing the right thing.

Significantly greater attention has been afforded ethics among public relations undergraduate curricula than graduate curricula. Industry leaders continue to support the need for master's degrees in public relations through communication schools rather than sending interested students to business schools (Shen and Toth 2008). Sockell (2013) opined that business schools, too, "are falling short" and that curricula need to be "ambitious ... about concepts of corporate social responsibility that go well beyond public relations and unvarnished self-interest." Beyond the college classroom, public relations' industry associations perpetually promote codes of ethics on websites and via seminars and workshops for practitioners. Public relations professors and instructors face four distinct hurdles when preparing for and creating ethics-CSR/Sustainability learning environments for public relations students.

Challenge 1: adjunct instructors and the publicity model

Several complex and related issues challenge college public relations curriculum directors to provide courses that will adequately prepare tomorrow's public relations professionals who also may work as CSR/Sustainability managers and team members. Findings of a recent study of college and university public relations program reliance on part-time, contingent, or adjunct faculty suggested that they transfer application of the publicity model to guide their work as publicists and media relations experts when teaching students how to promote clients' and organizations' products and services (Pompper 2011). I found that many research participants said they even bring their clients' projects to school so that students may work on them; opportunities that appeal greatly to students who have dreams of becoming publicists in the entertainment and sports industries. Indeed, CSR/Sustainability communication initiatives most often are considered press agentry, publicity, or media relations activities (David, Kline, and Dai 2005). Shortcomings of the publicity model must be exposed because what organizations need is ethical public relations counseling and two-way communication programs rather than publicity-greenwash.

Drawbacks to a publicity approach to CSR/Sustainability in the classroom include failure to provide students with critical thinking skills necessary for exploring ethical implications of dynamic, multi-dimensional issues. Encouraging college instructors to incorporate a human-centered worldview that considers implications of corporate decisions—beyond profit goals— represents a significant hurdle in ethics and social responsibility education (Giacalone and Thompson 2006). Martinson (2004) argued that "too many persons who call themselves public relations professionals do not respect the truth and do not respect those to whom particular communication efforts are directed" (p. 4). Turk (2006) concluded that college administrators, too, narrowly define public relations in terms of publicity rather than as organizations' ethical gauge, key to strategic planning, and builder of mutually beneficial two-way symmetrical relationships between organizations and stakeholders. Therefore, university public relations department and sequence directors likely find resistance from administrators when seeking resources to support the public relations learning environment—such as creating new classes and hiring fulltime, tenure-track scholar-professors of ethics-CSR/Sustainability.

Challenge 2: teaching students about CSR/Sustainability as ethical public relations

CSR/Sustainability seems a comfortable fit with public relations practice and scholarship precisely because of public relations' emphasis on high ethical standards. However, findings of a dated content analysis of six public relations textbooks, suggested only weak links connecting public relations ethics, CSR, and professionalism (Bivins 1989). This research must be updated. Argued here, and elsewhere, postmodern values in public relations provide sufficient foundation for enabling public relations professionals to serve as insider-activists (Holtzhausen 2000, 2014) when they labor as a moral compass on behalf of the public sphere *and* organizations. Undergraduate and graduate public relations students should learn about CSR/Sustainability as an integral component of ethical public relations.

Specific routes by which public relations educators navigate complex challenges associated with CSR/Sustainability and public relations in the classroom remains fairly uncharted territory—but some inroads are being carved. Martinson (2004) suggested that public relations instructors offer role differentiation lessons to help advocate for a client/organization without lying, cheating, or breaking the law for them. In other words, how do we teach public relations students to simultaneously remain loyal to the boss while also being ethical and true to the larger public sphere? Jenny Carty, Reporting and Governance Manager at Royal Bank of Scotland (RBS), earned a postgraduate diploma in sustainable development after her undergraduate degree in economics. She encouraged college professors to teach ethics with regard to CSR/Sustainability in ways that will make it practical for on-the-job application:

> I don't really see how a course in and of itself could train you for everything that sustainability encompasses ... We have to discover where we

have material impact ... examples of working closely with other parts of the bank. It means that it's important to know your sector and know where your biggest impacts *are* so that you can help someone to make a difference and try to lessen the bad impacts and try to have as many good ones as you can.

Also useful to public relations educators when imparting these lessons is an exploration of leadership styles. Aldoory and Toth's (2004) findings which advance public relations practitioners' preference for the transformational style emphasizes collective vision, a necessary goal when practicing public relations role differentiation and walking a tightrope of endeavoring to serve many. Finally, public relations classroom instructors will find useful Fitzpatrick and Gauthier's (2001) principles that blend public relations' mutual obligations to serve client organizations and the public interest: comparison of harms/benefits, respect/dignity for all people, and distributive justice such that benefits/burdens of actions or policies are fairly disseminated.

Challenge 3: integrating ethics-CSR/Sustainability across the curriculum versus a stand-alone course

Even though educators and practitioners concur that ethical-CSR/Sustainability is an important ingredient for the public relations curriculum, opinions are mixed as to whether these teachings should be mainstreamed across coursework or offered as a stand-alone course. The Commission on Public Relations Education (2012) recommended an incorporation of attention to codes of ethics and credibility for undergraduate public relations courses—and *mastery* of ethics at the graduate level. Moreover, this panel of experts recommended expanding public relations education about ethics beyond geographical and geopolitical borders and provide for an expanded "role of communication in society and the ethical challenges of global public relations." Too, both educators and practitioners endorse curricular attention to ethics codes of practice, CSR, credibility, and transparency (DiStaso, Stacks, and Botan 2009). Unfortunately, Austin and Toth (2011) found that only *one* among 21 master's degree programs actually required a public relations ethics course or offered an ethics elective. One suggested remedy for gaps and disparities among public relations curricula is to follow the lead of MBA programs in the USA because they adhere to a uniform model and standardized course offerings across university settings (Aldoory and Toth 2000). On the other hand, Sockell (2013) said that core competencies in business schools fail to integrate ethics and social responsibility into decision making across the curriculum and that isolated ethics classes may be too abstract or philosophical for applied careers where value-laden decisions are made every day on a range of issues with social responsibility implications.

There are many advantages to teaching public relations, globally, by integrating ethics instruction across the curriculum. Incorporating critical thinking skills with regard to ethics-CSR/Sustainability among all public relations courses closely mirrors the work-a-day environment (Christians and Covert 1980). Findings of a content analysis of universities' public relations program websites and interviews with instructors suggested a global preference for incorporating ethics training across curricula rather than offering a stand-alone course (Austin and Toth 2011). Earlier, Harrison (1990) found that 93 percent of public relations faculty reported including ethics in their course content and advised for integrating ethics across the curriculum. For business schools, Sockell (2013) advised that because it is the *people* within corporations who commit fraud, college faculty must move beyond the case study by somehow enabling students to develop their own tools for discovering and developing "personal values and a sense of individual responsibility" across the curriculum. Evidence of success in spreading ethics teaching across a curriculum are found in religion-based universities (Hutchison 2002) and in disciplines of business, public administration, medicine, and other hard sciences (McDonald 2004). In addition, Hutchison (2002) suggested that smaller university programs may find it an easier sell to integrate ethics across courses rather than trying to introduce a new course that might mean a zero-sum decision to cut some other course or to extend time-to-graduation for students. Separate ethics courses in business school settings do not necessarily translate to higher levels of ethical decision making among students, so Davis and Welton (1991) suggested integrating ethics into existing curricula. Reserving ethics for one distinct course could short-change the depth and breadth of issues required for global public relations practice (Creedon and Al-Khaja 2005).

On the other hand, advocates of teaching a stand-alone ethics course have suggested that this affords instructors the opportunity to provide in-depth explorations. For example, ethics courses in public relations can provide breadth, and offering it this way may prove simpler than doing battle with institutional hurdles associated with approvals for a new curriculum (Austin and Toth 2011). Austin and Toth (2011) also posited that ethics content in multiple public relations courses such as communication law or strategies/tactics have a tacked-on feeling which risks having those units cut when other topics/issues considered more timely or relevant surface. Even though Christians and Covert (1980) support across-the-curriculum ethics-CSR/Sustainability teaching, they also note that a sole dedicated course legitimates its emphasis and that the complex nature of contemporary decision making may require more concentrated attention. Interestingly, Gale and Bunton (2005) found that having taken a formal undergraduate ethics course translated to alumni members' awareness of ethical issues, boosted their ethical reasoning skills, and enabled ethics lessons to linger with them over time. Perhaps, ideally, public relations curricula at both undergraduate and graduate levels should attend to ethics across the core curriculum as well as to offer one course devoted exclusively to in-depth ethics in CSR/Sustainability.

Challenge 4: considering business schools' teaching of ethics and CSR/Sustainability

Without doubt, the search is on among corporations that seek to hire people who possess competencies and skills for counseling management about ethics and CSR/Sustainability. One research team referred to this as "upward influence" (Spreitzer, De Janasz, and Quinn 1999: 511); an imperative which emphasizes universities' role in preparing graduates for careers. Yet, Parsons (2004) opined that social responsibility may be a fad since it emerged as "the catch phrase of the 1990s, with ethics courses springing up all over MBA programs" (p. 157). Sometimes public relations instruction in communication schools is compared to the teaching of management, marketing, and branding in business schools—with ethics instruction possibly standing out as shared common ground for both disciplines. Public relations scholars focus on the management function and relationship building role among stakeholders, while business scholars tend to frame public relations as a support function and source for promotion and publicity. James Grunig (n.d.) considered this to be "one of the greatest challenges facing senior public relations executives today" and blamed institutionalization of public relations among marketing faculty and business school deans as "mak[ing] something look good when it isn't. Or it's trying to persuade us to do something that is really not in our best interest. Or it's trying to create favorable publicity in the media. And, you can't trust what a public relations person says. Or it's unethical and so on."

A comparison/contrast of US and European approaches to business school attention to ethics offers a revealing glimpse into curriculum development. To assess business school leaders' perspectives on CSR/Sustainability education in Europe, Matten and Moon's (2004) survey findings suggested that CSR is being "mainstreamed" into the core curriculum, a move consistent with encouragement provided by the UK government's CSR Academy (p. 323). CSR is a fairly recent development in Europe and one driver was US-based corporate scandals and finger pointing by the business press (Caulkin 2004) and academics (Adler 2002) at formative business schools' training. On the US side of the Atlantic, public relations practitioners are divided as to whether ethics-CSR/Sustainability classroom training is better coming from the public relations/communication college or the business school. A mid-Atlantic public relations agency vice president offered mixed reactions to the *home* debate and included advice for teaching CSR/Sustainability in upper-level undergraduate public relations courses:

> I don't think it comes at the Intro to PR level. I think students have to have an understanding of PR and the value of that before they get into one silo of PR which is CSR ... I also think it's a business adjunct subject because of the power of CSR to drive the bottom line ... It probably should have a home in PR as far as education goes. That's who's going to drive the point home in the real world; the PR professional's going to carry the flag for CSR.

Pedagogical directions for teaching ethics in CSR

Some recent teaching-oriented advice has been offered to supplement the public relations pedagogy literature. Cap (n.d.) applauded professional trade organizations for sponsoring codes of ethics to promote "honest, social responsibility and good governance," but added that these may mean nothing if executives fail to read them and live by them. Mahoney (2014) opined that the USA lags far behind Europe on many counts in addressing business ethics. At the 1998 National Communication Association (NCA) summer conference in the USA, van Leuven (1999) led a team which advanced four specific public relations major competencies—the very first one being ethics— so that students could "understand the parameters and frameworks utilized in ethical reasoning of professional issues. Discussions and coursework should increase knowledge, professional skills and a sense of true professionalism" (p. 82). Hutchison's (2002) evaluation of undergraduate public relations text-book attention to ethics-CSR/Sustainability recommended involving students in group presentations, developing socially responsible campaigns, and detailing ethical issues encountered while working internships. Other sets of findings have suggested that public relations instructors incorporate ethics content into service learning courses (Witmer, Silverman, and Gaschen 2009), reflect on current events and produce their own videos for class discussion (McWilliams and Nahavandi 2006), develop and invite students to play an "Ethics Bingo Game" to discern current ethical situations and professional ethical codes (Haywood, McMullen, and Wygal 2004), explore organizational contexts of ethical issues by examining narratives embedded in case studies and feature films (Moberg 2006), infuse class discussion with textbook case studies and dialogue about ethics discussions and questions addressed in chapters (Hutchison 2002), and use Socratic dialogue with students and invite them to keep a journal of ethics in the news—in addition to inviting guest speakers and arranging video conferences with them (van Leuven 1999).

Acquiring ethical CSR/Sustainability training on the job and beyond

At-work training and development programs for employees have a rich history and continue to evolve with emerging technological innovations. Traditional on-site employee development programs offer tailored alternative means to train employees about ethics–CSR/Sustainability beyond traditional university-setting learning environments. Research findings suggest that employer-sponsored workshops can prove highly effective in developing employees' leadership skills and managerial potential. In the CSR/Sustainability management space, customizable and flexible toolkits including ethics guidelines may be used to train employees so long as senior-level management buys in and the organizational culture is accepting of creative and innovative thinking (Knight 2006). Investigating IBM's corporate citizenship group, Deutsch (2008) found that a development exercise of pairing employees with philanthropic outreach activities provided fertile opportunities for developing employees' talents as ethical decision makers because they learn how to cope with change and gain increased social and cultural awareness. These employees may be classified as organizational assets, or "high potentials" (Ready, Conger, and Hill 2010).

Perhaps most formal among company development and training programs is the corporate university model. Allen (2002) defined this as: "[A]ny educational entity that is a strategic tool designed to assist its parent organization in achieving its goals by conducting activities that foster individual and organizational learning and knowledge" (p. 9). The number of corporate universities worldwide increased to 2000 in 2001 from only 400 in 1993 and multinational corporations hosting them include Boeing, Motorola, and Disney (Hearn 2002). Corporate universities are widely applauded for their flexibility and customization according to organizational cultures and needs, as well as quality and availability of technology for content delivery (El-Tannir 2002). One global financial institution's corporate university-trained employee teams by raising awareness of local social issues while simultaneously helping an NGO (Cisernos 2008). A desire to help employees learn first-hand about how and why socially responsible behavior happens and to enhance their decision-making skills has prompted some corporate university and executive training course directors to teach ethics via computer simulations, games, and case analyses, as well as infusing these traditional tools with meditation and yoga for social consciousness raising (Schneider, Zollo, and Manocha 2010). Policy studies organizations also offer formal programs in CSR/Sustainability, which include attention to ethics. Erin Fitzgerald, Senior Vice President, Sustainability at Innovation Center for US Dairy, explained how The Aspen Institute based in Washington, DC, in the USA helps:

> I'm a fellow ... One of the things that came up at the Aspen Institute is CSR and Sustainability. We created a new fellowship just for the CSR professional ... to give education and guidelines to the CSR professional to start embedding sustainability into the corporate strategy beyond just the CSR suite.

According to Mahoney (2014), some professors and pedagogical materials are more advanced than others—depending on one's geographic location—but added that institutions are morally responsible to the public sphere for promoting study of the ethics of business "just as much as the study of other dimensions and aspects of business" (p. 183). Moreover, ethics education constitutes an ongoing process; a lifetime of learning.

Discussion

This chapter's goal of exploring how/where/when public relations students acquire skills necessary for performing important responsibilities was examined in terms of integrating public relations ethics and CSR/Sustainability. Examined were ways that public relations managers prepare for ethics-CSR/Sustainability counseling and offered were insights into formal college classroom course-work and other on-the-job training such as that offered by *corporate universities*. Noted, in particular, are overlaps of CSR/Sustainability with regard to ethics, boundary spanning, and issues management. Elements of planning, research, collaborative decision making, and an ability to respect stakeholder positions also are important considerations in relationship building for the insider-activist—placing CSR/Sustainability squarely within the public relations arena.

Communication and ethics are the ties that bind the CSR/Sustainability-PR overlap. It was prophesied long ago that communication must be used to influence organizations to amend and adopt new policies and procedures in order to avoid a legitimacy gap (Sethi 1977). Indeed, this mantra is well visualized in the Venn diagram spheres of people, profit, and planet so widely used in conjunction with CSR. Heath (2013a) explained that a "legitimacy gap is that chasm between what an organization believes and does and what its key publics think it should believe" (p. 497). One of a public relations professor's chief responsibilities is to help students use communication and to view all public relations work through an ethics lens so that they may weigh the right thing to do against merely making an organization look good. Public relations professors set the tone for a career's worth of serving as an organizational conscience.

7 Measuring and reporting CSR/Sustainability

Organizations worldwide formally report on their CSR/Sustainability activities, goals, and achievements to demonstrate commitment and accountability. While no unifying theory has emerged among CSR/Sustainability reporting studies, the literature features three streams for understanding it: business case (good for profits), stakeholder accountability (proof preferred by certain groups and publics), and critical theory (critique of capitalist exploitation) (Brown and Fraser 2006). Some organizations, more than others, also report on *unac-*hieved goals to provide a more complete and transparent view; a tactic proven to yield stakeholder trust when explanations are offered for moving forward. Corporations operating in industries perceived as particularly risky to people and the natural environment may be accustomed to experiencing stakeholder skepticism, so it is especially important that *these* organizations act transparently in CSR/Sustainability reporting. This chapter explores these themes: CSR/Sustainability reporting; CSR/Sustainability evaluation and reporting challenges; public relations and CSR/Sustainability reporting; the quantitative/qualitative research methods debate; and improving CSR/Sustainability measurement and reporting.

CSR/Sustainability reporting

Some organizations rationalize a need for CSR/Sustainability reporting as response to stakeholder pressures. CSR/Sustainability reports may serve as tangible evidence of organizations' attention to a triple bottom line. While some corporations report on CSR/Sustainability programs in their traditional financial annual report formats, others produce stand-alone reports and post them on websites. Required reporting has progressive backing in Europe (Tschopp 2005) and France became the first nation in 2001 requiring public companies to produce CSR/Sustainability reports. Guidelines have improved for multinational corporations' CSR/Sustainability reporting in many parts of the world and among small and medium enterprises (SMEs), such as those in China. Tim Hui, Global Reporting Initiative (GRI) Director in China, described "top-level" companies' reporting as having "room for improvement," but praised the SMEs:

For small enterprises, interestingly, some of them have really done a good job with CSR or sustainability. For example, some really shabby small company which is a supplier of international buyer ... Wal-Mart ... they turn out to be very innovative in improving their social performance ... when they dye, say the Levi jeans, and they control drier temperature to save the cost. The outcome of this effort turned out to be both cost effective and environmentally friendly.

Numerous resources inspire voluntary CSR/Sustainability guidelines for organizations. The United Nations Global Compact, launched in 1999, is a non-legally-binding commitment for businesses worldwide to regularly report on progress toward achieving CSR/Sustainability goals ("Overview" 2013) and the World Business Council for Sustainable Development (2003) listed reporting benefits such as creating financial value, drawing talent, and attracting long-term capital and favorable financing. Also, the Sullivan Principles encourage corporations toward fair and equitable employment (Rolland and Bazzoni 2009) and the Brundtland Report of 1987 ("Our Common Future") is built upon outcomes of the United Nations Conference on the Human Environment. While voluntary guideline compliance can prove beneficial to corporations seeking benchmarks, of course, they lack enforcement powers.

Popular social investment mutual funds have heightened visibility of CSR/Sustainability ratings that further motivates companies to report on the environmental and social impacts of their operations. Investors, lobbyists, and NGOs rely heavily upon CSR and sustainability reports as part of their social investment mutual fund recommendations (Tschopp 2005) and need to know how particular companies attend to key issues such as child labor, health and safety, human rights, and other socio-environmental concerns. Beyond altruistic motives attached to protecting the natural environment and fostering equitable workplaces, corporations find that reporting on CSR/Sustainability efforts has financial benefits when businesses are positively ranked according to the Dow Jones Sustainability Index, FTSE4Good, UK 50 Index, the Dow Jones Sustainability Stoxx Index, the Calvert Social Index, and more (Márquez and Fombrun 2005). Socially responsible investment funds appeal to shareholders as a mechanism for pressuring corporations into more responsible practices (Ballou, Heitger, and Landes 2006) and to forming more ethical relationships with suppliers and politicians (Morsing and Schultz 2006). Investors value corporate social performance (Cheung 2011), but more often may use such indices to downgrade large profitable corporations that rank low on scales (Lourenço, Branco, Curto, *et al.* 2012).

Ratings and rankings

When researching a particular corporation's CSR/Sustainability record, investors and other stakeholders may choose among a number of rankings and ratings agencies. Some organizations blend external ratings and regulatory compliance guidelines (Castka, Bamber, Bamber, and Sharp 2004) or rely on templates such as PricewaterhouseCoopers' self-assessment reputational assurance framework to help companies manage their CSR and accountability processes (Frankental 2001). Reporting on corporate sustainability performance is considered "an investable concept" ("Corporate Sustainability" n.d.); one attractive to investors also interested in nonfinancial disclosures about business practices (Lourenço, Branco, Curto, *et al.* 2012). Yet, critics have suggested that paid-for management consulting and auditing assurance services firms' ratings introduces conflict of interest potential (Márquez and Fombrun 2005)— and none represent any internationally accepted global standard (Tschopp 2005). The most widely used CSR and sustainability guidelines and standards include:

1   The Global Reporting Index (GRI), launched in 1997, was initially developed by the United Nations, with guidelines from the Coalition for Environmentally Responsible Economies (CERES). The G4, fourth generation of GRI benchmarks, was introduced in 2014 following extensive consultation with investors, civil societies, and others. GRI Director, North America, Eric Israel explained, "We have close to 6000 companies producing sustainability reports and the majority of them, 80% or more, are using the GRI guidelines. Companies who are not using the GRI guidelines use *aspects* of the GRI guidelines ... they use the things that are convenient for them."

2   The Governance & Accountability Institute, Inc. (2014) serves as "the exclusive data partner" (p. 207) for GRI in the USA, UK, and Republic of Ireland and offers in its free report "top 10" and "bottom 10" frequencies of reported-on indicators. Hank Boerner, Chairman, Chief Strategist and Co-Founder of Governance & Accountability Institute, Inc. explained that some items are "easy" to report, such as financial information that already is assembled for the 10K annual filing that publicly traded US companies are required to submit to the Securities and Exchange Commission. Yet, Boerner added that the more complex sustainability indicators tend to be reported on less, such as "... male and female promotion rates ... that becomes a much less responded-to indicator and they go down to the bottom." Boerner said that the Governance & Accountability Institute's 2013 survey findings suggested that 72% of the S&P "... are doing something that we can call a report ... the actions, the program management steps, the teams we've organized, the achievements ... so we have a favorable story. Those arguments are good with the investor audience, also good with the supply chain audience."

3   The Institute of Social and Ethical Accountability (ISEA) AA1000 standard, since 2003, focuses on corporate financial accounting, social and environmental reporting processes according to impacts on multiple stakeholder groups, and integration of corporate values (ISEA 1999a, 1999b), considered a unique standard in assessing adherence to Accountability Principles (AccountAbility 2008).

4   The SA8000 developed by the Council on Economic Priorities Accred-
      itation, assesses performance on labor issues, health and safety, collective
      bargaining, discrimination, disciplinary practices, working hours, and
      compensation.
5   The International Standard on Assurance Engagements framework
      (ISAE100) is used to assess non-financial data such as corporations'
      attention to ethical considerations. It was released in 2000 and updated in
      2003 ("Sustainability Assurance" n.d.).
6   The ISO14001 standard also supports corporations' work in establishing
      environmental policy and development of programs ("ISO 14000" n.d.).

Reporting among NGOs and nonprofits

Nonprofits and NGOs are neither immune to nor excluded from the drive
toward transparency in social responsibility and sustainability reporting. One
hundred and five "nonprofit/services" around the world filed reports in 2013
("Sustainability Disclosure Database" 2014). CSR/Sustainability reporting
enables nonprofits to reverse reputational damage caused by misappropriation
of donor funds, questionable fundraising methods, and misuse of donors' personal
information—such as at the American Red Cross, the Nature Conservancy, and
the United Way (Waters 2005). Strategic corporate/nonprofit partnerships on
social issues like education, environment, health, and poverty include funding
for nonprofits, synergies which promote building on one another's strengths in
pursuit of a common purpose (Back 2011; Seitanidi and Crane 2009). Government cutbacks and a shift in social services provision from government to
nonprofits in many nations have made fundraising more important than ever.
Nonprofits seek to fill financial gaps by accepting more corporate dollars
through cause-marketing campaigns. CSR/Sustainability movement critics
worry, however, that nonprofits do not always report on partnerships with
corporations and become compromised (Seitanidi and Ryan 2007). John Bee,
Communication Manager, Public Affairs, Nestlé, headquartered in Switzerland,
explained that Creating Shared Value (CSV) programs and reporting represents several years of metamorphosis and that partnering with nonprofits has
been central to new ways of doing business at Nestlé:

> We, as an organization, have changed a lot over the last ten years. The
> report was what we were required to report on and not a great deal more.
> If we were challenged, then we'd challenge the challenger. I think that all
> changed in about 2010 when – you know, we were targeted by Green-
> peace on our use of palm oil. We got targeted and we got it wrong in the
> way we responded because we weren't as open and willing to engage as
> we should have been. Now, we learned pretty quickly and we turned it
> around … "What's the real root of this issue? It's not orangutans and Kit-
> Kat. It's deforestation. What can we do pro-actively to address that?" We
> formed a partnership with an organization called the Forest Trust to get

deforestation out of our supplies. By doing that and by then having Greenpeace applaud us for doing that – for getting it right – we were then able to apply that learning to different challenges that we were still grappling with and still are.

To avoid compromising a nonprofit's mission whilst accepting corporate funds, Susan Sabatino, Account Manager, Marketing Partnerships Team at the Nature Conservancy, explained:

[G]oals are to renew with the company if the partnership has worked out well. It's a two-way assessment. We'll assess how much we got out of the partnership—exposure through their channels, revenue we've received from them, how much of a heavy lift it's been for us. With some of our smaller partners, they have pretty high expectations for the partnership and those are often difficult for us to deliver upon because it's a small amount of revenue so we have to match up to what we put into it ... We have to be quite cautious about how much promotion we give a company. We can be subject to what's called Unrelated Business Income Tax (UBIT). If we do too much promotion for a company, if they're getting too much value from us related to the value we're getting from them, we could be exposed to that tax. We always have to be really careful when we're working with companies ... It's also about we're not here to promote a company. It's not our job. We need to be careful that we balance it out with our mission, as well.

NGOs and other nonprofits also use CSR/Sustainability reporting and databases to inform their agendas and to fuel debates for challenging corporations to improve operations. Boerner, at the Governance & Accountability Institute, explained that sometimes nonprofits fail to consider the scope of requests for data which could upset competitive environments if made public:

The more that these various global framers push, push, push to get to spread the range of what they're looking for and get more and more material information, I think the more pushback they're going to see as they come to companies and say "We'd like you to disclose the following." Companies will say, "Yes or it's OK," or "We're not comfortable with that. We'll give you some of it" – and "No, we're not going to give you any of it." The challenge is – mostly nonprofits and mostly not in the business world – who make up these frameworks and present them to the industrial leaders. That's a real challenge.

Nonprofit trade organizations also increasingly play an instrumental role in inspiring companies to participate in CSR/Sustainability measurement and reporting. Erin Fitzgerald, Senior Vice President, Sustainability at Innovation Center for US Dairy, explained these unique dynamics and contexts:

Everyone could go and do their own, but collectively there's a fundamental belief that we're stronger together if we can share best practices,
training, and tools. We can move faster. The challenge is how do you
report that collective change as an industry? We were the first industry
that ever set a voluntary greenhouse gas goal ... We see now that the
Apparel Coalition has done that – which is looking at child labor issues,
developing better textiles for products. We think that many other industry
sectors should band together and voluntarily address issues. There's a lot
of tremendous power in that. The second issue is "My gosh, how do
you start demonstrating progress?" We have had to develop a sustainability measuring system of our own. We follow GRI because there's no
industry standard actually for reporting on the sector. Then, we are
trying to encourage all of our members as a category to start voluntarily
reporting.

CSR/Sustainability evaluation and reporting challenges

Whether reports are compiled by using guidelines established within an
organization or by using outside resources, CSR/Sustainability evaluation and
reporting features multiple shortcomings. Companies often complain about
the cost and time spent filling out surveys and granting interviews with raters;
data used for compiling reports (Márquez and Fombrun 2005). Contracting
for an externally-produced CSR/Sustainability report is no guarantee that
findings will be positive, earn awards, increase sales, enhance reputation,
positively influence stakeholders, or stave off activists. CSR/Sustainability
report critiques cluster according to three themes. First, organizations provide
limited information about how operations and management decisions directly
affect stakeholders. Clarkson (1995) opined that *stakeholder satisfaction
should serve as the standard measure of CSR/Sustainability reporting.* Corporations infrequently nurture face-to-face dialog with external audiences to
discover operations' effects on quality of life, especially in developing nations
(Blowfield 2007). Second, CSR/Sustainability reports often attend more
to financial than social goals (Gray and Milne 2004) so that corporations'
focus on sustainability of the *business* rather than environmental sustainability leads to a "reporting-performance portrayal gap" (Adams 2004:
731). Forty multinational companies' environmental reports largely ignored
social impacts (Morhardt, Baird, and Freeman 2002: 225). In 2000, Shell was
among the first major UK corporations to issue a report assessing a company's social impact on multiple dimensions (Frankental 2001); this was
a follow-up to Royal Dutch/Shell's 1995 Brent Spar oil platform crisis
(Hoogheimstra 2000). Third, crafting of goals in CSR/Sustainability reporting
is critiqued. Providing all stakeholders—not just stockholders—with reliable
data as revealed through specific objectives, measurable outcomes, and anticipated achievement dates, goes a long way in establishing credibility and
building trust. Sometimes overly broad goals—as when a food manufacturer

pledges to "eradicate hunger"—are unrealistic and not measureable. Bee at Nestlé reflected on rhetoric of such goals:

> We don't like things like that, actually. We made a conscious decision we weren't going to go there. We're a Swiss company in a Swiss culture. Swiss culture is do it first, immaculately, flawlessly, and then report it back to the office ... [W]e're not going to gaze into a crystal ball because there are too many variables. We will tell you what is within our power to plan to do. We will set ourselves on the course to doing so. We also recognize that we do not have all the answers.

Conversely, low-balling at the outset means that organizations have a stronger likelihood of meeting certain goals so that they may publicize their achievements. Jennifer Pontzer, Co-owner of Concept Green, a US-based firm which provides sustainability consulting and support services, described unique cases when this strategy is acceptable: "[N]ear term goal of what you think you can meet works with behavior change and then gradually 'Let's set a goal that we're really going to have to think about how we can achieve it' ... Then there's the ten-year goal and 'Oh, we did it in three'." Study findings of content analyses of CSR/Sustainability reports suggest inattention to goal timetables or a defined end point for assessment, making most goals aspirational rather than realistic (Isaksson and Steimle 2009). Also, a practice of cherry-picking only positive results for CSR/Sustainability reports is inauthentic. Carrie Christopher, Co-owner Concept Green, a firm which provides sustainability consulting and support services, explained that transparency in reporting is a challenge: "There's an art and a science to it ... Fear of transparency. We don't want to feel bad about ourselves. We have blind spots. Opening a Pandora's box and looking at your flaws is never fun for anyone. The accountability can be very fuzzy." Consequently, some researchers have argued that considering CSR/Sustainability a *destination* short changes efforts to define, measure and report on goals because the journey may be ill-defined, never ending, or a chimera strategically promoted by organizations to avoid real accountability (Milne, Kearins, and Walton 2006).

Hence, providing an understanding of why organizations *do not report on* certain goal measures could substantively improve CSR/Sustainability reporting as a means for demonstrating authenticity and for building trust. By not reporting on specific issues such as gas emissions and social equity/human rights, some corporations falsely frame their operations as socially responsible and mislead stakeholders with one-sided views (Moneva, Archel, and Correa 2006). Additionally, companies that provide CSR and sustainability reports on their own website or other Internet-based depositories may be unable to resist revisionism (Adams 2004). Even though organizations have a unique opportunity for transparency by reporting on goals that they have *not* achieved with full explanations of circumstances and plans moving forward, very few actually do. Brenda Colatrella, Executive Director of Corporate

Responsibility at Merck, explained why reporting on *un*achieved goals is standard practice at this US-based pharmaceutical company: "We also want to acknowledge where we could have done better or something that failed." Jennifer Pontzer, Co-owner of Concept Green, a firm which provides sustainability consulting and support services, explained the benefits of total transparency in CSR/Sustainability reporting:

> It's a big part of the training courses we do. Within the GRI guidelines, there's a set of report principles for defining report quality and *balancing* is one of them ... not just talking about the good, that's easy ... With good sustainability reporting, you have what's called a disclosure of management approach ... If you're doing a strong job but just don't hit the goal and communicate the reasons why, those are the reports that build trust and are more genuine ... I would love to see the day when a company did not hit their greenhouse gas reductions and their stock plummeted. Maybe that's what we need, you know?

Sometimes organizations strategically decide to *not* report on certain goals. Boerner at G&AI explained that divulging data about energy use or waste-to-landfill could put some companies at a disadvantage should a competitor have access to those data: "So, while they have the information and it's good to have, they'll share it privately if asked, but they will not do it publicly ... We had an example given to us. The guy reverse engineered a competitor and then told us what that competitor was doing."

Finally, critiques of CSR/Sustainability reports have coalesced around flaws associated with economic, environmental and social auditing processes, standards, and metrics. Some external auditors' qualifications and ethical standards are unconvincing (Owen, Swift, Humphrey, *et al.* 2000) and there exist no universal guidelines. Moreover, use of lists such as Standard & Poor's represents only large corporations, leaving out CSR/Sustainability achievements among significant numbers of medium and small organizations, as well as nonprofits. Also, stronger environmental lobby groups may overpower weaker ones by advancing their own agendas in promoting specific guidelines (Larrinaga and Bebbington 2001). Consequently, the form of what is reported according to GRI and other agencies varies widely and simple check lists do not necessarily ensure accountability (Adams 2004). Annual and CSR reports of 108 Belgian corporations were incomplete and lacked detail and variety of information—such as vision/goals, management approach, performance indicators (Bouten, Everaert, van Liedekerke, De Moor, *et al.* 2011). Doug Bannerman, Leader Social Performance at Statoil, a Norway-based oil and gas production company, explained that changing the minds of critics may be futile: "If people are going to look at what we do in the CSR and sustainability space as nothing more than window dressing, then if that's the value they want to assign to it then that's probably the value it will have." Yet, Bannerman recommended using positive metrics that show value:

I think we've only ever had negative metrics, which is unfortunate – "If you don't do this, this horrible thing could potentially maybe happen" – like in a developing country, you might say "Yeah, well people are going to lock arms and lay down across the road and we won't be able to get trucks onto a construction site". For the most part, even for a project manager – in their mind, they're like "So, OK, I'm going to lose a million dollars a day. Whatever."

Establishing global standards and mandatory reporting on environmental, social, and financial goals could greatly boost credibility and stakeholder confidence in CSR/Sustainability, overall. Some academics have recommended that industries conduct themselves like the accounting profession; by attending to *assurance*—or, retaining an independent third party for review and verification of CSR/Sustainability. Assurance statements have become a standard fixture in 30% of European CSR reports, but only 7% in the USA (Coombs and Holladay 2012).

To address CSR/Sustainability reporting shortcomings, some organizations have subscribed to the concept of integrated reporting. This involves tracking value creation longitudinally so that reports may offer "concise communication about how an organization's strategy, governance, performance, and prospects, in the context of its external environment, lead to the creation of value in the short, medium, and long term" ("About IR" n.d.) According to Carol Adams, a senior researcher and professor of CSR/Sustainability on faculty at Monash University and Director of Integrated Horizons consultancy in Australia:

> Integrated reporting is a form of corporate reporting where organizations have to understand the sustainability implications of the work that they're doing. The social and environmental implications and the idea is that they tell the value creation story – which is broader than just looking at flows of money in and out. It goes beyond looking at the financial value that's being created by the organization. It looks at relationship value, for example, the people, the human capital – what's being contributed to human capital.

Scott Dille, Group Leader at Denmark-based Novo Nordisk, told of how an integrated reporting framework provides greater clarity when reporting on results at this healthcare company:

> We just stopped using GRI starting this year ... We are part of the UN Global Compact ... We've been trying to align our non-financial reporting with Sarbanes-Oxley requirements ... At the end of the day, too, there has to be accountability ... that extra motivation to drive better and better. That's one of the reasons we like integrated reporting because it exposes the relationship between things a bit more. Our CO_2 emissions

could have fallen dramatically from the previous year, but if it's not clear that's because we had falling sales and didn't produce as much, it's really not that interesting.

Public relations and CSR/Sustainability reporting

Public relations' role with regard to CSR/Sustainability reporting is seldom formally evaluated—notwithstanding condemnation of public relations as a tool of obfuscation commonly referred to as *greenwashing* or *spin* (Munshi and Kurian 2005). Twenty-three percent of US-based public relations professionals said that they lack measures for evaluating the value of CSR communications (Anonymous 2006). Epstein-Reeves (2011) argued for using the GRI standard to avoid producing a CSR report that "look[s] like an oversized, fluff marketing piece" (p. 2). As I have argued elsewhere, few corporate public relations managers actually follow through with measuring CSR/Sustainability programs beyond what is legally mandated for their industry (Pompper 2013), even though public relations counselors could make measurable contributions as communicators, boundary spanners, and insider-activists. What public relations practitioners *do* is become willing accomplices in sustaining negative slurs about the industry when they produce back-slapping publicity. CSR should not be simply "reduced to brand familiarity" (David, Kline, and Dai 2005: 297). Enduring are accusations of public relations' manufacture of "the appearance of its own goodness" (Roberts 2003: 263) through *good works narratives*. Reputation building work using one-way communication tools such as advertising, marketing, and publicity is less expensive than actual pursuit of CSR, Crouch (2006) emphasized. Cynthia Figge, COO and Co-Founder of CSRHub and Partner and Co-Founder of EKOS International, US, said: "It's really critical that the CSR report is not a marketing piece. People are really very clear on the difference ... A few years ago, Starbucks got criticized because their CSR report kinda smacked of too much marketing-speak."

Several public relations agencies now include CSR/Sustainability reporting expertise among their portfolio of services and serve as consultants, trainers, and publicists. Scott (2008) classified CSR consultancies providing assurance as a growth industry and Heath and Ni (2009) called CSR "a multi-billion dollar public relations specialty in the business world." Carrie Christopher, Co-owner of the Albuquerque-based consulting firm in the USA, Concept Green, explained that public relations and accounting firms offer the greatest competition for external CSR/Sustainability reporting services, but she sees this as a positive development: "We want the field to be full of ethical and educated and competent professionals because everybody wins." Joannides and Miller (n.d.) offered a sharply critical perspective of profit-centric consultancies providing CSR/Sustainability reporting standards and questioned their claims of *pioneering* and *leading worldwide authorities*. Very few public relations professionals interviewed for this book project agreed that they measure public relationships central to CSR/Sustainability reporting goals, most confessing that they only assess relationships insofar as they contribute to a small section of the corporate annual report, have a positive story to tell, or seek nonprofit partnerships.

Alignment of public relations with CSR/Sustainability measurement and reporting offers numerous benefits to organizations and stakeholders. Perhaps the most ardent champion of measurement and assessment in public relations, generally, has been Walter K. Lindenmann, a researcher and practitioner who served for many years as vice-president of research with Ketchum Public Relations in New York and has consulted with the Institute for Public Relations (IPR) in the USA. The IPR maintains a Commission on Public Relations Measurement & Evaluation, setting standards for the profession (White 1999). Jenny Carty, Reporting and Governance Manager at Royal Bank of Scotland (RBS), explained the importance of measurement: "The sustainability team here is 23 people strong ... We also conduct research and the purpose of the research is to feed into our policies ... So, for example, we're researching a paper on agriculture and the results of that research will feed into the scoping of the agricultural policy." Assessment of organization-public relationships gains credibility for organizations when data are collected and analyzed longitudinally; something that public relations practitioners are trained to do. Long-term relationships prove significantly more valuable to organizations than shallow short-term tactics and programs (Hon and Grunig 1999). Perhaps complicating efforts to further professionalize public relations for its ability to tangibly measure relationships is the ongoing practice of counting clips rather than as a normative touchstone for high ethical standards and insider-activism.

The quantitative/qualitative research methods debate

Methodological flaws in CSR/Sustainability reporting and manipulation of numbers used to quantify impacts and words used to describe them constitutes unethical behavior. Frankental (2001) opined that methodologies used for CSR/Sustainability reporting, generally, are poor and that organizations misuse techniques to accentuate, exaggerate, or avoid outcomes. Quantitative research methods are widely favored for CSR/Sustainability assessment even though numbers are as easy to misuse as language if the goal is to represent an organization favorably by selectively downplaying negative outcomes and promoting positive ones. Numbers represent an international language associated with finance, but organizations that confuse stakeholders by attaching numerical scores to descriptive variables and add categories to reports without actually doing more CSR amounts to manipulation (Morhardt, Baird, and Freeman 2002). Also, social impacts may not lend to numerical reporting and instead be better understood through words. Roberts (2003) concluded that perhaps social impacts are reported less frequently than financial impacts because they seem less quantifiable. Qualitative research methods prove especially helpful when assessing two-way dialog with stakeholders. Content analyzing feedback contained in blogs (Carson 2008) and corporate websites (Capriotti and Moreno 2007) reveals important stakeholder perceptions about corporate performance. Yet, many have criticized corporations for relying on narratives to tell their CSR/Sustainability story and one team opined that "qualitative statements about risk management ... are not reliable enough to audit" (Ballou, Heitger, and Landes 2006: 67). Doug Bannerman, Leader Social Performance at Statoil, a Norway-based oil and gas production company, critiqued measurement in CSR/Sustainability reporting:

[W]ith some of these big companies with deep, deep pockets, if somebody tells me they've spent $5 million on education, I'm like "Wow, that's a great number, but so what? What does that translate into? How many beneficiaries and what did that mean? ... [S]o, like how many kids went through that school? How many of those kids went to college? How many of those kids graduated from college? What kind of jobs did they get? How did their lives turn out?" ... [O]n the environmental side, it seems so much easier – and it's not because it hasn't been hard won. Like when you get into things like water management, emissions, that sort of stuff, it's crystal clear because you've got, "Here's what the regulation is," or "Here's what the company practice and policy is on this and we're measuring like crazy." Whereas on the social side, it still seems like the wild, wild west. It's like is it number of stakeholder meetings? Is it outcomes of stakeholder meetings? Is it community sentiment? Everyone sort of looks at me like, "How are we going to measure all this stuff?" I'm like, "I'm still trying to figure that out."

Bannerman at Statoil also critiqued GRI guidelines for de-emphasizing qualitative data such as conversations and negotiations between organizations and shareholders:

If you look at the environmental stuff, it's like "How much water?" "What's been the input to your product line, blah, blah, blah?" And then on the social side it's like "Do you have agreements with labor unions and stuff like that?" I'm like, OK, these are nice to know, but how to weight the stuff they're asking you to measure on the social? Are you actually making any kind of a difference? It's really hard to say.

Combining attributes of both quantitative and qualitative research method traditions well-serves CSR/Sustainability measurement and reporting. The communication audit method gained popularity during the 1980s and has been used extensively by public relations to benchmark communication management programs and for environmental scanning projects. For instance, organizations may assess CSR/Sustainability activities and stakeholder perceptions by combining survey, content analysis, interview, and focus group data. A CSR/Sustainability research team recommended a combination of qualitative and quantitative formal research methods which takes into account disclosed, perceived, and required commitment aspects—what they called a *CSR positioning matrix* which uses GRI indicators and the content analysis method (Calabrese, Costa, Menichini, *et al.* 2012). A useful research method for reporting on globalization effects is the multi-sited ethnography technique which involves multiple methods and enables a researcher to follow "a topic or social problem through different field sites geographically and/or socially" ("Multi-Sited Ethnography" n.d.).

Improving CSR/Sustainability measurement and reporting

Academics, communicators, and others have recommended CSR/Sustainability assessment, measurement and reporting enhancements. Suggestions cluster into three main categories: external oversight, internal guardianship, and integration of internal and external responsibility.

External oversight

Perhaps only legislation by a global regulatory body with punitive powers can hold organizations accountable for authentic CSR/Sustainability and reporting. While corporations may resist mandatory CSR/Sustainability reporting standards (Rodriguez and LeMaster 2007), global oversight could address voluntary measure shortcomings. Companies are legally required to report on aspects of ethical, social, and environmental impact in Australia, Denmark, France, the Netherlands, Norway, Sweden, and the USA. Tschopp (2005) called for regulatory bodies such as the Securities and Exchange Commission (SEC), the European Commission, the International Accounting Standards Board, or others to work for *worldwide consensus* on mandatory CSR/ Sustainability reporting systems that put social and environmental assessments on par with financial audits. An SEC seal of approval could take the form of strengthening and expanding requirements as outlined by the Sarbanes-Oxley Act (SOX) in the USA—even though SOX is neither as fraud-proof as hoped (Ballou, Heitger, and Landes 2006) nor as widely regarded among strategic communicators who doubt SOX's ability to eradicate unethical corporate behavior (Pompper 2014). In the USA, Estes' (1996) recommended a Corporate Accountability Act enforced by a Corporate Accountability Commission which would provide for mandatory stakeholder input. CSR/Sustainability reports which include reviews of external media reportage and stakeholder feedback provide a broader lens for transparent reporting. During an interview for this book project, senior CSR scholar and consultant Carol Adams reflected on her urging of companies to include such feedback in CSR/Sustainability reports (Adams 1999, 2004):

> I used to do the judging for the ACCA sustainability reporting awards. There was one year that Shell won it. This was while I was based in

the UK. What had happened was Shell had a lot of bad press about the Ngoni people, the Brent Spar platform – and that included negative feedback from stakeholders in its sustainability report two or three years afterwards … It was really being transparent – doing this to build trust back up. That's the main time I've seen it. It's not something you come across regularly, especially negative feedback. What I found with sustainability reporting is the least honest you are, the more you try to hide things or not reveal them in your sustainability report, the more the media will chase you.

Normative measures for global ethical codes of conduct for industries and consultation with the United Nations' Norms on the Responsibilities of Transnational Corporations has been recommended, too. Also, the news media in some nations point out wrongdoing in the public sphere, a watchdog function (Donohue, Tichenor, and Olien 1995).

Internal guardianship

Researchers have concluded that CSR/Sustainability is undervalued, internally, because initiatives are not well embedded across organizations. Integrating CSR/Sustainability inter-departmentally makes for easier reporting and greater value (Melo and Galan 2011). Few are organizations that administer CSR/Sustainability from an exclusive office, department, or cross-functional team (Anonymous 2006). Critics warned that placing CSR squarely within a public relations department can detract from perceptions of genuine commitment given the public relations field's reputation for publicity and philanthropy (Frankental 2001). Retaining third party public relations agencies to generate CSR/Sustainability publicity may exacerbate those perceptions. On the other hand, taking the actual CSR/Sustainability auditing process outside may foster a perception among stakeholders that organizations cannot be trusted to be honest (Moneva, Archel, and Correa 2006). Five specific recommendations are offered for internal CSR/Sustainability guardianship.

1   Embed CSR/Sustainability goals and reporting to create more ethical and committed organizations. Challenges are exacerbated by complexity of CSR/ Sustainability assessment and too few CSR/Sustainability professionals who understand organizational interconnectivity (Adams 2008). For instance, CSR/Sustainability reporting requires company-wide commitment (Peterson 2004b) with specific duties assigned while improving moral/ethical standards (Fraedrich, Thome, and Ferrell 1994).

2   Develop a social reporting system and institutionalize it to ensure that social goals are monitored and measured (Gond and Herrbach 2006). For-profit businesses already are attuned to reporting on financial goals,

but reporting on social and environmental goals may seem a daunting task, requiring significant systemic organizational change.

3   Put CSR/Sustainability measurement responsibilities in the same department to facilitate embedding processes, minimize confusion and costs, and ensure a one-stop source for data collection through reporting. Having one centralized CSR/Sustainability function requires infiltration throughout the organization and across its geographic borders. Yet, CSR/Sustainability reporting cannot happen in isolation, for it relies on multiple organizational functions (Adams 2008). Debated is the specific department where the CSR/Sustainability function should be housed. Some corporations liken CSR/Sustainability to charitable giving, so locate it with departments most closely aligned with socially responsible behaviors, such as community relations or public relations. Locating CSR/Sustainability reporting responsibilities in public relations departments has received mixed reactions. Even though public relations may be seen as "a conductor of positive publicity and responder to negative publicity," the function is ill-favored for the highest-level corporate decision making (Benn, Todd, and Pendleton 2010). Public relations' lack of say at the top limits counselors' ability to play a key role in CSR/Sustainability management, philanthropy, value, and communication (Kim and Reber 2008). As I have argued elsewhere, scrutiny of CSR/Sustainability elements in mission statements with possible linkages to corporate financial performance emphasizes a need for public relations to play a central role in CSR/Sustainability (Jung and Pompper 2014).

4   Accept that CSR/Sustainability and the importance of reporting is much more than image/reputation management, a concept equated with greenwash. CSR/Sustainability reporting must be supported by authentic actions and commitment to ongoing transparency and improvement. For many corporations, this translates to radical overhaul of managerial culture and internal governance (Adams 2004) and extending concern beyond stockholder wealth (O'Dwyer 2003).

5   Adopt from the public relations literature a crisis management mode of thinking when organizing for CSR/Sustainability measurement and reporting. Measurement of relationships in CSR/Sustainability contexts shares much with research used to deal with short-term crises and reputation risk management. For example, Coombs' (1998) concept of "crisis responsibility" (p. 180) draws substantive parallels with CSR/Sustainability management – such as clarifying an organization's role in mitigating a crisis situation that may be related to lack of CSR/Sustainability commitment. Hideki Suzuki, Senior Corporate Governance Analyst at Bloomberg, a privately held financial software, data, and media company headquartered in New York City, applauded companies' willingness to report on CSR/Sustainability: "Unless you disclose, people cannot know

anything. We don't even know if they're managing those risks unless you disclose. By disclosing, we at least know that you're trying to manage the risks." Jennifer Pontzer, Co-owner of Concept Green, a firm which provides sustainability consulting and support services, urged for social goal reporting, too: "So, we've seen gradual changes in the evolution – in the shifting from a company reporting its financials to a gradual increase in non-financial reporting ..." Hank Boerner of Governance & Accountability Institute, Inc., explained risk management connections: "The risk management person might be looking at audits and insurance coverage to argue for better premiums. It [sustainability] gets interpreted an awful lot. So, corporations that affect a radical overhaul of internal procedures ... put themselves in a more accountable and socially responsible position; a good thing for stakeholders and organizations."

Integrating internal and external approaches

Combining inside-out/outside-in approaches may work best for heightened accountability and enhanced relationship building with stakeholders. This "double-path approach" could take the form of including key stakeholder group representatives on CSR/Sustainability planning and assessment teams (Herzig and Schaltegger 2011: 151), steps that match stakeholder expectations with CSR activities (Brown and Forster 2013). Using CSR/Sustainability as a relationship-building tool with employees and local stakeholders enabled corporations in Spain to report on improved workforce safety (Huertas and Capriotti 2008). Empowering diverse stakeholders to participate in CSR/ Sustainability strategic decision making and auditing processes increases transparency and communicates a deep respect for stakeholders; a loop reminiscent of public relations environmental monitoring or scanning. Moreover, this orientation could help to remedy damage done to the public relations industry reputation as merely a publicity or philanthropy mechanism.

Discussion

Measurement of and reporting on CSR/Sustainability goals persists as an essential step for holding organizations accountable to stakeholders and the larger public sphere. However, challenges of accountability, ethics, credibility, and complexity demand ongoing improvement. In particular, managers avoid assessment when stakeholder demands for social and environmental measures are perceived as a drain on the corporate bottom line or reveal anything negative. Of the three streams of literature attending to CSR reporting, academics across multiple disciplines *and* practitioners most often rely on business case and stakeholder accountability frameworks to convince corporations of CSR reporting's merits. On the other hand, critical theory reveals capitalism's propensity for exploiting the most vulnerable populations and avoiding transparency; the most useful approach for calling out offensive organizations and working with them to affect positive change. Ongoing deference to the business case framework and its marketing orientation short changes public relations' normativity and postmodern capabilities. Public relations researchers too infrequently use critical theory to discuss negative outcomes of specific economic systems; venues where they potentially could make a substantive impact in encouraging corporations' CSR/Sustainability assessment and reporting behaviors—as well as in advancing the public relations insider-activist function. Gans (1979) opined that the news industry operates within and ultimately supports the capitalist enterprise, but critically urged businesses to compete responsibly and to "refrain from unreasonable profits and gross exploitation of workers and customers" (p. 46). Nearly a quarter century later, Gans (2003) called for citizens to "democratize the economy" by enabling people who are impacted by businesses to be represented on company boards and committees (p. 121). Also, discovering and reporting on internal and external stakeholder perceptions requires more than simply numbers. Quantitative/qualitative mixed-method approaches should be considered, rather than defaulting to a dichotomy wherein one or the other is viewed as superior/ substandard. I argue that public relations professionals as insider-activists simultaneously should urge corporate managers to look upon CSR/Sustainability as a charge for deep systemic change to organizational infrastructures, transparency in reporting, and governance for meaningful, respectful relationships.

Precisely whom should be assigned CSR/Sustainability reporting— corporations themselves or third party authorities has been debated extensively by academics, think tanks, accountants, and business leaders. Motives and degrees of willingness to share truthful, transparent views for CSR/Sustainability assessment reporting are called into question and self-interest and fear clouds the view. In the USA, Estes (1996) considered the high stakes of CSR decisions and drafted the Corporate Accountability Act; "an act that might be proposed to Congress to require full and fair corporate disclosure to stakeholders" (p. 245). Even though the Act falls short of spelling out specific assessments, tools, and operationalization of CSR/Sustainability, it does provide governance guidelines for making assessment data publically available and for inviting wide swaths of stakeholders to participate in corporate accountability proceedings. No doubt, corporations would balk at reduced efficiencies anticipated with inclusion of outside stakeholders in corporate governance associated with CSR/ Sustainability. For the common good, however, some disruption of autonomy could be a step in the right direction. Clearly, public relations can play a key role in CSR/Sustainability assessment and reporting as part of its communication management and relationship building functions.

8 Reforming organizations
Insider perspectives in three parts

Professionals working to install CSR/Sustainability processes in organizations and those who work in industries designed to report on or support those efforts have witnessed varying degrees of success. Opportunities for reflection about recalibration of organizational mindsets ultimately reveal suggestions for how to reform organizations to make them more committed to CSR/Sustainability and more ethical. Some public relations researchers have opined that there exist too few recommendations or scholarship about precisely how public relations practitioners might go about improving their standing in organizations as counselors to top management (e.g., Reber and Berger 2006). This chapter addresses that gap with regard to CSR/Sustainability.

When working in a CSR/Sustainability context, public relations counselors should enact the insider-activist role by endeavoring to serve as a change agent promoting and driving change ethically, across organizational culture and its systems. Public relations' insider-activist role can challenge dominant worldviews such as *profit above all else*, as well as unjust practices linked to differential power that often result in negative impacts on the public sphere (Holtzhausen 2014; Holtzhausen and Voto 2002) which CSR/Sustainability programs are designed to avoid or reverse. The following insights shared by CSR/Sustainability insiders offer unique perspectives and encourage public relations practitioners to use their boundary-spanning and leadership potential to counsel organizations toward cross-functional, collaborative processes required to support embedded CSR/Sustainability; a reformation for some organizations. In offering practical advice to help public relations counselors embrace their inner activist and change agent, this chapter explores insider perspectives for organizational reform in three parts, according to this book's central themes of: critically exploring the interplay among public relations, communication, and CSR/sustainability; navigating ethical dilemmas in CSR/sustainability work; and moving beyond the business case—how the public relations profession contributes to CSR/Sustainability.

Critically exploring the interplay among public relations, communication, and CSR/Sustainability

Because corporations are designed to maximize profits—and most non-profit organizations emphasize fundraising—organizational infrastructures, government, and economic systems supporting those efforts can override attention to the *people* and *planet* spheres of Elkington's (1999) triple bottom-line model. This finding has emerged throughout the past few decades of CSR/Sustainability studies and was underscored during interviews conducted for this book. Even though most organizations' websites profess attention to all three spheres in equal measure, quite simply, profit rules. Particularly in capitalist economies, corporate boards of directors are duty bound to stock-holders (Cunningham 1999). Even though boards of directors may carefully consider a company's actions in terms of effects on public interests—including employees, communities, and others—such considerations are seldom legally binding. Banerjee (2008) opined that this translates to social concerns receiving limited authentic attention from corporate boards of directors.

Even though public relations is so much more than publicity, organizations frame public relations almost exclusively as a means to maximize positive news and to minimize negative news via traditional and social media. Organizations empower public relations to share stories about activities and programs designed to demonstrate corporate commitment to people and the planet. A staunch CSR critic, Reich (2008), argued that this strategy constitutes a deception designed to limit corporate accountability for misconduct, reduce criticism, and to offset likelihood for increased regulation, legislation, or lawsuits that ultimately could result in required CSR performance standards in nations such as the USA. A senior public relations scholar opined that organizations "congratulat[ing] themselves" for CSR performance through "self-serving awards" are more about *seeming good* than *being good* (Heath and Ni 2009, italics added). Because such programs and promises result in only superficial attention rather than solid leadership and management, corporations are accused of *greenwash* and of *talking the talk without walking the walk*—especially among companies that already have a bad reputation, because they can become a magnet for groups seeking to expose deception and selfish manipulations; hidden motives of CSR programs (Szykman, Bloom, and Blazing 2004). Kim (2013) opined that people do not want to associate with companies which they perceive as engaged with confusing, deceptive, or manipulative CSR practices. Research findings have suggested that such companies experience a backlash effect when they self-promote environmental initiatives (Yoon, Gürhan-Canli, Schwarz 2006). For sure, people's reaction toward strategies of communicating CSR motives is often one of skepticism; a precursor to attitude formation and behavioral intentions (David, Kline, and Dai 2005; Kim and Choi 2012).

When suspected of profit-centric motives and lacking accountability to people and the planet, organizations jeopardize relationships with all manner of savvy stakeholders who can discern when CSR/Sustainability initiatives are inauthentic or not embedded across corporate platforms. May (2009) characterized this phenomenon as *blowback* when stakeholders resist and public relations practitioners are charged to deal with the fallout. Some researchers have encouraged corporations to attend to the people and planet spheres of the triple bottom-line model through use of the business case—in anticipation of reward from shareholders in the form of positive word of mouth and ultimately, sales. Duhé (2005) found that reputation enhancement which can result from earned respect for commitment to social responsibility is "value enhancement" that may bolster financial performance (p. 74). Findings of our content analysis of Fortune 500 corporation mission statements suggested that higher-performing corporations attended more to stakeholders *and* to market/profit/product than lesser-performing corporations (Jung and Pompper 2014).

Research findings about employee resistance suggest several key points relevant to integration or embedding of CSR/Sustainability across organizations. Employees can sabotage, impede, or delay organizational goals when they perceive that management seeks to control them in unfair ways. For example, socializing employees to new systems and dynamics associated with sustainability programs may be resisted when employees feel that their continued employment status is at risk should they fail to adapt (Casey 1999). Researchers critique such moves in terms of ethical implications (Legge 1998), normative control (Ashforth and Vaidyanath 2002), employee activism (Lips-Wiersma and Morris 2009), and "corporate totalitarianism" (Chomsky 1995). Affecting culture change in organizations requires solid communication, education, and participation; all tasks which may benefit from having a professional public relations communicator on the team.

Location, location, location

A key entry point for critically examining the interplay among public relations, communication, and CSR/sustainability is to identify where these functions are housed in organizations. As mentioned in Chapter 7, location and reporting chain amidst corporate hierarchies can prove quite telling when seeking to assess degree of commitment and importance bestowed upon CSR/Sustainability in any given organization. As explained by Hideki Suzuki, Senior Corporate Governance Analyst at Bloomberg, a privately held financial software, data, and media company headquartered in New York City, CSR/Sustainability managers reporting to the highest levels of power in a corporation—the CEO or a board of directors—exemplifies an authentic company-wide commitment to embedded CSR/Sustainability wherein policies and decisions have the approval and full weight of top management. Suzuki said:

> The CSR managers get to present to the board and talk CSR in terms of P&L and then they can pinpoint and say, "Here is what you need to do – not only for the good of the company, but for the reputation. You can actually save money or make money by being sustainable." Whereas, if they just ultimately report to the head of PR, they're obviously thinking of this as a PR issue.

Often, public relations practitioners may regularly communicate a lack of knowledge about or inattention to sustainability issues in the larger business context with investors, effects that could be off-putting to investors. In a recorded interview distributed via YouTube, Suzuki explained that investors evaluate companies in terms of ESG (environmental, social, and corporate governance); nuances of the triple bottom-line emphasis on people and planet, as well as profit (3BL Media 2013).

Discussions with insiders about where CSR/Sustainability management is housed in corporate settings proved quite revealing about perceptions of the public relations function. Many professionals interviewed for this book explained that they consider public relations more as filling a publicity function than one of counseling top management or stakeholder relationship building. Jenny Carty, Reporting and Governance Manager at Royal Bank of Scotland (RBS), explained that avoiding perceptions and realities of one-way communication is especially important in the finance industry and at RBS, in particular, since the company was bailed out in 2008 and now is government owned:

> Sustainability in RBS sits within the communication department. In terms of governance, we report in to the head of communications and we also report in to a sustainability committee. The committee is a board-level committee so there are members of our executive committee as well as non-executives from the board ... [W]e have a really robust and well-developed sustainability governance at RBS ... I would imagine that the reason we don't have a team titled public relations is ... the perception of spin doctors and people paid to improve reputation. That obviously would not sit well – the fact that we would pay people to improve our reputation – as a publicly-owned company, that wouldn't be appropriate. I know public relations is more than that ... There was a recent poll done on the least favorite brand in the UK. The least favorable sectors were energy sectors that were right down there at the bottom because of soaring energy prices. And then after that it was banking.

Brenda Colatrella, Executive Director, Corporate Responsibility at Merck & Co., Inc., shared a similar insider perspective about perceptions of public relations in the CSR/Sustainability space:

> Our PR/communication function is separate. I actually don't see us as a PR function. I think it's much more about behavior and responsible practices and all that good stuff. I won't say I don't think it's important to talk about what we're doing – to put information into the public domain ... I think it's important that we make folks aware of what we do, why we do it, and how we do it ... I actually view it as more educational than where people will typically think of PR.

Similarly, Karen Sommer, Director of Global Public Affairs and coordinator of CSR/Sustainability reporting at Johnson Controls, Inc., said that connections between public relations and CSR are indirect at this technology company:

> They are a dotted line ... The corporate communication folks are reaching out to us when things are coming up and us going knocking on their door with things we can share. When they need a story for this that and the other thing, there's really an open door policy, a really great relationship between the functions. For me, it's second nature.

In other words, public relations at some companies plays no role in CSR/ Sustainability policy making and primarily is used for publicity. At Johnson Controls, Sommer explained:

> From my perspective, getting more recognition for our company, the things that we are doing, PR's going to be part of that. They're not necessarily at the table helping us make decisions. It's more of us reaching out to them needing their help...We've got a whole arm of folks who are responsible – government relations perspective, they are part of that conversation about policy making.

What's old is new again: public relations thinking

Beyond publicity tasks, public relations supports CSR/Sustainability efforts at corporations, trade groups, and nonprofits in other multiple ways, both externally and internally. Public relations managers may serve an important role simply by helping organizations to understand the scope, breadth, and opportunities associated with CSR/Sustainability programs and reporting. Concept Green LLC, a New Mexico-based consulting group in the USA helps companies to develop, implement, and measure sustainability programs because some companies find the hurdle of just getting started too much, while others simply have failed to overcome the pitfalls of "greenwash and wasted efforts" ("Concept Green" n.d.). Jennifer Pontzer, Concept Green Co-owner, elaborated:

> When initially talking with prospective clients, we talk about really understanding where they are and then working together on where they want to go. It can be overwhelming. There are so many areas, when you start with what's going on in the world, and how does my organization fit in? What are the impacts of my organization? Where do I have control? Where do I have influence? We use the GRI reporting framework and working in sustainability of doing materiality assessments, helping companies to understand where the significant impacts are – positive and negative impacts. When we get in the field and talk about impacts, we automatically think about the negatives, but there's a lot of value created by organizations and the work that they do. This isn't just fixing all the

things that are wrong. Also, part of sustainable development is understanding positive impacts and how can you continue to do that and enhance them while you're working to mitigate the negative impact. Just the initial hurdle of getting started – but once they do, it takes time and to be able to prioritize, that's key. Being OK with not being perfect in all areas.

Public relations plays an important role during internal CSR/Sustainability employee ethics training at Novo Nordisk, a healthcare company headquartered in Denmark. Here, a Sustainability Committee is headed by Novo Nordisk's Vice President of Corporate Relations. Scott Dille, Group Leader, explained that the company emphasizes ethical decision making as both an individual and as an organizational responsibility:

> On the one hand, we're all just public citizens with our own opinions and beliefs about decisions that governmental or global bodies should be making. At the same time, we shift through the door and we're inside the company and then we have that identity. But really when it comes to CSR, these are very similar the way you're talking and feeling about them inside or outside the workplace. So, there is a reason to discuss and engage around them, but see how they're relevant from an open orders perspective or from an industry perspective – not just our responsibility as a private-sector body.

Dille described a "two-step workshop" process used at Novo Nordisk wherein managers participate in ethics workshops and then later duplicate the session with their direct reports, by using:

> ... internal case studies on ways to engage internal discourse around sustainability – just due to the fact that discourse creation of either what is ethical or the right thing to do from a sustainability perspective. You look at that being a gray area and use case studies to engage internally in the organization – kind of let people know why and how decisions were made by getting them to articulate how *they* would make the decision.

Ethics and CSR/Sustainability workshops such as this offer public relations practitioners the opportunity to educate and inspire employees on decision making and the merits of ethical behavior. Indeed, behavioral patterns can be taught and organizational training programs including case studies, films, group discussion, role playing, and self-assessment have proven effective tools. This educator role for public relations counselors in CSR/Sustainability settings underscores the function's influence in decision-making processes and relationship building which exemplify excellent communication (Grunig, Grunig, and Dozier 2002).

From a nonprofit perspective, two-way communication with residents and community members about environmental impacts offers public relations practitioners the chance to develop and enhance relationships through listening, education, and action. Gloria Horning, an independent documentary filmmaker and news reporter, organizes Louisiana and north Florida residents in the US to raise awareness of concerns about landfill runoff and eyesores linked to pulp paper mills, industrial products suppliers, petrochemical refineries, and distilleries. In her documentary, *Southern Voices for Change*, Horning (2014) explored socio-economic facets of the David versus Goliath fight of lower-income African-Americans doing battle with big corporations. She regularly attends local government meetings with officials and corporate representatives to ensure that all voices are heard. "We had a great meeting last night" Horning explained. "It was a big town hall meeting and all the players were there. They tried to bullshit the people and the people didn't take it ... What you think is a locally-owned landfill ... I followed the chain and it goes all the way to Houston." Horning's documentary features interviews with residents living alongside the landfills, as well as with legendary consumer advocate Erin Brockovich, who battled Pacific Gas & Electric for polluting water in a small community in California in 1993, and with environmental activist Lois Gibbs, who fought governments and corporations over Love Canal, NY, pollution in the late 1970s, and with Dr Robert Bullard, who is considered to be the "father of environmental justice" ("Core Staff" n.d.).

Public relations in the insider-activist role

A public relations professional's potential as insider-activist could find no better proving ground than the CSR/Sustainability space. Possibilities for public relations practitioners in acquainting organizations with responsibilities to stakeholders and helping organizations to build relationships and develop plans for ethical problem solving and opportunities are functions organic to the insider-activist, postmodern role of public relations (Holtzhausen, 2000, 2014; Holtzhausen and Voto 2002). Actively reporting on or crusading about CSR/Sustainability provides a service to organizations, investors, employees, and other stakeholders. Public relations counselors also might consider actively reaching out to build relationships with investor groups that also seek to "promote more sustainable and just practices," such as the Interfaith Center on Corporate Responsibility; a coalition of faith and values-driven members representing 300 organizations ("About ICCR" n.d.). Eric Israel, Director Global Reporting Initiative (GRI) North America spoke of CSR/Sustainability reporting's weight with investors:

> If companies still don't get it that something is changing, whether that is through regulations or supply chain, or whatever, I would be very worried if I was an investor. I would be very reluctant. It took a while for human kind to accept that the world was not flat, that it was round. It's that kind of paradigm, that kind of belief that is very difficult for organizations if they want to prepare themselves for the future.

Public relations practitioners, as counselors and insider-activists, have a responsibility to persuade top management of the importance attached to transparency, ethics, and authenticity in CSR/Sustainability policies, programming, and reporting.

CSR/Sustainability reporting has matured globally; it is no longer a novelty or some future trend on the horizon. Today, public relations practitioners are well-positioned to fulfill an internal-activist role and it is imperative that they support reporting measures. At Humana, the corporate communications department inspired the US-based healthcare company's CSR launch, as explained by Jim Turner, Director, Corporate Communications: "We convened a group here back at the beginning of 2009. We sort of formalized our approach to CSR and it was our Corporate Communications department that brought people together and created our CSR platform." At Campbell's Soup, David Stangis, Vice President of Public Affairs and Corporate Responsibility, explained the evolution of intra-organizational attention to CSR/Sustainability and a new role for public affairs there:

> [C]ommunications people are completely different today … CSR is forward-looking, proactive … a trend-spotting function. And I don't think the world has trained a lot of PR people to be there. They're worried about managing messages today. It's just part of the way they're trained. It's part of the way the world focuses on them. I think it's different today. It's different in *this* company. When I first got here and I started talking about being more proactive in communicating what we do in taking leadership positions on key policy topics that are important to Campbell, or leading as Campbell … having our own message. You know, that's uncomfortable at first; uncomfortable for any company that's used to bobbing and weaving and reacting to everything that's there – doing a great job on everything – but it's different than being proactive.

CSR/Sustainability leadership at the trade group, Innovation Center for US Dairy, concurred about positive changes in public relations' role inside organizations. Erin Coffield, Vice President, Health and Wellness Communications framed public relations' communication function as a key public service arm for CSR/Sustainability efforts:

> What PR does is it helps to tell the story … [T]he public wants to know where their food comes from and how it's made and that it's good for them and for the planet. All of this business technical work that we're doing helps us to tell that story in a transparent and authentic way. I think there's a symbiotic relationship between communications and the work that we're doing to really live that triple bottom line.

Externally, public relations counselors also have an activist role to play in relationship building between corporations and nonprofits or NGOs. For example,

Scott D. Tattar, Senior Vice President, Director of Public Relations & CSR at LevLane, a Philadelphia-based advertising and public relations firm, said:

> Business is the biggest driver of social change. They have the resources and the power to make real changes in the community ... [W]e try to identify community opportunities for our for-profit clients, like Taco Bell. We represented hundreds of them, pool their money, and pour it into the community to support education; mostly kids below the four-year college line; kids in high schools struggling. We created the "Taco Bell Goes to School Workshop," so they can connect with real, potential employers, and community colleges.

While some critics might call this variety of relationship building too self-serving given a profit motive and context of seeking to increase fast food sales among under-served populations, Tattar defended such activities, explaining that competitors such as McDonald's have successfully employed tactics like this for many years, adding:

> In order to have a successful CSR program and have it funded, a company must feel good that it's going to affect their bottom line in a positive way. You can't expect them to fork over money for a good cause unless it's going to come back and help them. And I understand that. I'm not embarrassed by it and I encourage my clients to stand up tall when it comes to that.

On the other hand, Ihlen (2013) persuasively argued that public relations, when employed in this manner for CSR/Sustainability ends, "set[s] up storefronts for corporations in an attempt to 'gussy up' their images" (p. 209) and begs the question, does attempting to hide a profit motive diminish a corporation's reputation? Because some stakeholder groups regard CSR programs as marketing stunts, some corporations describe their CSR programs as motivated by a desire to do good (Forehand and Grier 2003). Yet, stakeholder skepticism of CSR programs may be prevented or reduced when companies acknowledge self-serving motives *in conjunction with* society-serving motives (Kim 2013).

Partnerships between corporations and nonprofits also call for public relations to play an activist role as part of relationship building. Susan Sabatino, Account Manager, Marketing Partnerships Team at the Nature Conservancy described her work with transportation company, CSX Corporation, as "working with them to change their practices to make them more sustainable" and by actively providing an environmental scanning function. Sabatino explained:

> I keep ongoing monitoring with them to see if any major issues arise with that brand and keep my finger on the pulse of what's going on with them.

Are there any headlines with CSX? I track what they're doing around the CSR space, too. CSX funds our education program… we do grants out to schools. We had an event with them and we did a press release saying that the event was sponsored by CSX.

Across CSR/Sustainability efforts, public relations practitioners have become eternal boundary spanners who perform invaluable service to organizations internally as educators and organizers—and externally as relationship builders. Across all roles which benefit the larger public sphere, communication and a commitment to ethics remain critical.

Navigating ethical dilemmas in CSR/Sustainability work

In addition to serving as activists for organizations, public relations practitioners' training in high ethical standards positions them well for serving as organizational sentries; always on the lookout for ethics infractions and potential ethics lapses. Overall, presenting only one-sided CSR/Sustainability success stories—without formally admitting to or explaining challenges in reporting—further fuels greenwash accusations and could constitute ethics breaches.

A multinational food company with first-hand experience navigating one of the most explosive and media-focused ethical issues of the late 2000s, Nestlé was targeted by activists. Greenpeace and others protested the company's unethical use of palm oil, a candy ingredient acquired from a supplier accused of deforestation and destroying orangutan habitat in Indonesia's rainforests in 2010 ("Nestlé Doesn't Deserve a Break" 2010). John Bee, Communication Manager, Public Affairs, Nestlé, headquartered in Switzerland, said: "We, as an organization, have changed a lot over the past ten years … [W]e weren't as open and willing to engage as we should have been." Bee has resolved that sometimes a steep learning curve is required before organizations realize that CSR/Sustainability requires drastic organizational change and a new mindset. What Bee described constitutes a set of circumstances where public relations counselors acting as the insider-activist must "negotiate their way through their obligation to transparency with the public, which benefits a democratic society, and their obligation to the organization to be sustainable" (Holtzhausen 2014: 239).

Among all CSR/Sustainability managers, public relations practitioners, and other professionals interviewed for this book, some were more willing than others to share specific examples of ethical dilemmas encountered in their organizations. Ihlen (2013) opined that corporations consider public relations as a tool for "establish[ing] truths about their CSR engagement" (p. 210). Yet, how do public relations counselors negotiate power differentials between organizations and members of the public sphere? Perhaps dynamics which most test public relations counselors' mettle involve recommendations *against* an organization's proposal that may superficially seem consistent with goals, but ultimately could prove detrimental to the larger public sphere. Recalling a recent meeting discussion at the pharmaceutical company, Merck & Co., Inc. headquartered in the USA, Brenda Colatrella, Executive Director, Corporate Responsibility, explained that she "wasn't really satisfied with the dating on the product" that colleagues wanted to donate. Colatrella said that it is her responsibility to point out potential risks and then to use those moments to educate others about potential downsides to something that may seem merely a simple act of philanthropy:

> Even though it subscribed to the WHO guidelines, which we subscribe to – which was greater than 12 months of dating, I knew that the area they were looking to go into with that product was very challenging in terms of proper clearance through the regulatory authorities and the government ... It took a good couple of emails back and forth and ... once I got on the phone, I explained my concerns more fully and he said, "OK I get it. I was just looking at this as it's a product that's relevant for the conditions that exist in that country. But, I had no idea what it takes to actually donate." I think sometimes, there's just a naïve approach to donation.

At the Nature Conservancy, Nancy Sabatino, Account Manager, Marketing Partnerships Team, described established policies and "a full risk assessment" process for discerning with whom the nonprofit organization will partner and more particularly, those it considers unethical and *will not* partner, as evaluated by a formal risk assessment committee. Sabatino elaborated:

> We have certain standards that we have to meet with every company ... particularly risky industries for us – anything aligned with things like mining, fracking, any energy companies. Obviously with our mission, these are really high risk industries for us ... automobiles, transportation industry ... the tobacco industry ... firearms and ammunition companies ... companies in the defense industry ... energy or petrochemicals. We never do anything around pornographic, lewd imagery, anything like that. So we do have our no-go industries that we don't work with on the marketing partnership team.

Ethical considerations also are given considerable attention at Johnson Controls, a US-based technology company, where employees participate in annual ethics training and certification. Karen Sommer, Director of Global Public Affairs, explained that ethical standards have become engrained as part of the organizational culture because employees are taught to discern among tasks that they "don't feel good ... [and] should be raising a red flag."

Perhaps less obvious are ethical considerations associated with establishing and reporting on CSR/Sustainability goals, selectively reporting on only the goals that reflect positively on an organization—while omitting goals not met or that could reflect negatively on the organization. At the Concept Green consulting firm, Co-owners Jennifer Pontzer and Carrie Christopher called this practice "cherry picking in reporting on goals;" one that they consider unethical. Most public relations practitioners interviewed agreed that reporting on unaccomplished CSR/Sustainability goals presents a hurdle that is often ignored—even though research findings suggest that stakeholders highly esteem transparency and honesty in CSR/Sustainability reporting as a building block toward trust (Christensen and Langer 2009). Furthermore, Hideki Suzuki at Bloomberg explained that from his vantage point as a corporate governance analyst working with many public relations and CSR/Sustainability managers, goals are "conservative so that they can achieve those goals." Suzuki added:

> Let's say a company is going to be conflict free and clean of all the social issues for example, all the child labor, discrimination and all that stuff. They probably can't do that for a lot of legal reasons ... I'm sure they have good lawyers who are preventing them from saying anything in the report ... I think there's no harm in showing people you're doing the best you can even if you can't definitively say, "My supply chain is squeaky clean." No one's going to be able to say that, anyway ... A company like Nintendo is not known for their CSR activities ... they sort of gave up because it's just insane for them to be chasing down suppliers' suppliers and *their* suppliers. It's an infinite chain that they just couldn't pursue. At least they were honest about it.

Research findings suggest that some stakeholder groups may lean toward trusting organizations that are open and sincere about their CSR/Sustainability programs' motives (Forehand and Grier 2003). During an interview for this book, Carol Adams, a senior researcher and professor of CSR/Sustainability on faculty at Monash University and Director of Integrated Horizons consultancy in Australia, opined that the first step in formally reporting on an unmet CSR/Sustainability goal may be the hardest: "Once you've done it you realize that the world doesn't fall apart and actually it helps develop trust. You tend to keep on doing it unless you get a change in senior managers and you get someone else in who's a bit wary of doing it."

Moving beyond the business case: how the public relations profession contributes to CSR/Sustainability

In nations with capitalist economic systems, such as those in the USA, short-term thinking inspired by the perpetual chase toward quarterly profit reporting and a business case argument where responsibility is linked to commercial concerns often leads organizations into shortsighted actions. This is a given for public relations counselors who face uphill battles when trying to convince top management to adopt more long-term views, wherein decisions made today with regard to CSR/Sustainability issues will have longer-term implications for the future. Economically, there is mounting evidence that CSR/Sustainability activities reduce costs and risk to companies, as well as lend a competitive edge and create internal synergies (Salazar and Husted 2008). Even when start-up costs attached to CSR/Sustainability programs and reports may mean a short-term financial hit, the long-term benefits associated with transparency and reputation and trust-building could be well worth the investment. Beyond the business case, however, we know that sidestepping harm and improving well-being for people and the planet are earmarks of corporate good citizenship (Grunig 2000b).

Both public relations and CSR/Sustainability involve organizations' ethical and moral obligations to protect and enhance the public sphere. Even though profit "is and will always be the overarching motive of corporations" (Ihlen 2013: 209), public relations and CSR/Sustainability practitioners maintain a sharp focus on all three triple bottom-line spheres of responsibilities to people, planet, and profit. John Bee, Communication Manager, Public Affairs, Nestlé, knows firsthand about the importance of counseling upper management on ethics and strategic thinking required to maximize CSR/Sustainability. Transparency about CSR/Sustainability goal setting and degrees of accomplishment remain sensitive issues for senior management, however. While reporting on a goal not yet accomplished could be perceived by the investment community as a sign of weakness, other stakeholders may see it as a sign of integrity and transparency. Unfortunately, Bee opined, corporate managements may "not yet be in the comfort zone to do that" because perceived risk and the short-term business case measure endures—but he believes his counsel is making a positive impact:

> We have done [reported a "failure"]. Yes. We report where we're not where we need to be. Stakeholders, they actually don't believe you if you say you've got it all under control. You're better off saying "Look, here's where we've got talent" … salt, sugar, fat – technologically, we could phase those out, but the product will taste awful and nobody will choose it … We have to address the two things side by side and sometimes we don't know how to. That's the sort of thing you'll see in our report … With CSR, you should also be able to examine yourself to see the degree to which you're not meeting the expectation of the people who are looking at what you do; the opinion leaders … If you look at our stakeholder base, it's kind of everybody in the world, one billion plus products every single day of the year. That means that one billion purchasing decisions are made in our favor. That means that an exponential number of interactions on those purchasing decisions are made by anyone – from our own trade union workers, to faith leaders, to NGOs, academics, the government, you name it! They have an opinion about what we do.

Cynthia Figge at CSRHub suggested that rationales for senior managements' reluctance to report fully on unmet CSR/Sustainability goals vary as widely as the contexts for each organization—depending upon industry, company, size, nation, region, etc.:

> I think companies that are working hard on this issue ... where they've set public goals and they're falling short of them and they're not being super forthright about it. Maybe they're disclosing it, but maybe it's harder to find it, etc., in terms of ways it's presented. They're probably doing that because they're trying to maintain in the market a position of leadership ... So it's really hard to disclose where you're falling behind ... [T]hey're going to talk about where they did better. They may talk about if they had really *serious* issues. Companies are learning that it's better to be forthright and open about those things and what they're doing to turn that around ... There's no good that comes from not being transparent. But let's say you set really rigorous goals about reduction of water consumption and didn't make it. The information may be available, but it's not going to be highlighted. I just think that that's kind of a natural thing. Also, I think some companies, depending on their industry and pressure with standards ... If a company is lagging, might even be external, might not be internal goals ... If you're disadvantaged for whatever reasons – geographically, your energy mix, or because your access to recycled material – you're going to be less likely to be totally forthright about that. It's a competitive issue."

At the Norway-owned petroleum company, Statoil, Doug Bannerman currently serves as Leader Social Performance and earlier in his career worked as a sustainability consultant. He explained that lawyers often counsel against transparency about unmet sustainability goals because the information is "discoverable" and investor relations professionals also advise against sharing too much due to concerns about revealing "market influencing" information that could negatively impact stock price. Bannerman recalled conversations with clients when he worked as a consultant:

> I was nose deep into sustainability reporting and I would say to companies "These reports come across as 'Look how fantastic we are and you're leaving yourself no wiggle room. If you're great at everything, what are you going to say next year'?" There seems to be a real hesitance to say "Hey, we set a goal for ourselves this year doing x and oops, we blew it or we didn't even get around to it and here's what we learned from this incident and here's what we'll do in the future." As nice as it would be to have that narrative and be able to talk about it, I think lawyers are terrified if you'd ever go out to the public and say you didn't do something well. So, I will blame them ... [To IR people] I'm like, "What if it makes our stock go up?" What then?

Using communication vehicles, public relations counselors may support greater degrees of transparency in CSR/Sustainability reports and other communiqués with narratives offering full explanations for goals not yet accomplished and plans for moving forward. Such activities greatly contribute to perceptions of organizational reputation but must be genuine and properly positioned as part of ongoing public communication about CSR/Sustainability so as not to come off as greenwash. Hideki Suzuki, Senior Corporate Governance Analyst at Bloomberg, said that most of the public relations practitioners he works with perform investor relations tasks, but may be missing the larger picture of what CSR/Sustainability means for their companies. Suzuki explained: "In a lot of corporate contacts I talk to, they work with investor relations and all I hear is, 'How do we get to be a Dow Jones Sustainability member? What do we need to do?' They clearly just care about doing their job as an IR rep. Not so much about doing something greater."

Beyond offering full disclosure on *all* formal, published CSR/Sustainability goals, public relations has a higher threshold to meet in terms of building relationships, trust, and reputation for organizations. Counselors should persuade management on the virtues of setting higher expectations beyond simply what is expected for complying with CSR/Sustainability guidelines from implementation through reporting. Brenda Colatrella, Executive Director, Corporate Responsibility at Merck & Co., Inc., said:

> [I]f you're not working in an environment or culture that values CSR, your job will be a heck of a lot harder. If you have buy-in from the top – which, happily, we have here – you're going to struggle to make folks in your organization understand what this means and why it's important. A lot of times organizations just take it for granted – "Well, of course we're acting responsibly!" Some people feel that way and to some degree that's true – "wouldn't be in business if we weren't acting responsibly" – but what we're talking about here is sort of aiming for that bar that's beyond compliance. It's looking at: "What do we need to do to build trust?" In a healthcare company, building trust is really critical for us. So what can we do to build trust and make it clear that one of our primary foci is to behave in a responsible manner and meet the needs of patients.

In China, companies are increasingly working to comply with labor laws, proper treatment of workers, and work conditions for pregnant women—and even though Chinese business managers may consider mere compliance with laws to be *outstanding* CSR performance, too few take CSR/Sustainability any further, according to Timothy Hui, Director Global Reporting Initiative (GRI) China. Hui explained: "People still need to understand that CSR practice is not just compliance. It's above and beyond what the law requires." Greenwashing is a common theme across Chinese state-owned companies' CSR reports. Hui added that he applauds the Central Government and the Communist Party's willingness to encourage government-owned media to disclose "the dark side of factories" as a means for shaming owners into more deeply-embedded and genuine CSR/Sustainability commitments.

Opportunities are abundant in China for public relations—or guanxi—to establish connections and relationships when counseling organizations on the merits of CSR/Sustainability to benefit the organization through reputation enhancement, as well as the planet and people.

Discussion

Public relations scholars and practitioners have worked long to establish the profession as a management function and to position those who practice public relations as ethical leaders and counselors. Framing public relations practice as a means for affecting intra-organizational behavior change (Choi and Choi 2009) could have significant utility in the CSR/Sustainability space. Insider perspectives in three parts, as presented in this chapter, promote a focus on issues central to the dynamics and complexity of public relations with CSR/Sustainability: critically exploring the interplay among public relations, communication, and CSR/sustainability; navigating ethical dilemmas in CSR/sustainability work; and moving beyond the business case—how the public relations profession contributes to CSR/Sustainability. Shared are voices of professionals who work in CSR/Sustainability arenas, including public relations, marketing, and media; specialists who urge for reformation among organizations, ethically, and with an eye on *all three bottom lines* of people, planet, and profit.

Examining the interplay among public relations and other professionals engaged in the CSR/Sustainability space helps to illuminate and critique public relations and to enhance understandings of its potential as a practice for insider-activism. Discovering the degree to which some CSR/Sustainability professionals frame public relations as publicity and greenwash—both within organizations and from without—calls for improved behavior among professionals, information campaigns on behalf of our trade organizations worldwide, and curriculum improvement in the college classroom. Moreover, by geographically locating public relations practitioners far from the key decision makers in organizations and intellectually from CSR/Sustainability planning and reporting tasks, public relations is significantly disadvantaged from realizing its full potential. Ethics training workshops and seminars that sensitize employees to the scope of organizational impact on people, planet, and profit certainly are a positive step.

Encouraging public relations' potential as insider-activism supporting CSR/Sustainability efforts may seem radical to some organizations at first blush. However, the prospect of greater support for embedding CSR/Sustainability throughout organizational hierarchies and across systems could prove palatable to organizations still embarking upon the shift in mindset—away from CSR/Sustainability as some fluffy "nice to do" future project to an ethical, authentic, fully integrated "must do" paradigm shift for reforming organizations right now. In stating his position that "corporations make good people do bad things," Estes (1996) argued that corporations should provide information "reflecting the national impact of corporate actions" (p. 230). Again, here is where public relations counselors may perform an important service to both corporations and the rest of the public sphere. Collectively, this book's central themes support new directions for public relations leadership by fulfilling an insider-activist role; one with implications for interplay with CSR/Sustainability, for navigating ethical dilemmas, and for moving beyond business case arguments that have contributed to public relations' diminished status, exclusively, as a publicity function.

9 Considering the future of public relations and links with CSR/Sustainability

Public relations practitioners need a larger skill set to successfully handle multiple complex challenges in organizations and the larger public sphere when it comes to CSR/Sustainability. Insider activism work requires a commitment to high ethical standards, awareness, courage, impeccable communication skills, cultural sensitivity, ongoing learning, ability to build authentic relationships, and resistance to dependence on the one-way asymmetrical publicity model. To help meet the charge, this book offers insights gained by critically exploring points of overlap among public relations and CSR/Sustainability and by amplifying voices of professionals working in CSR/Sustainability spaces. As noted throughout this book, public relations offers several assets for supporting CSR/Sustainability policy making and programming. However, the greatest challenges include limited (often negative) perceptions of the public relations profession and its enduring attachment to publicity and use of philanthropy; outcomes linked to greenwashing. Moreover, organizational dynamics create obstacles for public relations counselors—such as not having a seat at the senior management table and being placed in low- to mid-level ranked hierarchical positions. Public relations often lacks organizational status to do much more than follow orders. An ability to blow the whistle on ethics breaches which threaten organizations and stakeholders supports CSR/Sustainability and the public relations insider-activist role. Other negative forces include work cultures which thrive on groupthink and favor consensus over dissensus. A desire for unanimity in some organizations inadvertently trumps consideration of alternate solutions to problems and opportunities (Janis 1982). In Japan, it is said that *the nail that sticks out gets hammered down* (Hashi 2012). CSR/Sustainability thrives on creative thinking, courage to be unique, and willingness to nurture and implement new ideas.

Ironically, a major disconnect has been revealed between researchers' findings and behind-the-scenes perspectives offered in this book. While an overview of the public relations literature suggests that public relations plays a significant role in CSR/Sustainability (e.g., Kim and Reber 2008; Moreno, Zerfass, Tench, *et al.* 2009), professionals interviewed for this book characterized public relations' current role in CSR/Sustainability in highly limited ways. What public relations practitioners say they do and what other professionals working in the CSR/Sustainability space perceive and observe them doing does not measure up. Even the public relations professionals narrowly defined their CSR/Sustainability role in terms of promoting organizations' *good works* stories, developing marketing relationships, or recruiting employee volunteers for service projects. Furthermore, public relations' role as organizational conscience and educator among internal stakeholders means standing up for what's right oceans and land masses away. Moloney (2006) drew from Tedlow's (1979) conclusion that public relations people are more likely to fail than to succeed in attempting to reform organizations when he posited that "only a few have the capacity to undertake such a career-limiting and ethically challenging project" (p. 105).

While the insider-activist role for transforming organizations into more just and moral places may be an aspirational goal for public relations at present, it is a campaign worth waging. Introduction of the insider-activist role to the public relations literature via postmodern theorizing (Holtzhausen 2000, 2014; Holtzhausen and Voto 2002) finds practical application in the CSR/ Sustainability arena. This may be the only route to influencing balance among the triple bottom-line model's spheres of people, planet, and profit. The framework offered in this chapter clarifies the two-way symmetrical model of excellent public relations as one of shared power—rather than having organizations occupy one end of a communication continuum and *everyone/thing else* at the other. In CSR/Sustainability contexts, large degrees of power are undeniably economic and political—and must be more evenly distributed globally for benefit of the public sphere. Some have suggested dropping the social (people and planet) from the triple bottom-line model, arguing that the social is *implied* in all environmental and business ethics contexts. Corporations' profit-centric efforts continue to overshadow social goals, a course which desperately requires correction. This chapter ties together threads explored throughout this book in these subsections: negotiating challenges of economic system underpinnings, flaws inherent in the business case model, inspiring infrastructural change for real responsibility and sustainability, on more government oversight, a progressive movement toward global ethics, and public relations praxis.

Negotiating challenges of economic system underpinnings

Three inter-related outcomes of capitalism have important implications for the success of CSR/Sustainability programs and public relations' role. First, severe demarcations of power imbalances emerge globally when multinational corporations respond to competitive pressures. Second, quarterly earnings reporting procedures in a free market economy encourage and sustain short-term strategizing rather than cultivating a long-term authentic commitment to CSR/Sustainability implementation and reporting. Third, competitive pressures and the drive to attract investors emerge as a pervasive overlay in free-market economies.

Capitalism's zero-sum dilemma

Dating back to the seventeenth and eighteenth centuries, the economic and political power wielded by concentrated capital of the Dutch and British "Indies" companies set a historic pattern for colonialism which constituted might over right. Today, the corporation is classified as the most powerful global institution (Cheney, Roper, and May 2007) and is considered by some to have taken on pathologies of a clinically diagnosed psychopath— consistent with the legal definition of a corporation as "a person" in the USA (Bakan 2003). In CSR/Sustainability contexts, the quest for earnings often supersedes any concern for indigenous peoples or environmental damage— as when leading economic powers consume more than their share of natural resources and subjugate developing nations. By addressing some problems through wealth generation, capitalism simultaneously creates other issues.

The *sustainable capitalism* framework could offer a means for accommodating capitalism's paradox by infusing it with equitable balancing of people, planet, and profit. This means holding multinational corporations accountable for their public sphere footprint and for monitoring authenticity in meeting CSR/Sustainability commitments via social audits. Elkington (1999), who also co-founded the London-based consulting firm, SustainAbility, in 1987, endorsed this route. Furthermore, the objective of holding corporations accountable, as expressed by public relations senior scholars, "is not to dislodge capitalism but to improve it, to make it better" (Starck and Kruckeberg 2003: 31). As noted in Chapter 1, the American economist, Milton Friedman (1970) argued that corporations operating in capitalist economic systems primarily are responsible to stockholders. So, to divert profits into costs used for purposes other than profit maximization (e.g., charitable support for the poor, improving the environment) has been likened to stealing from stockholders. Even though those who define CSR as charitable giving have been critiqued as using a manipulative strategy designed to *put a human face on capitalism*, Friedman's (1970) argument suggests that decisions about use of business profits in such ways should be made by stockholders rather than a corporate board of directors, CEO, or any other executives or managers.

Short-term strategy versus long-term authenticity: chasing the earnings statement

The short-term framework of reporting earnings quarterly drives corporations operating in a free market, but also thwarts CSR/Sustainability programs and reporting since these require long-term care. CSR/Sustainability makes "good business sense for some corporations, in some sectors, on some issues, under certain circumstances" (Ihlen 2013: 209). Of course, many organizations still operate with little or no regard for CSR/Sustainability. Bhattacharya (2013) opined that across organizations, sustainability departments tend to be "outshouted" by other departments with shorter-term pressures. Because quarter-by-quarter financial goal setting may preclude the long-term view required for embedding CSR/Sustainability across all organizational platforms, public relations insider-activists could play a central role in minimizing fear/risk associated with transparency and raising awareness about the benefits of ethical, long-range perspectives on organizations' impact on people, planet, and profit. Cynthia Figge, COO and Co-Founder of CSRHub, a repository of CSR/Sustainability ratings and information "on nearly 8900 companies from 135 industries in 102 countries" ("About CSRHub" n.d.), concurred that CEOs and boards fear investor backlash associated with transparency in the near term:

> It's complicated … I've seen this because I've done so many first reports … Once they're over that hurdle and see that they're not necessarily going to be punished by the market because they have been more transparent, then there's a greater likelihood that they will actually disclose. But it is a journey. It's not "Oh, we see this as clear evidence that we're being rewarded for transparency, let's reveal more."

Carrie Christopher, Co-owner Concept Green, a US-based firm which provides sustainability consulting and support services, explained that CSR/Sustainability is essentially about building long-term value in organizations; a paradigm shift that some are reluctant to embrace for fear of cutting into profits: "Some don't know where to start … shareholders and the general public, regulators, insurers, investors … there's a kind of a convergence of different interests and demands for the US corporations to make some big changes." According to Jennifer Pontzer, Concept Green Co-owner:

> [I]t took a while for some of the leading companies to truly demonstrate and have the strong business cases. This is like risk management – better performing companies really looking at the long view … the companies that were really bringing sustainability into their overall strategy … It's more about long-term return and that's a difficult case for many to make at the executive and board level … Some companies have to really shift how they do business – the good thing is that they find a lot of wonderful opportunities that they might not have thought about or realized they had strong expertise in areas that they can really leverage.

John Bee, Communication Manager, Public Affairs, Nestlé, headquartered in Switzerland, explained that top management recognizes a self interest in protecting the natural environment to grow raw materials required for its food manufacturing business, but also considers long-term social needs:

> That's nutrition, wellness and health to our consumers. Looking after water resources and developing rural communities … We need to identify

the social needs inherent in those three focus areas and find business solutions to provide for-profit answers to those challenges. That's the way we look at these things. We don't think it's valid to give back to society or anything like that, we think that it's better to take a proactive stance.

Some corporations apply a mixed motives interpretation of time with regard to CSR/Sustainability. Brenda Colatrella, Executive Director, Corporate Responsibility at Merck in the USA, explained:

> I think it's challenging sometimes for corporations to jumble the short-term view versus the long-term vision ... If you can focus on the long term, at least always have that in your line of sight, you will also be able to achieve some of your short-term goals. It's the long-term sustainability of companies that's really going to make a difference in the long run. You can achieve your short-term gains, but if you're not here in ten years, what does it mean? ... It's no longer going to be that CSR is a nice thing to do or nice to have. I think we're already there. It's going to be a business imperative ... CSR is actually good for the business ... I am a firm believer that it really drives the business and makes it more sustainable.

At Campbell's Soup in the USA, Vice President Public Affairs and Corporate Responsibility, David Stangis, agreed that attention to both short and long-term CSR goals is required:

> We're kind of in this vicious loop where the world is looking for "What did you do on the top line? What did you do on the bottom line?" every quarter. You can't avoid that conversation today. It's a publicly-traded company. Even if you get to the bottom line – which is where a lot of our sustainability initiatives end up paying off, cost savings and increased efficiency, the entire tradeable marketplace in terms of equity is focused on the top line. It's how can we best leverage this (CSR) for both the top line and the bottom line both near-term and long-term. That's why I think the evangelism only works so well. That's why you see people really understanding that there's a lot more to this than coming in and trying to convince a company to be more green or to be a better corporate citizen. You have to prove it. You're not going to be around—I mean you'll be around for a while, but you're not going to be vital to the company if you can't prove your value or the value of the system you're putting in place.

The long versus short-term perspective debate also has implications for public relations practitioners who use communication to build relationships with stakeholders. Specifically, communicating about a company's good works and the launch of a first sustainability report presents an opportunity for public relations to *tell a story* and ultimately to enhance sales and reputation, as Fitzgerald at Innovation Center for US Dairy, explained:

> That is a tricky point ... They [consumers] don't expect you to have all the answers. That's the great thing about sustainability reporting is that the more people do it, you're publicly disclosing things and we should reward people for publicly disclosing things. That's how we start sharing stories and case studies and best practices. I think a lot of companies are afraid to do a sustainability report because they're so afraid of getting sued or whatever ... What we want to see is in the dairy category everyone starting to track their performance and measure. That's lifting all boats. Ultimately, a big vision is that we'd be able to track our industry performance over time.

Competitive pressures and appealing to investors

Publicly-traded companies operating within a free-market economy carefully consider business case arguments when any proposed deep organizational change is considered. Corporations tend to enact operational changes only if these are going to be good for business and not create alarm among investors and stockholders. Hence, institutional investors exert significant power and increasingly challenge corporate decision makers' autonomy; a "disturbance on the corporate boundary" (Roberts 2001: 22). That any changes lead to social sustainability and/or minimize negative environmental impact is merely secondary (Munshi and Kurian 2005). Laura Mandell, Vice President, Sustainability Communications at Innovation Center for US Dairy, predicted that because economics is of utmost importance, sustainability reporting eventually will merge with financial reporting.

The business-and-society relationship debate has spawned a *corporate citizenship* conceptual framework which has prompted some for-profit businesses to incorporate social concerns with profit issues. This term gained favor in the 1990s, as an alternative to *business ethics* and *CSR* since both may suggest to some that ethics and responsibility are missing in business operations (van Luijk 2001). *Citizenship* implies that corporations are on even footing with and have the same rights as people in society and that all are inter-dependent (Waddell 2000). Business leaders have suggested that companies express their citizenship through programs which address stakeholders and social needs. Birch (2001) identified 12 generic principles of corporate citizenship, including sustainable capitalism, attention to a triple bottom line, longtermism, transparency, accountability, and sharing responsibility. Some of Birch's (2001) other corporate citizenship values directly relate to the public relations function, such as: employee and stakeholder empowerment, communication, engagement, and dialogue. Yet, critics consider *corporate citizenship* as rhetoric embedded with a paradox which simply masks corporations' preference for framing their own issues rather than enabling others to impose upon business any checklists or guidelines for what *they* consider to be socially responsible (Matten, Crane, and Chapple 2003).

Public relations communicators also conform to free-market conventions when engaging in investor relations, operating as "blind servants" to those in power (Holtzhausen 2014: xvi). According to Christopher at Concept Green, it is impossible to ignore economic realities: "I've worked in institutional investing and I've sat in on a lot of those quarterly earnings discussions and you say, 'We didn't hit our target. There goes the stock price'." Convincing corporate management to overcome this anxiety is a hard sell, Christopher at Concept Green explained: "[W]hat they don't understand is that setting goals, making goals, reporting progress to goals initiates a dialog and it shows humility and credibility."

Flaws inherent in the business case model

Even though organizations want to be perceived as ethical and may use business case arguments to persuade for CSR/Sustainability support, some stakeholders keenly observe inauthenticity, double standard, public relations spin, and greenwash. CSR/Sustainability debates have opened new spaces for dialogue about business-society relations that did not exist on a large scale 25 years ago. Importantly, the transformative potential of organizations and interested stakeholders to work together for positive change is significant. Perhaps some Fortune 500 companies are reaping social-financial link benefits (Jung and Pompper 2014). However, any connections between CSR/Sustainability, consumers, and potential organizational rewards in the form of increased sales or enhanced reputation are tenuous. Vogel (2005) characterized the business case as overblown since consumers only consider patronizing companies whom they consider responsible or sustainable once price and quality factors are satisfied.

Perhaps the most significant flaw in the business case argument, as framed by critics, is multinational corporations' overwhelming economic and political power. Waddock (2007) referred to a "dark side" to big box superstores' impact on local communities, such as Wal-Mart, Home Depot, and CVS, resulting in "social ills just by virtue of their success" (pp. 74–75). Such dynamics include a perpetual push for expansion, focus on internal efficiency while externalizing costs to local taxpayers, and control over employees, markets, and consumer preferences. These effects loom large over CSR's transformative potential (Spence 2007). Bader (2014a) wrote of her experiences working on CSR projects inside BP and shared excerpts with *Fortune* magazine:

> Of course companies have to justify expenditures. But when value is measured only in short-term returns, human rights are at risk. General Motors and every other company would do well to put the "business case"

in its rightful place: behind considerations of safety and the sustainability of people and our planet.

Christopher Gowan, a lead US-based attorney representing the people of Ecuador in their lawsuit against Chevron (which acquired Texaco) for polluting water and land in conjunction with oil extraction operations, explained that some multinational corporations simply have the resources to outspend and the sheer size to intimidate:

> The biggest problem in this case is that you have a justice system that is so expensive and a litigant that has literally an untapped budget ... It's an unbelievable 1) discrepancy in resources and 2) not only are they very well funded, but they're also very well organized ... It's utterly and completely absurd. If you just look at the trial, they had in the courtroom live streaming transcriptions, they had ten lawyers, translators, a huge room command center, and they had all their laptops. All of these things we didn't have. We didn't even have a level playing field in the courtroom. Literally, their table had more stuff than ours did because we couldn't afford it. The extent of just filing papers – five copies of every brief – and responding to every single ridiculous thing that they filed. The problem is that the justice system in America has become so expensive that you just can't afford. It's just become impossible to take on one of these corporations. Because of that, they can get away with not being responsible.

Inspiring infrastructural change for real responsibility and sustainability

As popularity of environmental and social fund investments grows and lobbyists and NGOs exert increasing pressure, corporations' business case for shifting into the CSR/Sustainability paradigm with balanced attention to economic, environmental, and social issues seems more straightforward. CSR can enhance a business–society relationship only if corporations consider all stakeholders and embed social responsibility vertically and horizontally across organizations (Frankental 2001). An authentic global CSR/Sustainability approach requires listening to *all* stakeholders' voices—even the most unempowered groups—and transparently assessing and reporting on goals. As noted by other CSR researchers, "unchecked corporate power is problematic for democratic society" (Cheney, Roper, and May 2007: 3).

Moreover, the public relations profession is overdue for a reputation metamorphosis, and helping organizations transform to an authentic CSR/Sustainability commitment offers the insider-activist a proving ground. The insider-activist role incorporates what Meyerson (2001) called "quiet catalysts" (p. 166) for inspiring change, resisting traditions and norms, building supportive coalitions, and recommending specific actions for gradual and forward social change. Public relations counselors should be able to address the challenge if they have been trained to embrace diverse stakeholder groups, conduct research, guide stewardship initiatives, span boundaries, build relationships, monitor social and traditional media watchdogs, and develop counseling skills used to enable top management to recalibrate its ego. The public relations insider-activist backed by high ethical standards could write a new chapter for a profession increasingly considered negatively and narrowly. Also, reconceptualizing public relations and establishing this new vantage point offers practitioners the opportunity to embody and reshape the two-way symmetrical excellence model so that organizations and stakeholders are more evenly distributed along the power continuum. Encouraged is a Western European multi-stakeholder approach that goes beyond simply attending to stockholders (Crane and Matten 2004) because external forces charge companies to behave in socially responsible ways by attending to social goals (de Gilder, Schuyt, and Breedijk 2005), forming liaisons with nonprofits (Hoare 2004), and earning respect for being socially responsible (van Luijk 2000). Indeed, the most important stakeholder is society (Starck and Kruckeberg 2003)—a truism which guides public relations practitioners as the embodiment of an organizational conscience for insider-activism.

In particular, least-admired industries must be inspired to embrace social values in conjunction with profit seeking, reform infrastructures, and knock down silos to enjoin even the most diverse departments in building new organizational cultures where CSR/Sustainability may take root. As veteran corporate communicators working for a US-based petroleum company recommended, CSR must be lived from the inside out, trust among stakeholders must be earned, giving back to communities must be recognized as the right thing to do, transparency must become the norm, and external criticism and new ideas must be welcomed (Spangler and Pompper 2011). Reflecting on how an unnamed multinational corporation experienced a sea change in perspective about stakeholders and CSR, Doug Bannerman, Leader Social Performance at Statoil, a Norway-based oil and gas production company, said:

> I think they went from a period of basically, "Who the hell are these human rights activists? They're not stakeholders because they're not shareholders" ... You've got to think, like, they had CSR people that they were bringing into the company at that point. Imagine what it was like for those people if that was the environment they were coming into? "I'm going to be a change agent and it's going to be great working here," and then they were told, "Those people aren't going to tell us how to run our company" ... So they've come leaps and bounds.

A specific infrastructural change that could help organizations to consider social indicators equally on par with financial indicators would be for CSR/Sustainability and public relations managers to embrace new measurement tools. Bannerman at Statoil opined: "I'm hoping that it gets more rigorous and that we see more metrics attached to it... That's the one thing I find really, personally, frustrating is that when you see people trying to measure social impact it usually boils down to philanthropy numbers and it drives me nuts." Nancy Mancilla, CEO and Co-founder of ISOS Group, a CSR consulting firm in the USA, concurred that companies are very slowly adjusting attention in reporting beyond financials by assessing social dimensions of CSR efforts: "The environment has captured initial attention, but the people aspect is only starting to catch on. Somehow people are less comfortable with how they feel about other people ... As comfort levels in organizations increase, it will become easier." Jeff Leinaweaver of Global Zen Sustainability in the USA, concurred: "It's the social side that's the next frontier and it's the real scary one."

On more external oversight

Some critics feel that corporations simply have too much power—and with too little oversight cannot be trusted to act voluntarily in the public interest through self-regulation. Deregulation and globalization trends have exacerbated these dynamics. Waddock (2007) crystallized a "paradox of corporate citizenship" (p. 76) as success and enormous growth, but where resources are used for corporations' own purposes (until scandals are exposed) instead of providing for the good of the wider public sphere. Therefore, external oversight via legal/governmental regulations with violation penalties are considered necessary in some nations. While governments certainly may be capable of limiting businesses that fail to hold up their end of the business-society contract in their drive toward profits, Munshi and Kurian (2005) lamented that "they rarely do" (p. 517). Spence (2007) also concurred that business may be incapable of fully considering environmental and social impact, and also argued for mandatory regulation or even redesigned economic systems.

In the USA, for example, Estes (1996) endorsed the ethical investing movement as a mechanism for rewarding responsible corporations but also recommended that the US Congress adopt the Corporate Accountability Act. It would be enforced by a new Corporate Accountability Commission and this group would solicit stakeholder feedback about corporations' compliance with social responsibilities. Because corporations' reports to the Commission would be publicly available, processes could force greater transparency and accountability for a more balanced view of creating wealth for stockholders without harming other shareholders; qualities that Estes (1996) said he saw too little of in the course of his career as a chief financial officer at software development and publishing companies. Mandatory requirements that corporations be held to standards to protect people and the natural environment could help to reverse corporations' record of exploitation and destruction in developing nations (Munshi and Kurian 2005). Global Reporting Initiative (GRI) North America director, Eric Israel, noted that stock exchanges also can serve as a regulatory body of sorts and explained how 44 stock exchanges around the globe are considering sustainability measures as requirements for listing on certain stock exchanges. He also pointed to the *Risky Business report* (Gordon 2014), produced by an independent, bipartisan consortium of government, business, and academic leaders, urging businesses to take responsibility and act sustainably:

> Our goal with the Risky Business Project is not to confront the doubters. Rather, it is to bring American business and government – doubters and believers alike – together to look squarely at the potential risks posed by climate change, and to consider whether it's time to take out an insurance policy of our own.

The public relations insider-activist must resist institutionalized injustices routinely committed against stakeholders. Estes (1996) opined that enforced government oversight should force corporations to act authentically as good citizens "instead of doing good deeds merely for their public relations value" (p. 242). Holtzhausen (2014) reminded us that public relations practitioners often are charged to protect corporate interests in developing countries which are often "exploited by world powers, much like the big oil companies are doing in Africa today" (p. 240). In China, Global Reporting Initiative (GRI) director, Tim Hui, explained that a national CSR performance and reporting standard is being drafted and may be put into place during 2015. Hui told of how China's president has visited the African continent multiple times and has called for improved social responsibility efforts on behalf of Chinese companies that do business there:

> A lot of the time, this responsibility for sustainability doesn't happen by itself or it doesn't happen by the market. That's where government is in the best position to play its role to make things happen – especially when a market mechanism is not fully there yet … If we want this trend to be really healthy and minimize mistakes and maximize lessons, we really need to nurture and to put together a clear cut policy orientation from the Central Government level so that all other ministries under the state council would have a clear-cut direction to move ahead.

A progressive movement toward global ethics

The business-responsibility-to-society framework offers a development agenda as part of a progressive movement. Elkington (1999), inspired by Hans Küng, Swiss theologian and director of the Global Ethic Foundation based in Tübingen, Germany, noted that globalization and accumulation of wealth under capitalism may be inevitable. However, he advocated for control, responsibility, and a global ethic which supports a basic social contract rather than endangers it. Given globalization of capital, why not globalization of ethics? As addressed in Chapter 7, the United Nations Global Compact of 1999 offers a non-legally-binding commitment for businesses worldwide to adopt socially responsible and sustainable policies and to regularly report on progress ("Overview of the UN Global Impact" 2013). Hank Boerner, Chairman, Chief Strategist and Co-Founder of Governance & Accountability Institute, Inc. (G&AI) opined:

> The Compact is aspirational. It would be good to not have child labor and be able to say, "We're a citizen and we agree that we shouldn't have child labor." Compliance in these voluntary schemes is very easy if you're a wordsmith. You can massage what the company is or is not doing until they're caught doing it. I'm reminded of Apple. Apple products are so iconic for young people and educators over the years. The *New York Times* had the team in China looking at supply chain and they discovered – sometimes these things are serendipitous, they discovered that Foxconn, which is the large supplier for Apple, Samsung, and others was stretching safety nets in factories to catch suicidal workers. That's a big story.

Küng called for a global ethic which, "means a fundamental consensus on binding values, irrevocable standards and personal attitudes which can be shared by people of all religions and also by nonbelievers ... [S]ustainable capitalism will depend on a shared understanding not only of the importance of values but also of the adoption of specific principles" (cited in Elkington 1999: 143). Yet, where the charge grows murky is when one considers *Whose morality? Whose values? Whose ethics?* will guide the development of a global ethic or global principles. Boerner added:

> We have trouble with that now in terms of negotiating treaties like the WTO – which to some extent holds companies accountable. If Chinese solar manufacturers flood the market, we can go through the WTO or act unilaterally to deal with those companies. But again, you're reflecting the culture. So, emerging countries like China, India, and Turkey and others – bricks in the mist, and so forth – saying, "Well it's all well and good for you as an advanced society to tell us what's good for us, but we have to raise our people up. And so we're going to do what you did 100 years ago." In fact, I had this said to me by a client who was in the news a lot, Mikhail Khodorkovsky, he was the richest man in Russia ... [W]e did a lot of work with him ... I asked him some questions about how he operated and he said, "You know, you criticize us, but look at your Robber Barons of the 1800s and the trusts and the concentration of power both politically and economically and look at your wild wild west 1929 stock exchange and in 2008. How can you tell us that you're *advanced*?" He has a point. Whose standard do you apply? Ethics is such a touchy subject.

Multinational corporations' philanthropic-oriented CSR programs are critiqued for being more about strategically paving the way for smooth manufacturing than for genuine CSR. For some researchers, this brand of philanthropy has been interpreted as *corporate social leadership* and includes examples such as Coca-Cola distributing health information for peoples of the African continent (Hilton and Gibbons 2002). Consultant Jeff Leinaweaver of Global Zen Sustainability, headquartered in the USA, critiqued colonial overtones of such projects as not really addressing change required to operate a sustainable business:

> This is rampant in CSR ... *Compassionate prejudice* is lots of companies seeing CSR, sustainability as campaigns to save the Africans. Save fill-in-the-blank of someone who's usually not white, usually someone not in America that they're helping. They'll find some kind of sad story that they'll be highlighting how they've rescued them – a hero/savior kind of thing going on – and you see this a lot! ... I see the CSR people not questioning the level of greenwashing that nobody actually realizes that they're doing. It's just about happy campaign. I remember working on a CSR report for a big bank and these reports are supposed to be about transparency and not just happy anecdotes. When we got through it and highlighting certain things, all the PR people wanted was the magic. I think people forget that it takes a second for people to look at these stories, that a lot of people put a lot of time into to create what I call the anti-story or kind of a counter-story. People take one look at it and say that "It's all BS. I don't believe any of it." I think these ethics are really important and people needing to understand sustainability is a really big deal – understanding CSR is a really big deal. Once you get on the elevator or escalator, you can't get off of it. I think that for people who are just starting, it's great. But after a while, you run out of low-hanging fruit. I think we're starting to get to that point. This will be a real make or break as to whether or not PR can help.

Multinational corporations have no easy task in negotiating between *moral relativists* who argue for application of local standards and *moral imperialists* who support a single global standard for ethics (Elkington 1999). Social implications for all concerned must be carefully considered, since corporate policies and behaviors cannot escape the social, ethical, moral, and cultural consequences of the business-in-society relationship (Birch 2001).

Public relations' environmental scanning duties must include scrutiny of social values and norms in communities and nations where multinational corporations operate. Public relations practitioners are duty-bound to prescribe and practice ethical behavior (Starck and Kruckeberg 2003) in conjunction with standards held by indigenous peoples. Public relations researchers have emphasized the importance of developing "ethical accents" (Pratt 1993: 230) and perspectives which correspond with normative worldviews of indigenous societies; stakeholders living and working in countries where corporations operate (Pratt 2003). A key consideration with regard to ethics associated with global CSR/Sustainability is corporations' increasing use of temporary agency employment which reframes the social contract and calls into question *who determines the collective good to be served in a global world* (Townsley and Stohl 2003). Findings for a study of CSR-and-religious-denomination overlap suggested that religious groups more broadly and diversely define businesses' social responsibilities than non-religious groups (Brammer, Williams, and Zinkin 2007). The Interfaith Centre on Corporate Responsibility, an organization committed to using the "power of persuasion backed by economic pressure from consumers and investors to hold corporations accountable," has drawn from spiritual and ethical values of Christianity, Islam, and Judaism to provide guidelines for ethical international business behavior ("About ICCR" n.d.).

Media that fulfill a watchdog function also may assist in affecting a type of global ethics with regard to CSR/Sustainability. Theorists have recognized media's role in forming public opinion and news media historically have supported progressive agendas in democratic nations. Even though critics have suggested that overlap of capitalism with democracy receives insufficient scrutiny (e.g., Almond 1991), journalism scholars long have examined news media as fora for exposing inhumane work environments and insufficient consumer protections (Ihlen 2013). Journalists uphold social order maintenance (Gans 1979) and serve as democracy guardians (Donohue, Tichenor, and Olien 1995); subjective values which also may be interpreted as means for shaming and publicizing organizations' unethical behavior. So, news media coverage may fulfill a global ethics role.

Public relations praxis

Potential for positive synergies remains high when enjoined public relations and CSR/Sustainability efforts advance both financial and social goals. According to Habermas' (1989) teachings on social justice, public relations practice in Europe emphasizes the active participation of individuals and groups as members of the public sphere, an important message which bears amplification across public relations practice globally. For decades, public relations scholars have encouraged practitioners to serve as an ethical conscience of organizations and to use their expertise in building relationships, managing conflict, navigating reputation, and communicating with publics. Unfortunately, practitioners work amidst a public sphere which perceives that organizations have failed to deliver on too many promises (Lehman 2007) and are considered "deceptive, or greedy"—leading to cynicism and disbelief when public relations advances narratives about corporate good works (Surma 2006: 48). Yet, with public relations performing a heightened role as internal-activist and change agent, organizations could be poised to reform mindsets and infrastructures essential to authentic transformation which embraces transparency, ethics, responsibility, and sustainability. David

Stangis, Campbell's Soup Vice President of Public Affairs and Corporate Responsibility, shared thoughts of a horizontal model of internal corporate sustainability commitment:

> I still think you're going to have a small little brain trust – almost a consulting group – it might be in corporate strategy … it might be its own little corporate affairs function like it is here and we had at Intel … That's the future … thought leaders, the voice that works with the CEO and the board and the groups that do the reporting and the data … [For example] we're working on the first procurement sustainability strategy for the company in its 146-year history. So procurement is running its own … everything we buy, all of the ingredients, sustainable agriculture. We're making new metrics and strategies in our sustainable agriculture world – the packaging group which is in R&D – they're setting up their own sustainability strategy.

For public relations to fulfill its maximum potential as a management function in support of CSR/Sustainability, however, actions must speak louder than words. Internal public relations managers must be willing to slip from the golden handcuffs and assume the role of whistleblower in the event of ethical violations – not unlike Wendell Potter, former CIGNA vice president of corporate communications, who refused to use public relations on behalf of the health insurance giant to stonewall national healthcare reform legislation in the USA (Hornick and Quijano 2009). Operating postmodernly, public relations also must break out of its perceived low-status mold of one-way communication through publicity and philanthropy by filling an internal-activist role. Banerjee (2008) warned that because CSR practices and decisions are established at highest organizational levels, public relations lacks agency in CSR implementation. Public relations must be seen as credible and more than an image-building tool (Surma 2006), as engaging with a self-preoccupied "ethics of narcissus" (Roberts 2001: 125), or representing "a hallmark of shallow practice" (Ihlen 2013: 209). Organizational structure impacts moral decision making from individualistic, as well as communal standpoints. Organizations can be highly complex, also prone to decentralized decision making (Grunig and Hunt 1984) which can lead to turf conflict and confusion. In particular, tensions with advertising and marketing teams which conflate branding with CSR must be navigated and public relations must stave off encroachment threats. Jeff Leinaweaver, owner of the US-based consulting firm, Global Zen Sustainability, expressed mixed feelings about public relations' role in organizations' sustainability programs:

> I have seen a lot of problems because PR gets involved or feels like it's their domain … They have every opportunity to lead this conversation … PR needs to understand how deeply internal this goes … Their job is to

understand the reinvention and how to talk about that and understand the risks. But for those who have companies who aren't willing to do that or are scared of it, it's absolutely the relationship between PR and CSR is greenwashing. Beyond that, a bigger issue that I see is that once a lot of these people obtain a job and get a title called CSR Director, they start being put on circuits where people start looking at them like experts in the field of Sustainability or CSR and there's a high degree of illiteracy out there around what the real issues are. There's also a high degree of inability to name that elephant in the room once people have titles and people assume that identity ... A lot of people have grown into positions internally where they've just organically become a part of – like suddenly the CFO says we have a budget, you PR folks, we'll give you a fulltime head. A lot of people are just appointed in that position and it starts from there. If they look at sustainability as just recycling, employee engagement ... Not just campaigns that throw money at people. How's that authentic? ... If PR people are truly that engaged employee, part of the ethics is really *challenging* all of this stuff.

Carol Adams, a senior researcher and professor of CSR/Sustainability on faculty at Monash University and Director of Integrated Horizons consultancy in Australia, has written extensively about "radical overhaul of corporate governance structures" required to affect mandatory requirements for corporations to report on ethical, social, and environmental issues (Adams 2004: 752). When asked *what this might look like*, she had this to say:

It's a good question. There's overhauls and there's changes, and then there's *radical* overhauls – which I think is something that's quite different. What is really needed is organizations where the senior managers actually talk and work and can work across the functional silos of the organization and try to understand each other's languages and perspectives and work collaboratively. I think that is a real challenge for large organizations and for individual leaders.

To prepare public relations students for a career of working collaboratively on CSR/Sustainability programs across organizations, fulfilling the internal-activist role, and making ethical decisions, numerous suggestions for college classroom and curricular updates are offered. Recommended for curriculum is: a historical overview of social problems and change, emphasis on critical thinking skills, ethical case studies and problem solving, requirements for a second language or two, and practice conducting social audits. In addition, practical job search advice for college students must include investigating organizations' value systems so that graduates may compare these with their own deeply-held beliefs. Leinaweaver of the Zen Sustainability consulting firm suggested deeper investigations of potential employers' organization structures:

Millennials want to be with companies that care. This is really important. You see this meshing between employee engagement, recruitment, and PR ... Sometimes they are too quick for a checklist and a lot of blaming the older generation for the mess that the planet is in – sometimes overt and sometimes subtle. They're the saving generation. You're always going to have that. What they're starting to find is that it's a lot harder to change once you're part of it and realize you've been complicit. A lot of companies are bringing in young people who are bright eyed and willing to work hard, but are now in the position of having to hold the mirror up to themselves. Ask themselves, "How am I complicit? How am I part of this?" I think that's a huge hurdle. Huge ethics issue ... The PR people in other countries speak three languages and they're the same age and they understand the cultural complexities of language and how language matters.

Few of the professionals interviewed for this book had majored in CSR/ Sustainability as college students, but rather studied: biology/chemistry, business, communication, economics, engineering, environmental health/toxicology, journalism, law, philosophy, public relations, and other disciplines. Today, colleges and universities increasingly offer courses in CSR and sustainability— especially in business schools. Stangis at Campbell's Soup, shared perceptions of job interview conversations:

I remember having a conversation with somebody who was doing a master's degree in environmental sustainability – an executive master's – and they asked me, "What kind of degrees are you looking for?" – and I'm back to the core competencies. They were like, "Really? I'm sitting here and invested all this time and you're going to hire somebody with a science background or a communications background or a supply chain background? Sustainability – I know how to do that." I say, "Well ... "

Organizations must recognize that Millennials have concerns about organizations' value systems and are attracted to companies with a conscience. Jim Turner, Director Corporate Communications at Humana in the USA, explained:

More and more companies are devoting more resources to people who are focused exclusively on CSR. That's one great example of why I see it growing in importance and why I think it will continue to. Employees want to know their employer is committed to making the places they live and work better... We hear more questions related to CSR in interviews now than ever. People are doing their homework before they consider coming to work for a company like Humana, or our competitors, or anyone else. They want to know that they're coming to work for a company that is demonstrably committed to its local communities and the people it serves and want more than just a corporation that provides goods and services, but rather is part of the fabric of all the communities.

Discussion

Linkages between public relations and CSR/Sustainability seem organic, and with some key changes, public relations could be a major driver of organizational reform required to advance responsibility- and sustainability-thinking. Overall, the capitalist economic structure and its conventions (e.g., quarterly earnings reporting) pose significant challenges for a public relations' insider-activist role. While the business case model has proven useful in convincing some organizational members to adopt CSR/Sustainability, a significant downside has been a depreciation of the social goals of protecting people and the planet. Should governments and industries adopt mandatory requirements for CSR/Sustainability, public relations could be a major ally for integrating those changes across organizational silos. Moreover, ongoing scrutiny of ideas for global ethics while recognizing unique qualities of multiple cultures is necessary; a sensitivity that public relations practitioners are trained to support. This is a postmodern perspective conducive to enacting the insider-activist public relations role. Finally, public relations practitioners must take action in helping to transform work cultures so that progressive movements which support CSR/Sustainability advance beyond mere talk. Public relations cannot be perceived as a "prosthesis" artificially attached to the organizational body (Roberts 2003: 250). Value that CSR/Sustainability brings to organizations must be fully embedded. Likewise, public relations can support organizational transformation by spearheading regular social audits as part of ongoing benchmarking for measurement and reporting on CSR/Sustainability goals.

Rather than focusing exclusively on one-way publicity activities, public relations' insider-activist role means further developing and enhancing mutually-beneficial relationships among organizations and multiple stakeholders. Corporate philanthropy and community projects as window dressing are exposed for the greenwash techniques that they are. A story shared by Doug Bannerman, Leader Social Performance at Statoil, crystallized the importance of authentic relationships with communities:

> I work at a very operational level with our assets folks to basically say to them, "Look, you've got to either earn or keep your social license and here's how we do it." You've got to engage with local stakeholders. We have to create benefits beyond the folks that are getting royalty checks. Those are the kind of conversations we have... What I try to do is just be very pragmatic. I don't say like, you know, "We're not here to save the world, we're not giving away puppies." You need these rock solid relationships for the following reasons. Or, yes, we're creating millionaires through royalty checks, but you've got a whole community of people that

their roads are getting trashed or they see a truck going by their door every ten minutes, so what's in it for them? So, we've got to think about other things they can do in the community. Then the light bulb eventually goes off.

Should organizations slowly reform beyond short-termism and eventually adopt what Estes (1996) called enlightened self-interest, or very long-term profitability, public relations practitioners enacting the insider-activist role may be relied upon to systematically enable organizations to reform and consequently to affect positive social change.

Bibliography

3BL Media. (2013). 'Ethical Sourcing Forum 2013 – An Interview With Hideki Suzuki, Bloomberg, ESG Data Analyst.' 22 March. Available online at: www.youtube.com/watch?v=ea27ipmFI50&feature=youtube_gdata_player (accessed 13 July 2014).

Aasland, D. G. (2004). 'On the Ethics Behind "Business Ethics."' *Journal of Business Ethics*, 53(1–2): 3–8.

"About CSRHub" (n.d.). Available online at: www.csrhub.com/content/about-csrhub/ (accessed 15 July 2014).

"About ICCR" (n.d.). Available online at: www.iccr.org/about-iccr (accessed 18 February 2014).

"About IR" (n.d.). *Integrated Reporting*. Available online at: www.theiirc.org/the-iirc/about/ (accessed 29 April 2014).

AccountAbility. (2008). 'AA1000 Assurance Standard.' Available online at: www.accountability.org/standards/aa1000as/index.html (accessed 2 April 2014).

Accounting Standards Steering Committee (1975). *The Corporate Report*. ICAEW: London.

Adams, C. A. (1999). *The Nature And Processes of Corporate Reporting on Ethical Issues*. London: Chartered Institute of Management

Adams, C. A. (2002). 'Factors Influencing Corporate Social and Ethical Reporting: Moving on From Extant Theories.' *Accounting, Auditing & Accountability Journal*, 15(2): 223–250.

Adams, C. (2004). 'The Ethical, Social and Environmental Reporting-performance Portrayal Gap.' *Accounting Auditing & Accountability Journal*, 17(5): 731–757.

Adams, C. (2008). 'A Commentary On: Corporate Social Responsibility Reporting and Reputation Risk Management.' *Accounting, Auditing & Accountability Journal*, 21(3): 265–370.

Adeola, F. O. (2001). 'Environmental Injustice and Human Rights Abuse: The States, MNCs, and Repression Of Minority Groups in the World System.' *Human Ecology Review*, 8(1): 39–59.

Adler, P. S. (2002). 'Corporate Scandals: It's Time for Reflection in Business Schools.' *Academy of Management Executive*, 16(3): 148–149.

Aguinis, H. and Glavas, A. (2012). 'What We Know and Don't Know About Corporate Social Responsibility: A Review And Research Agenda.' *Journal of Management*, 38(4): 932–968.

Aldoory, L. and Toth, E. L. (2000). 'An Exploratory Look at Graduate Public Relations Education.' *Public Relations Review*, 26(1): 115–125.

Aldoory, L. and Toth, E. (2004). 'Leadership and Gender In Public Relations: Perceived Effectiveness Of Transformational and Transactional Leadership Styles.' *Journal of Public Relations Research*, 16: 157–183.

Ali, S. (2013). "Authenticity on Social Media." In *Encyclopedia of Public Relations*, 2nd edn, p. 52. Thousand Oaks, CA: Sage.

Allen, M. (2002). *The Corporate University Handbook: Designing, Managing, and Growing A Successful Program*. New York: American Management Association.

Allen, T. (2013). 'From the Heart: MCO Employees Save Lives With Soap.' Available online at: www.blogsouthwest.com/from-the-heart-mco-employees-save-lives-with-soap/ (accessed 4 August 2013).

Almond, G. (1991). 'Capitalism and Democracy.' *Political Science and Politics*, 24: 467–474.

Andreoni, J. (1990). 'Impure Altruism and Donations to Public Goods: A Theory Of Warm-glow Giving.' *The Economic Journal*, 100: 464–477.

Anonymous (2005). 'The Union of Concerned Executives: CSR as Practiced Means Many Different Things.' *The Economist*. 20 January. Available online at: www.economist.com/node/3555194 (accessed 2 June 2014).

Anonymous (2006). 'New Survey Charts the State of CSR.' *PR News,* 62(25): 1.

'Apple and Procurement" (n.d.). Available online at: www.apple.com/procurement/ (accessed 23 February 2014).

Arenas, D., Lozano, J. M., and Albareda, L. (2009). 'The Role of NGOs in CSR: Mutual Perceptions Among Stakeholders.' *Journal of Business Ethics*, 88(1): 175–197.

Arnold, M. (2001, July 12). 'Walking the Ethical Tightrope.' *Marketing*, 17.

Arya, B. and Salk, J. (2006). 'Cross Sector Alliance Learning and Effectiveness of Voluntary Codes of Corporate Social Responsibility.' *Business Ethics Quarterly*, 16(2): 211–234.

Ashforth, B. E. and Vaidyanath, D. (2002). 'Work Organizations as Secular Religions.' *Journal of Management Inquiry*, 11(4): 359–370.

Austin, L. L. and Toth, E. L. (2011). 'Exploring Ethics Education in Global Public Relations Curricula: Analysis of International Curricula Descriptions and Interviews With Public Relations Educators.' *Public Relations Review*, 37: 506–512.

Austin, J. E. (2000). *The Collaboration Challenge: How Nonprofits and Businesses Succeed Through Strategic Alliances*. San Francisco, CA: Fossey-Bass Publishers.

Axelson, B. (2013). 'Walmart Asks Workers to Donate Food to Fellow Employees for Thanksgiving.' Available online at: www.syracuse.com/news/index.ssf/2013/11/walmart_asks_workers_to_donate_food_to_fellow_employees_for_thanksgiving.html (accessed 25 December 2013).

Back, L. (2011). 'Does CSR Threaten the Nonprofit Sector?' Available online at: www.triplepundit.com/2011/02/csr-threaten-nonprofit-sector/ (accessed 28 July 2014).

Backhaus, K. B., Stone, B. A., and Heiner, K. (2002). 'Exploring the Relationship Between Corporate Social Performance and Employer Attractiveness.' *Business & Society*, 41: 292–318.

Bader, C. (2014a). 'Corporate America Doesn't Need a "Business Case" to Do Good.' Available online at: http://fortune.com/2014/04/04/corporate-america-doesnt-need-a-business-case-to-do-good/ (accessed 20 June 2014).

Bader, C. (2014b). *The Evolution of a Corporate Idealist: When Girl Meets Oil*. Brookline, MA: Bibliomotion.

Baijia, L. (2013). 'Apple's PR Crisis in China provides lessons.' *China Daily USA.* 3 April. Available online at: http://usa.chinadaily.com.cn/epaper/2013-04/03/content_ 16373193.htm (accessed 17 July 2014).

Bakan, J. (2003). *The Corporation: The Pathological Pursuit of Profit and Power.* London: Constable.

Baker, M. (2008). 'Arguments Against Corporate Social Responsibility.' Available online at: www.mallenbaker.net/csr/against.php#antiprofit (accessed 24 June 2014).

Ballou, B., Heitger, D., and Landes, C. (2006). 'The Future of Corporate Sustainability reporting.' *Journal of Accountancy,* 202(6): 65–74.

Banerjee, S. (2008). 'Corporate Social Responsibility: The Good, the Bad and the Ugly.' *Critical Sociology,* 34(1): 51–79.

Bansal, P. and Roth, K. (2000). 'Why Companies Go Green: A Model of Ecological Responsiveness.' *Academy of Management Journal,* 43: 717–736.

Bardhan, N. and Weaver, C. K. (2011). "Introduction: Public Relations in Global Cultural Contexts." In N. Bardhan and C. K. Weaver (ed.), *Public Relations in Global Cultural Contexts,* p. 1–28. New York: Routledge.

Basil, D. Z., Runte, M. S., Easwaramoorthy, M., and Barr, C. (2008). 'Company Support for Employee Volunteering: A National Survey of Companies in Canada.' *Journal of Business Ethics,* 85: 387–398.

Bauman, Z. (1993). *Postmodern Ethics.* Cambridge, MA: Blackwell.

Beaver, W R. (2005). 'Battling Wal-Mart: How Communities Can Respond.' *Business and Society Review,* 110(2): 159–169.

Becker, G. S. (1993). *Human Capital: A Theoretical and Empirical Analysis, With Special Reference to Education,* 3rd edn. Chicago, IL: University of Chicago Press.

Beder, S. (2000). *Global Spin: The Corporate Assault on Environmentalism.* Foxhole, Dartington: Green Books.

Ben-Porath, Y. (1980). 'The F-connection: Families, Friends, and Firms, and the Organization of Exchange.' *Population Development Review,* 6(1): 1–30.

Benn, S., Todd, L. R., and Pendleton, J. (2010). 'Public Relations Leadership in Corporate Social Responsibility.' *Journal of Business Ethics,* 96: 403–423.

Berger, B. (2008). 'Employee-organizational Communications.' Available online at: www.instituteforpr.org/topics/employee-organizational-communications/ (accessed 3 September 2014).

Berger, B. K. and Reber, B. H. (2006). *Gaining Influence in Public Relations: The Role of Resistance in Practice.* Mahwah, NJ: Lawrence Erlbaum Associates.

Berkley, R. A. and Watson, G. (2009). 'The Employer–employee Relationship as a Building Block for Ethics and Corporate Social Responsibility.' *Employee Responsibilities and Rights Journal,* 21(4): 275–277.

Best, S. & Kellner, D. (2001). *The Postmodern Adventure. Science, Technology, and Cultural Studies at the Third Millennium.* New York: Guilford.

Bhattacharya, C. B. (2013, September). 'Awakening the Green Self: Corporate Responsibility and the Role of the Stakeholder.' Keynote address presented at The 2nd International CSR Communication Conference, Aarhus University, Denmark.

Bhattacharya, C. B. and Sen, S. (2004). 'Doing Better at doing Good: When, Why, and How Consumers Respond to Corporate Social Initiatives.' *California Management Review,* 47(1): 9–24.

Birch, D. (2001). "Corporate Citizenship: Rethinking Business Beyond Corporate Social Responsibility." In J. Andriof and M. McIntosh (eds), *Perspectives on Corporate Citizenship,* pp. 53–65. Sheffield: Greenleaf Publishing.

Bivins, T. H. (1989). 'Are Public Relations Texts Covering Ethics Adequately?' *Journal of Mass Media Ethics*, 4(1): 39–52.

Bivins, T. H. (2006). "Responsibility and Accountability." In K. Fitzpatrick and C. Bronstein (eds), *Ethics in Public Relations: Responsible Advocacy*, pp. 19–38. Thousand Oaks, CA: Sage.

Black, L. D. and Härtel, C. E. J. (2004). 'The Five Capabilities of Socially Responsible Companies.' *Journal of Public Affairs*, 4(2): 25–144.

Blazovich, J. and Smith, L. M. (2011). 'Ethical Corporate Citizenship: Does it Pay?' *Research on Professional Responsibility and Ethics in Accounting*, 15: 127–163.

Blowfield, M. (2007). 'Reasons to Be Cheerful? What We Know About CSR's Impact.' *Third World Quarterly*, 28: 683–695.

Boardman, C. M. and Kato, H. K. (2003). *The Confucian Roots of Business Kyosei*. Netherlands, Dordrecht: Springer Science & Business Media.

Boje, D. M., Adler, T. R., and Black, J. A. (2005). 'Theatrical Facades and Agents in a Synthesized Analysis From Enron Theatre: Implications to Transaction Cost and Agency Theories.' *Tamara. Journal of Critical Postmodern Organization Science*, 3(2): 39–56.

Bonyton, L. A. (2002). 'Professionalism and Social Responsibility: Foundations of Public Relations Ethics.' *Communication Yearbook*, 26: 230–265.

Bortree, D. S. & Seltzer, D. (2009). 'Dialogic Strategies and Outcomes: An Analysis of Environmental Advocacy Groups' Facebook Profiles.' *Public Relations Review*, 35: 317–319.

Botan, C. (1993). 'A Human Nature Approach to Image and Ethics in International Public Relations.' *Journal of Public Relations Research*, 5(2): 71–81.

Bourdieu, P. (1990). *The Logic of Practice*. Stanford, CA: Stanford University Press.

Bouten, L., Everaert, P., Van Liedekerke, L., De Moor, L., and Christiaens, J. (2011). 'Corporate Social Responsibility Reporting: A Comprehensive Picture?" *Accounting Forum*, 35: 187–204.

Bowen, H. R. (1953). *Social Responsibilities of the Businessman*. New York: Harper.

Bowen, S. A. (2008). 'A State of Neglect: Public Relations as "Corporate Conscience" or Ethics Counsel.' *Journal of Public Relations Research*, 20: 271–296.

Bowen, S. A. (2013). 'Corporate social responsibility.' In *Encyclopedia of Public Relations*, 2nd ed, pp. 304–306. Thousand Oaks, CA: Sage.

Bowmann-Larsen, L. and Wiggen, O. (2004). *Responsibility in World Business: Managing Harmful Side-effects of Corporate Activity*. Tokyo: United Nations University Press.

Brammer, S., Millington, A., and Rayton, B. (2007). 'The Contribution of Corporate Social Responsibility to Organizational Commitment.' *International Journal of Human Resource Management,* 18(10): 1701–1719.

Brammer, S., Williams, G., and Zinkin, J. (2007). 'Religion and Attitudes to Corporate Social Responsibility in a Large Cross-country Sample.' *Journal of Business Ethics*, 71(3): 229–243.

Breitbarth, T., Harris, P., and Insch, A. (2010). 'Pictures at an Exhibition Revisited. Reflections on a Typology of Images Used in the Construction of Corporate Social Responsibility and Sustainability in Non-financial Corporate Reporting.' *Journal of Public Affairs*, 10: 238–257.

Broom, G. M. (1982). 'A Comparison of Sex Roles in Public Relations.' *Public Relations Review*, 8: 17–22.

Broom, G. M. and Dozier, D. M. (1986). 'Advancement for Public Relations Role Models.' *Public Relations Review*, 12(1): 37–56.

Broom, G. M. and Sha, B.-L. (2013). *Cutlip & Center's Effective Public Relations*, 11th edn. New York: Pearson.

Brown, J. and Forster, W. R. (2013). 'CSR and Stakeholder Theory: A Tale of Adam Smith.' *Journal of Business Ethics*, 112: 301–312.

Brown, J. and Fraser, M. (2006). 'Approaches and Perspectives In Social and Environmental Accounting: An Overview of the Conceptual Landscape.' *Business Strategy and the Environment*, 15: 103–117.

Brown, R. E. (2008). 'Sea Change: Santa Barbara and the Eruption of Corporate Social Responsibility.' *Public Relations Review*, 34(1): 1–8.

Bruce, I. (1994). *Meeting Need: Successful Charity Marketing*. Hemel Hempstead: CSA Publishing.

Burns, J. L. (2000). 'Hitting the Wall: Nike and International Labor Practices.' Harvard Business School Case Study N 1–700–047. Boston, MA: Harvard Business School Publishing.

Bussell, H. and Forbes, D. (2002). 'Understanding the Volunteer Market: The What, Where, Who and Why of Volunteering.' *International Journal of Nonprofit and Voluntary Sector Marketing*, 7(3): 244–257.

Calabrese, A., Costa, R., Menichini, T., and Rosati, F. (2012). 'A Positioning Matrix to Assess and to Develop CSR Strategies.' *World Academy of Science, Engineering and Technology*, 69: 642–648.

Cameron, G. T., Wilcox, D., Reber, B. H., and Shin, J. H. (2007). *Public Relations Today: Managing Competition and Conflict*. Boston, MA: Allyn & Bacon.

Cancel, A. E., Cameron, G. T., Sallot, L. M., and Mitrook, M. A. (1997). 'It Depends: A Contingency Theory of Accommodation in Public Relations.' *Journal of Public Relations Research*, 9: 31–63.

"Canon's Corporate Philosophy of Kyosei" (2014). Available online at: www.canon.com/ir/strategies/philosophy.html (accessed 3 August 2014).

Cap, K. (n.d.). 'Discussions at Seneca.' *International Public Relations Association*. Available online at: www.ipra.org/itl/04/2010/who-really-needs-a-code-of-ethics (accessed 29 June 2014).

Capriotti, P. (2007). 'Risk Communication Strategies in the Chemical Industry in Spain: An Examination of the Web Content of Companies on Issues Related to Chemical Risk.' *Journal of Communication Management*, 11(2): 150–169.

Capriotti, P. and Moreno, A. (2007). 'Corporate Citizenship and Public Relations: The Importance and Interactivity of Social Responsibility Issues on Corporate Websites.' *Public Relations Review*, 33: 84–91.

Carnegie, A. (1900). *The Gospel of Wealth, and Other Timely Essays*. New York: Century.

Carroll, A. B. (1979). 'A Three-dimensional Conceptual Model of Corporate Social Performance.' *Academy of Management Review*, 4(4): 497–505.

Carroll, A. B. (1991). 'The Pyramid of Corporate Social Responsibility: Toward the Moral Management of Organizational Stakeholders.' *Business Horizons*, July–August.

Carroll, A. B. (1994). 'Social Issues in Management Research.' *Business and Society*, 33(1): 5–25.

Carroll, A. B. (2004). 'Managing Ethically With Global Stakeholders: A Present and Future Challenge.' *Academy of Management Executive*, 18(2): 114–120.

Carroll, A. B. (2006). 'Trust is the Key When Rating Great Workplaces.' 29 July. Available online at: http://onlineathens.com/stories/073006/business_20060730047.shtml (accessed 3 Seprember 2014).

Carson, D. (2008). 'The Blogosphere as a Market Research Tool for Tourism Destinations: A Case Study of Australia's Northern Territory.' *Journal of Vacation Marketing*, 14(2): 111–119.

Carson, E. D. (1999). 'On Defining and Measuring Volunteering in the United States and Abroad.' *Law and Contemporary Problems*, 62(4): 67–71.

Casey, C. (1999). 'Come, Join Our Family: Discipline and Integration in Corporate Organizational Culture.' *Human Relations*, 52(2): 155–178

Casmir, F. (1993). 'Third-culture Building: A Paradigm Shift for International and Intercultural Communication.' *Communication Yearbook*, 16: 407–428.

Castka, P., Bamber, C. J., Bamber, D. J., and Sharp, J. M. (2004). 'Integrating Corporate Social Responsibility (CSR) Into ISO Management Systems – in Search of a Feasible CSR Management System Framework.' *The TQM Magazine*, 16(3): 216–224.

Caulkin, S. (2004). 'Business Schools for Scandal.' *The Observer*, 28 March, 9.

Center for Media and Democracy (n.d.). Available online at: www.sourcewatch.org/index.php/Center_for_Media_and_Democracy (accessed 13 August 2014).

Chapple, W. and Moon, J. (2005). 'Corporate Social Responsibility (CSR) in Asia: A Seven-country Study of CSR Web Site Reporting.' *Business and Society*, 44(4): 415–441.

Chase, W. H. (1982, December 1). 'Issue Management Conference – A Special Report.' *Corporate Public Issues and Their Management*, 7: 1–2.

Cheney, G., Roper, J., and May, S. (2007). "Overview." In S. May, G. Cheney, and J. Roper (eds), *The Debate Over Corporate Social Responsibility*, pp. 3–12. New York: Oxford University Press.

Cherrier, H., Russell, S., and Fielding, K. (2012). 'Corporate Environmentalism and Top Management Identity Negotiation.' *Journal of Organisational Change Management*, 25(4): 518–534.

Cheung, A. (2011). 'Do Stock Investors Value Corporate Sustainability? Evidence From an Event Study.' *Journal of Business Ethics*, 99(2): 145–165.

Chevron (n.d.). 'The Power of Human Energy.' Available online at: www.chevron.com/ (accessed 10 February 2014).

Choi, J. and Choi, Y. (2009). 'Behavioral Dimensions of Public Relations Leadership in Organizations.' *Journal of Communication Management*, 13(4): 292–309.

Chomsky, N. (1995). 'Corporate Totalitarianism.' Lecture. 22 June. Available online at: https://play.spotify.com/track/4oYfdp0Hew81CaaYswTW8b?play=true&utm_source=open.spotify.com&utm_medium=open (accessed 12 September 2014).

Christians, C. G. and Covert, C. L. (1980). *Teaching Ethics in Journalism Education*. Hastings-on-Hudson, NY: The Hastings Center.

Christensen, L. T. and Langer, R. (2009). "Public Relations and the Strategic Use of Transparency: Consistency, Hypocrisy, and Corporate Change." In R. L. Heath, E. L. Toth, and D. Waymer (eds), *Rhetorical and Critical Approaches to Public Relations II*, pp. 129–153. New York: Routledge.

Cisernos, G. (2008). 'How CSR Can Help Management Development.' *European Foundation for Management Development (EFMD) Global Focus*, 2(2): 38–39.

Clark, C. E. (2000). 'Differences Between Public Relations and Corporate Social Responsibility: An analysis.' *Public Relations Review*, 26(3): 363–380.

Clark, J. M. (1916). 'The Changing Basis of Economic Responsibility.' *Journal of Political Economy*, 24: 209–229.

Clarkson, M. B. E. (1995). 'A Stakeholder Framework for Analyzing And Evaluating Corporate Social Performance.' *Academy of Management Review*, 20(1): 92–117.

Clary, E. G. and Snyder, M. (2002). 'Community Involvement: Opportunities and Challenges in Socializing Adults to Participate in Society.'*Journal of Social Issues*, 58: 581–591.

Cloud, D. L. (2007). "Corporate Social Responsibility as Oxymoron: Universalization and Exploitation at Boeing." In S. May, G. Cheney, and J. Roper (eds), *The Debate Over Corporate Social Responsibility*, pp. 219–231. New York: Oxford University Press.

Coleman, J. S. (1988). 'Social Capital in the Creation of Human Capital.' *American Journal of Sociology*, 94(Suppl.) S95–S120.

"Comment policy" (n.d.). *Disney Post* – The Official Blog of the Walt Disney Company. Available online at: https://thewaltdisneycompany.com/blog (accessed 17 August 2014).

Commission on Public Relations Education (2012). *Standards for a Master's Degree in Public Relations: Educating for Complexity. The Report of the Commission on Public Relations Education.* New York: Public Relations Society of America. Available online at: www.commpred.org/_uploads/report5-full.pdf (accessed 5 Sepromber 2014).

Concept Green (n.d.) 'Here's What We Do, and How We Can Help Your Organization.' Available online at: www.conceptgreen.net/services (accessed 13 July 2014).

Conley, J. M. and Williams, C. A. (2005). 'Engage, Embed, and Embellish: Theory Versus Practice in the Corporate Social Responsibility Movement.' *Journal of Corporation Law*, 31(1): 1–38.

Connolly-Ahern, C. and Broadway, S. C. (2007). 'The Importance of Appearing Competent: An Analysis of Corporate Impression Management Strategies on the World Wide Web." *Public Relations Review*, 33: 343–345.

Coombs, W. T. (1998). 'An Analytic Framework for Crisis Situations: Better Responses for a Better Understanding of the Situation.' *Journal of Public Relations Research*, 10(3): 177–191.

Coombs, W. T. and Holladay, S. J. (2012). *Managing Corporate Social Responsibility: A Communication Approach.* Malden, MA: Wiley-Blackwell.

"Core Staff" (n.d.). Environmental Justice Resource Center at Clark Atlanta University. Available online at: www.ejrc.cau.edu/staff.html (accessed 13 July 2014).

Cornelissen, J. P. (2004). *Corporate Communications: Theory and Practice.* London: Sage.

CorpWatch (2001). 'Greenwash Fact Sheet.' Available online at: www.corpwatch.org/article.php?id=242 (accessed 1 June 2014).

"Corporate responsibility" (n.d.). Chevron. Available online at: www.chevron.com/corporateresponsibility/ (accessed 9 September 2014).

"Corporate Sustainability" (n.d.). Dow Jones Sustainability Indices. Available online at: www.sustainability-indices.com/sustainability-assessment/corporate-sustainability.jsp (accessed 5 May 2014).

Corredor-Ruiz, J. (2000). 'The Function of Public Relations in the Stability and Social Equilibrium of Organizations.' *Alacaurp*, 1: 12–16.

Corvellec, H. and Hultman, J. (2012). 'From Less Filling to "Wasting LESs:" Societal Narratives, Socio-materiality, and Organizations.' *Journal of Organizational Change Management*, 25(2): 297–314.

Cowperthwaite, G. (Producer & Director). (2013). *Blackfish* (Motion picture). USA: Magnolia Pictures.

Cox, R. (2013). *Environmental Communication and the Public Sphere*, 3rd edn. Thousand Oaks, CA: Sage.

Crane, A. and Matten, D. (2004). *Business Ethics: A European Perspective.* New York: Oxford University Press.

Creedon, P. and Al-Khaja, M. (2005). 'Public Relations and Globalization: Building a Case for Cultural Competency in Public Relations Education.' *Public Relations Review*, 31(3): 344–354.

Crouch, C. (2006). 'Modeling the Firm In Its Market and Organizational Environment: Methodologies for Studying Corporate Social Responsibility.' *Organization Studies*, 27: 1533–1551.

Crowson, P. (2009). 'Adding Public Value: The Limits of Corporate Responsibility.' *Resources Policy*, 34(3): 105–111.

Cunningham, L. (1999) 'Corporate Governance Roundtable.' *Cornell Law Review*, 84(5): 1289–1295.

Curtin, P. A. and Boynton, L. A. (2001). "Ethics in Public Relations: Theory and Practice." In R. L. Heath (ed.), *The Handbook of Public Relations*, pp. 411–421. Thousand Oaks, CA: Sage.

Curtis, J. E., Baer, D. E., and Grabb, E. G. (2001). 'Nations of Joiners: Explaining Voluntary Association Membership in Democratic Societies.' *American Sociological Review*, 66(6): 783–805.

Daugherty, E. (2001). 'Public Relations and Social Responsibility.' In R. L. Heath (ed.), *Handbook of Public Relations*, pp. 389–402. Thousand Oaks, CA: Sage.

David, P., Kline, S., and Dai, Y. (2005). 'Corporate Social Responsibility Practices, Corporate Identity and Purchase Intention: Viability of a Dual-process Model.' *Journal of Public Relations Research*, 17(3): 291–313.

Davis, J. and Welton, R. (1991). 'Professional Ethics: Business Students' Perceptions.' *Journal of Business Ethics*, 10(6): 451–463.

Davis, K. (1960). 'Can Business Afford to Ignore Social Responsibilities?" *California Management Review*, 2: 70–76.

Dawkins, J. (2004). 'Corporate Responsibility: The Communication Challenge.' *Journal of Communication Management*, 9(2): 108–119.

De Bakker, F., Groenewegen, P., and den Hond, F. (2005). 'A Bibliometric Analysis of 30 Years of Research and Theory on Corporate Social Responsibility and Corporate Social Performance.' *Business & Society*, 44(3): 283–317.

de Gilder, D., Schuyt, T. N. M., and Breedijk, M. (2005). 'Effects of an Employee volunteering Program on the Work Force: The ABN-AMRO Case.' *Journal of Business Ethics*, 61(2): 143–152.

DeLeon, J.R., Bonfiglio, M., Stratton, R., and Berlinger, J. (Producers) and Berlinger, J. (Director). (2009). *Crude: The Real Price of Oil* (Motion picture). United States: Entendre Films.

Dellarocas, C. (2006). 'Strategic Manipulation of Internet Opinion Forums: Implications for Consumers and Firms.' *Management Science*, 52(10): 1577–1593.

DeLorme, D. E. and Fedler, F. (2003). 'Journalists' Hostility Toward Public Relations: An Historical Analysis.' *Public Relations Review*, 29: 99–124.

De Moya, M. and Jain, R. (2013). 'When Tourists Are Your "Friends:" Exploring the Brand Personality of Mexico and Brazil on Facebook.' *Public Relations Review*, 39: 23–29.

Deutsch, C. H. (2008). 'Training Meets Philanthropy at IBM.' *International Herald Tribune*, 26 March, p. 11.

Dhanesh, G. (2012). 'Relationship Maintenance Strategies: Does CSR Fit the Bill?' May. Paper presented at the International Communication Association Conference, Phoenix, AZ.

DiStaso, M., Stacks, D., and Botan, C. (2009). 'State of Public Relations Education in the United States: 2006 Report on a National Survey of Executives and Academics.' *Public Relations Review*, 35: 254–269.

Doane, D. (2005). 'The Myth of CSR: On Philanthropy.' *Global Policy Forum*. Available online at: www.globalpolicy.org/socecon/tncs/2005/1104myth.htm (accessed 1 September 2013).

Doh, J. P. and Guay, R. R. (2006). 'Corporate Social Responsibility, Public Policy, and NGO Activism in Europe and the United States: An Institutional-stakeholder Perspective.' *Journal of Management Studies*, 43: 47–73.

"Dollar for Doer Statistics" (2013). Available online at: http://doublethedonation.com/blog/2013/01/dollars-for-doers-grants-definition/ (accessed 30 December 2013).

Donohue, G. A., Tichenor, P. J., and Olien, C. N. (1995). 'A Guard Dog Perspective on the Role of Media.' *Journal of Communication*, 42: 115–132.

Doppelt, R. (2003). 'The Seven Sustainability Blunders.' *The Systems Thinker*, 14(5): 1–7.

Dozier, D. M. (1983). 'Toward a Reconciliation of Role Conflict in Public Relations research.' May. Paper Presented at the Meeting of the Western Communications Educators Conference, Fullerton, CA.

Dozier, D. M. and Lauzen, M. M. (2000). 'Liberating the Intellectual Domain From the Practice: Public Relations, Activism, and the Role of the Scholar.' *Journal of Public Relations Research*, 12(1): 3–22.

Du, S., Bhattacharya, C. B., and Sen, S. (2007). 'Reaping Relationship Rewards From Corporate Social Responsibility: The Role of Competitive Positioning.' *International Journal of Research in Marketing*, 24: 224–241.

Duhé, S. C. (2005, March 10–13). "Communicating with Corporate Insiders: A Political Economic Analysis of Firm Reputation for Social Responsibility and its Contribution to the Bottom Line." In M. L. Watson (ed.), *The Impact of PR in Creating a More Ethical World: Why Can't We All Get Along?* Paper Presented at the 8th International Public Relations Research Conference, Miami University, South Miami, FL, p. 74.

Dutta, M. J. and Pal, M. (2011). "Public Relations and Marginalization in a Global Context." In N. Bardhan and C. K. Weaver (eds), *Public Relations in Global Cultural Contexts: Multi-paradigmatic Perspectives*, pp. 195–225. New York: Routledge.

Earth Charter Initiative (n.d.). 'FAQ, What is the Earth Charter?' Available online at: www.earthcharterinaction.org/content/pages/FAQ.html#5 (accessed 11 June 2014).

Easterly, W. (2014). 'Bill Gates' Misguided Capitalism.' Available online at: www.huffingtonpost.com/william-easterly/bill-gates-misguided-capi_b_110289.html (accessed 3 December 2014).

Eisenegger, M. and Schranz, M. (2014). 'Reputation Management and Corporate Social Responsibility.' In Ø. Ihlen, J. L. Bartlett, and S. May (eds) *The handbook of Communication and Corporate Social Responsibility*, pp. 128–146. Malden, MA: Wiley-Blackwell.

Elkington, J. (1999). *Cannibals With Forks: The Triple Bottom Line of the 21st Century Business.* Oxford: Capstone.

El-Tannir, A. A. (2002). 'The Corporate University Model for Continuous Learning, Training and Development.' *Education + Training*, 44(2): 76–81.

Engholm, C. (1991) *When Business East Meets Business West: The Guide to Practice and Protocol in the Pacific Rim.* New York: Wiley.

Environmental Protection Agency (EPA) (n.d.) 'Environmental Justice Program and Civil Rights.' Available online at: www.epa.gov/region1/ej/ (accessed 10 February 2014).

Epstein-Reeves, J. (2011). 'How to Create On-point CSR Reports That Pop.' *PR News.* 14 February. Available online at: www.prnewsonline.com/topics/corporate-responsi bility/2011/02/14/how-to-create-on-point-csr-reports-that-pop/ (accessed 24 June 2013).

Esrock, S. and Leichty, G. (2000). 'Organization of Corporate Web Pages: Publics and Functions.' *Public Relations Review*, 26(3): 327–344.

Estes, R. (1996). *Tyranny of the Bottom Line: Why Corporations Make Good People Do Bad Things.* San Francisco, CA: Berrett-Koehler Publishers.

European Commission (2011). *Communication From the Commission of the European Parliament, the Council, the European Economic and Social Committee and the Committee of the Regions: A Renewed EU Strategy 2011–14 for Corporate Social Responsibility.* Brussels: European Commission.

Ewen, S. (1996). *PR! A Social History of Spin.* New York: Basic Books.

Fairclough, G. (2002). 'Study Slams Philip Morris Ads Telling Teens Not to Smoke – How a Market Researcher Who Dedicated Years to Cigarette Sales Came to Create Antismoking Ads.' *Wall Street Journal.* 24 May (Eastern edition), p. 1.

Fieseler, C., Fleck, M., and Meckel, M. (2010). Corporate Social Responsibility in the Blogosphere. *Journal of Business Ethics*, 91: 599–614.

Fineman, S. (2001). 'Fashioning the Environment.' *Organization*, 8: 17–31.

Fitzpatrick, K. R. (1996a). 'Public Relations and the Law: A Survey or Practitioners.' *Public Relations Review*, 22: 1–6.

Fitzpatrick, K. R. (1996b). 'The Role of Public Relations in the Institutionalization of Ethics.' *Public Relations Review*, 22: 249–258.

Fitzpatrick, K. and Bronstein, C. (2006). "Introduction: Toward a Definitional Framework for Responsible Advocacy." In K. Fitzpatrick and C. Bronstein (eds), *Ethics in Public Relations: Responsible Advocacy*, pp. ix–xiv. Thousand Oaks, CA: Sage.

Fitzpatrick, K. R. and Gauthier, C. (2001). 'Toward a Professional Responsibility Theory of Public Relations Ethics.' *Journal of Mass Media Ethics*, 16(2–3): 193–212.

Flynn, F. J. (2005). 'Identity Orientations and Forms of Social Exchange in Organizations.' *Academy of Management Review*, 30: 737–750.

Forehand, M. R. and Grier, S. (2003). 'When is Honesty the Best Policy? The Effect of Stated Company Intent on Consumer Skepticism.' *Journal of Consumer Psychology*, 13: 349–356.

Foster, M. and Meinhard, A. (2002). 'Corporate Social Responsibility in the Canadian Context: The New Role of Corporations in Community Involvement and Social Issues.' Centre for Voluntary Sector Studies, Ryerson University, *Working Paper, Number 20.*

Foucault, M. (1980). *Power/knowledge: Selected Interviews and Other Writings, 1972–1977.* (Edited and translated by C. Gordon.) New York: Pantheon. Frederick.

Fraedrich, J., Thome, D. M., and Ferrell, O. C. (1994). 'Assessing the Application of Cognitive Moral Development Theory to Business Ethics.' *Journal of Business Ethics*, 13: 829–838.

Frankental, P. (2001). 'Corporate Social Responsibility: A PR Invention?' *Corporate Communications*, 6(1): 18–23.

Frederick, W. C. (1986). 'Toward CSR3: Why Ethical Analysis is Indispensable and Unavoidable in Corporate Affairs.' *California Management Review*, 28: 126–141.

Frederick, W. C. (1994). 'From CSR1 to CSR2: The Maturing of Business-and-society Thought.' *Business and Society*, 33(2): 150–164.

Frederick, W. C. (1998). 'Moving to CSR4.' *Business and Society*, 37(1): 40–60.

Freeman, R., Wicks, A., and Parmar, B. (2004). 'Stakeholder Theory and the Corporate Objective Revisited.' *Organization Science*, 15(3): 364–369.

Freeman, R. B. (1997). 'Working for Nothing: The Supply of Volunteer Labor.'*Journal of Labor Economics*, 15(1): S140–S166.

Freitag, A. (2007). 'Staking Claim: Public Relations Leaders Needed to Shape CSR Policies.' *Public Relations Quarterly*, 52(1): 37–40.

French, W. A. and Granrose, J. (1995). *Practical Business Ethics.* Englewood Cliffs, NJ: Prentice Hall.

Friedman, M. (1970). 'The Social Responsibility of Business is to Increase Its Profits.' *New York Times Magazine*, 13 September, 32–33, 122, 126.

FrynasJ. G. (2005). 'The False Developmental Promise of Corporate Social Responsibility: Evidence From Multinational Oil Companies.' *International Affairs*, 81(3): 581–598.

Gale, K. and Bunton, K. (2005). 'Assessing the Impact of Ethics Instruction on Advertising and Public Relations Graduates.' *Journalism & Mass Communication Educator*, 60(3): 272–285.

Gallicano, T. D., Brett, K., and Hopp, T. (2013). 'Is Ghost Blogging Like Speechwriting? A Survey of Practitioners About the Ethics of Ghost Blogging.' *Public Relations Journal*, 7(3). Available online at: www.prsa.org/intelligence/ prjournal/documents/ 2013_gallicano.pdf (accessed 19 March 2014).

Gans, H. J. (1979). *Deciding What's News.* New York: Pantheon.

Gans, H. J. (2003). *Democracy and the News.* New York: Oxford University Press.

Garriga, E. and Melé, D. (2004). 'Corporate Social Responsibility Theories: Mapping the Territory.' *Journal of Business Ethics*, 53: 51–71.

Gebler, D. (2006). 'Creating an Ethical Culture.' *Strategic Finance*, 87(11): 28–34.

Gerow, C. (2013). 'Mobil CEO Did More Than Just Advertise.' *Region's Business: A Journal of Business & Politics.* Available online at: http://philadelphia.regionsbusi ness.com/print-edition-commentary/mobil-ceo-did-more-than-just-advertise/ (accessed 22 January 2014).

Gertten, F. (Director) (2009). *Bananas!* (Motion picture). Sweden: WB Film.

Giacalone, R. A. and Thompson, K. R. (2006). 'Business Ethics and Social Responsibility Education: Shifting the Worldview.' *Academy of Management Learning & Education*, 5(3): 266–277.

Giddens, A. (1984). *The Constitution of Society: Outline of the Theory of Structuration.* Cambridge, MA: Polity Press.

Glavas, A. and Piderit, S. K. (2009). 'How Does Doing Good Matter? Effects of Corporate Citizenship on Employees.' *Journal of Corporate Citizenship*, 36: 51–70.

Godes, D. and Mayzlin, D. (2004). 'Using Online Conversations to Study Word-of-mouth Communication.' *Marketing Science*, 23(4): 545–560.

Golden, L. L. (1968). *Only By Public Consent: American Corporations Search for Favorable Opinion.* New York: Hawthorne Books.

Goldfarb, A. (2009). 'Golden Handcuffs' Can Hold Key to Locking Up Top Executives.' *Fenton Report.* 22 March. Available online at: www.fentonreport.com/entrepreneurs/% E2%80%9Cgolden-handcuffs%E2%80%9D-can-hold-key-to-locking-up-top-executives (accessed 20 June 2014).

Gond, J. and Herrbach, O. (2006). 'Social Reporting as an Organizational Learning Tool? A Theoretical Framework.' *Journal of Business Ethics*, 65(4): 359–371.

Gordon, K. (2014). 'Risky Business: The Economic Risks of Climate Change in the United States.' Available online at: http://riskybusiness.org/report/overview/execu tive-summary (accessed 24 July 2014).

Governance & Accountability Institute, Inc. (2014). *Sustainability – What Matters?* New York: Governance & Accountability Institute, Inc.

Gray, J. and Laidlaw, H. (2004). 'Improving the Measurement of Communication Satisfaction.' *Management Communication Quarterly*, 17: 425–448.

Gray, R. and Milne, M. (2004). "Towards Reporting on the Triple Bottom Line: Mirages, Methods and Myths." In A. Henriques and J. Richardson (eds), *The Triple Bottom Line: Does it All Add Up?* London: Earthscan.

Gregory, A. (2003). 'The Ethics of Engagement in the UK Public Sector: A Case in Point.' *Journal of Communication Management*, 8(1): 83–94.

Greenwood, C. (2012). 'Whistleblowing in Public Relations: Ethical Dilemma or Role Responsibility.' August. Paper presented at the annual meeting of the Association for Education in Journalism and Mass Communication, Chicago, IL. Available online at: http://citation.allacademic.com/meta/p_mla_apa_research_citation/5/8/2/3/3/p582339_index.html (accessed 20 June 2014).

Grunig, J. E. (n.d.). 'The Arthur W. Page Center.' Available online at: http://thepagecenter.comm.psu.edu/index.php/challengesaccomplishments/892-james-grunig (accessed 12 February 2014).

Grunig, J. E. (1992). *Excellence in Public Relations and Communication Management*. Hillsdale, NJ: Lawrence Erlbaum Associates.

Grunig, J. E. (1993). 'Image and Substance: From Symbolic to Behavioral Relationships.' *Public Relations Review*, 19(2): 121–139.

Grunig, J. E. (2000a). "Two-way Symmetrical Public Relations: Past, Present, Future." In R. L. Heath (ed.), *The Handbook of Public Relations*, pp. 11–30. Thousand Oaks, CA: Sage.

Grunig, J. E. (2000b). 'Collectivism, Collaboration, and Societal Corporatism as Core Professional Values in Public Relations.' *Journal of Public Relations Research*, 12: 23–48.

Grunig, J. E. (2001). "Two Way Symmetrical Public Relations: Past, Present and Future." In R. L. Heath (ed.), *Handbook of Public Relations*, pp. 11–30. Thousand Oaks, CA: Sage.

Grunig, J. E. and Grunig, L. A. (1992). "Models of Public Relations and Communication." In J. E. Grunig (ed.) *Excellence in Public Relations and Communication Management*, pp. 285–325. Mahwah, NJ: Lawrence Erlbaum.

Grunig, J. E., Grunig, L. A., and Ehling, W. P. (1992). "What is an Effective Organization?" In J. E. Grunig (ed.), *Excellence Public Relations and Communication Management: Contributions to Effective Organizations*, pp. 65–89. Hillsdale, NJ: Lawrence Erlbaum Associates.

Grunig, J. E. and Huang, Y. H. (2000). "From Organizational Effectiveness to Relationship Indicators: Antecedents Of Relationships, Public Relations Strategies, and Relationship Outcomes." In J. A. Ledingham and S. D. Bruning (eds), *Public Relations as Relationship Management. A Relational Approach to the Study and Practice of Public Relations*, pp. 23–54. Mahwah, NJ: Lawrence Erlbaum Associates.

Grunig, J. E. and Hunt, T. (1984). *Managing Public Relations*. New York: Holt, Rinehart & Winston.

Grunig, J. E. and Repper, F. C. (1992). "Strategic Management, Publics, and Issues." In J. E. Grunig, D. M. Dozier, W. P. Ehling, L. A. Grunig, F. C. Repper, and J. White (eds), *Excellence in Public Relations and Communications Management*, pp. 117–157. Hillsdale, NJ: Lawrence Erlbaum.

Grunig, L. A. (1986). 'Activism and Organizational Response: Contemporary Cases of Collective Behavior.' Paper presented to the Association for Education in Journalism and Mass Communication, Norman, OK.

Grunig, L. A. (1992). "Activism: How it Limits the Effectiveness of Organizations and How Excellent Public Relations Departments Respond." In J. E. Grunig (ed.), *Excellence in Public Relations and Communication Management*, pp. 503–530. Hillsdale, NJ: Lawrence Erlbaum.

Grunig, L. A., Grunig, J. E., and Dozier, D. (2002). *Excellent Public Relations and Effective Organizations: A Study Of Communication Management in Three Countries*. Mahwah, NJ: Lawrence Erlbaum Associates.

Grunig, L. A., Toth, E. L., and Hon, L. (2000). 'Feminist Values in Public Relations.' *Journal of Public Relations Research*, 12(1): 49–68.

Guay, T., Doh, J. P., and Sinclair, G. (2004). 'Non-governmental Organizations, Shareholder Activism, and Socially Responsible Investments: Ethical, Strategic, And Governance Implications.' *Journal of Business Ethics*, 52: 125–139.

Guillory, J. E. and Sundar, S. S. (2014). 'How Does Web Site Interactivity Affect Tour perceptions of an Organization?' *Journal of Public Relations Research*, 26: 44–61.

Habermas, J. (1989). *The Structural Transformation of the Public Sphere: An Inquiry Into a Category of Bourgeois Society*. Trans. T. Burger. Cambridge, MA: MIT Press.

Halverson, R. (2004). 'Accessing, Documenting, and Communicating Practical Wisdom: The Phronesis of School Leadership Practice.' *American Journal of Education*, 111(1): 90–112.

Hamann, R., Agbazue, T., Kapelus, P., and Hein, A. (2005). 'Universalizing Corporate Social Responsibility?' *Business and Society Review*, 110(1): 1–19.

Hannegan, C. (2004). 'Employees as Reputation Makers.' *Strategic Communication Management*, 8(6): 5.

Hargie, O. and Tourish, D. (2009). *Auditing Organizational Communication*. London: Routledge.

Harrison, S. L. (1990). 'Ethics and Moral Issues in Public Relations Curricula.' *Journalism Educator*, 45(3): 32–38.

Hashi (2012). 'The Nail That Sticks Up.' Available online at: www.tofugu.com/2012/09/13/the-nail-that-sticks-up/ (accessed 22 July 2014).

Haywood, M. E., McMullen, D. A., and Wygal, D. E. (2004). 'Using Games to Enhance Student Understanding of Professional and Ethical Responsibilities.' *Issues in Accounting Education*, 19(1): 85–99.

Hearn, D. R. (2002). 'Education in the Workplace: An Examination of Corporate University Models.' Available online at: www.newfoundations.com/OrgTheory/Hearn721.html (accessed 5 January 2014).

Heath, R. L. (1997). *Strategic Issues Management: Organizations and Public Policy Challenges*. Thousand Oaks, CA: Sage.

Heath, R. L. (2001). "A Rhetorical Enactment Rationale for Public Relations." In R. Heath (ed.), *Handbook of Public Relations*, pp. 31–50. Thousand Oaks, CA: Sage.

Heath, R. L. (2013a). "Issues Management." In *Encyclopedia Of Public Relations*, 2nd edn, pp. 495–498. Thousand Oaks, CA: Sage.

Heath, R. L. (2013b). "Counseling." In *Encyclopedia of Public Relations*, 2nd edn, pp. 213–214. Thousand Oaks, CA: Sage.

Heath, R. L. and Coombs, T. (2006). *Today's Public Relations an Introduction*. Thousand Oaks, CA: Sage.

Heath, R. L. and Ni, L. (2009). 'Corporate Social Responsibility: Three R's.' Available online at: www.instituteforpr.org/topics/corporate-social-responsibility-three-rs/ (accessed 11 May 2013).

Heath, R. L. and Ryan, M. R. (1989). 'Public Relations' Role in Defining Corporate Social Responsibility.' *Journal of Mass Media Ethics*, 4(1): 21–38.

Henderson, D. (2001). *Misguided Virtue: False Notion of Corporate Social Responsibility.* London: Institute of Economic Affairs.

Hendry, J. (2001). 'Missing the Target: Normative Stakeholder Theory and the Corporate Governance Debate.' *Business Ethics Quarterly*, 11(1): 159–176.

Herzig, C. and Schaltegger, S. (2011). "Corporate sustainability reporting." In J. Godemann, and G. Michelsen (eds), *Sustainability Communication: Interdisciplinary Perspectives and Theoretical Foundation*, pp. 151–169. Dordrecht, Netherlands: Springer.

Hess, D. N., Rogovsky, N., and Dunfree, T. W. (2002). 'The Next Wave Of Corporate Community Involvement: Corporate Social Initiatives.' *California Management Review*, 44: 110–125.

Hiebert, R. E. (2013). "Ivy Lee." In *Encyclopedia of Public Relations*, 2nd edn, pp. 512–516. Thousand Oaks, CA: Sage.

Hilton, S. and Gibbons, G. (2002). *Good Business: Your World Needs You.* London: Texere.

Hoare, S. (2004). 'Social Workers.' *Human Resources*, November, 40–43.

Holland, L. and Gibbon, J. (2001). "Processes in Social and Ethical Accountability." In J. Andriof and M. McIntosh (eds), *Perspectives on Corporate Citizenship*, pp. 278–295. Sheffield, UK: Greenleaf Publishing.

Holtzhausen, D. R. (2000). 'Postmodern Values in Public Relations.' *Journal of Public Relations Research*, 12(1): 93–114.

Holtzhausen, D. R. (2002). 'A Postmodern Critique of Public Relations Theory and Research.' *Communication*, 28(1): 29–38.

Holtzhausen, D. R. (2014). *Public Relations as Activism: Postmodern Approaches to Theory and Practice.* New York: Routledge.

Holtzhausen, D. R., Peterson, B. K., and Tindall, N. T. J. (2009). 'Exploding the Myth of the Symmetrical/Asymmetrical Dichotomy: Public Relations Models in the New South Africa.' *Journal of Public Relations Research*, 15(4): 305–341.

Holtzhausen, D. and Voto, R. (2002). 'Resistance From the Margins: The Postmodern Public Relations Practitioner as Organizational Activist.' *Journal of Public Relations Research*, 14: 57–84.

"Home Depot" (n.d.). 'CSR Case Study: The Home Depot Giving Back to Communities.' Available online at: /www.commdev.org/files/1073_file_hd_e.pdf (accessed 20 December 2013).

Hon, L. and Grunig, J. E. (1999). 'Guidelines for Measuring Relationships in Public Relations.' Available online at: www.instituteforpr.org/topics/measuring-relationships/ (accessed 2 April 2014).

Hooghiemstra, R. (2000). 'Corporate Communication and Impression Management – New Perspectives Why Companies Engage in Corporate Social Reporting.' *Journal of Business Ethics*, 27: 55–68.

Hornick, E. and Quijano, E. (2009). 'Whistle-blower: Health Care Industry Engaging in PR Tactics.' Available online at: www.cnn.com/2009/POLITICS/08/12/health.industry.whistleblower/index.html (accessed 19 August 2014).

Horning, G. (2014). 'Southern Voices for Change' (documentary). Available online at: www.youtube.com/watch?v=0MI8dcgBjNY&feature=youtube (accessed 13 July 2014).

Houghton, S. M., Gabel, J. T. A., and Williams, D. W. (2008). 'Connecting the Two Faces of CSR: Does Employee Volunteerism Improve Compliance?' *Journal of Business Ethics*, 87: 477–494.

Huertas, A., and Capriotti, P. (2008). 'Using Corporate Social Responsibility as a Public relations Tool in a Local Community.' *Building Bridges in a Global Economy*, 2: 51–56.

"Human Rights Impacts of Oil Pollution: Ecuador" (n.d.). Available online at: www.business-humanrights.org/Documents/Oilpollution/Ecuador/Culture (accessed 29 June 2014).

Hutchison, L. L. (2002). 'Teaching Ethics Across the Public Relations Curriculum.' *Public Relations Review*, 28: 301–309.

Ihlen, Ø. (2008). 'Mapping the Environment for Corporate Social Responsibility: Stakeholders, Publics and the Public Sphere.' *Corporate Communications: An International Journal*, 13(2): 135–146.

Ihlen, Ø. (2013). "Corporate Social Responsibility." In *Encyclopedia of Public Relations*, 2nd edn, pp. 206–210. Thousand Oaks, CA: Sage.

Inkpen, A. C. (2002). "Strategic Alliances." In M. A. Hitt, R. E. Freeman, and J. S. Harrison (eds), *The Blackwell Handbook of Strategic Management*, pp. 409–432. Oxford: Blackwell Publishing.

Isaksson, R. and Steimle, U. (2009). 'What Does GRI-reporting Tell us About Corporate Sustainability?' *The TQM Journal*, 21(2): 168–181.

ISEA (1999a). *AccountAbility 1000 (AA1000): A Foundation Standard in Social and Ethical Accounting, Auditing and Reporting*. London: ISEA.

ISEA (1999b). *AccountAbility 1000 (AA1000): Framework: Standard, Guidelines and Professional Qualification*. London: ISEA.

"ISO 14000" (n.d.). Available online at: www.iso.org/iso/home/standards/management-standards/iso14000.htm (accessed 5 May 2014).

Jahdi, K. S. and Acikdilli, G. (2009) 'Marketing Communications and Corporate Social Responsibility (CSR): Marriage of Convenience or Shotgun Wedding?" *Journal of Business Ethics*, 88: 103–113.

Jain, R. and Winner, L. H. (2013–2014). 'Are We Teaching Them to Be CSR Managers? Examining Students' Expectations of Practitioner Roles in CSR.' *Teaching Public Relations Monograph*, 88.

Jamali, D. and Keshishian, T. (2009). 'Uneasy Alliances: Lessons Learned From Partnerships Between Businesses and NGOs in the Context of CSR.' *Journal of Business Ethics*, 84(2): 277–295.

Janis, I. L. (1982). *Groupthink*. Boston, MA: Houghton Mifflin.

Jarvis, C. (2011). 'Dollars for Doers: The Incentive Nobody Wants."' Available online at: www.realizedworth.com/2011/11/dollars-for-doers-incentive-nobody.html (accessed 1 September 2013).

Jensen, J. (1997). *Ethical Issues in the Communication Process*. Mahwah, NJ: Lawrence Erlbaum Associates.

Jo, S. and Shim, S. (2005). 'Paradigm Shift of Employee Communication: The Effect of Management Communication on Trusting Relationships.' *Public Relations Review*, 31: 277–280.

Joannides, V. and Miller, B. (n.d.). 'Authorship and Authority – Competing Claims Within Corporate Social Responsibility Report Guidance Providers.' Available online at: http://docs.business.auckland.ac.nz/doc/bob-miller.pdf (accessed 22 March 2014).

Jonas, H. (1984). *The imperative of responsibility.* Chicago, IL: The University of Chicago Press.

Jones, D. (2005). 'CEOs Refuse to Get Tangled Up in Messy Blogs.' *USA Today.* 10 May. Available online at: http://usatoday30.usatoday.com/money/companies/mana gement/2005-05-09-blog-cover_x.htm (accessed 9 March 2014).

Jones, D. A. (2010). 'Does Serving the Community Also Serve the Company? Using organizational Identification and Social Exchange Theories to Understand Employee Responses to a Volunteerism Programme.' *Journal of Occupational and Organizational Psychology,* 83: 857–878.

Joutsenvirta, M. and Uusitalo, L. (2010). 'Cultural Competences: An Important Resource in the Industry-NGO Dialog.' *Journal of Business Ethics,* 91(3): 379–390.

Jung, T. and Pompper, D. (2014). 'Assessing Instrumentality Of Mission Statements and Social-financial Performance Links: Corporate Social Responsibility as Context.' *International Journal of Strategic Communication,* 8(2): 79–99.

Katu, R. (1997). 'The Path of Kyosei.' *Harvard Business Review,* 75(4): 55–63.

Kelleher, T. (2010). 'Editor's Note.' *Journal of Public Relations Research,* 22(3): 239–240.

Kelly, K. S. (2001). "Stewardship: The Fifth Step in the Public Relations Process." In R. L. Heath (ed.), *Handbook of Public Relations,* pp. 279–289. Thousand Oaks, CA: Sage.

Kenner, R. (Producer and Director). (2008). *Food, Inc.* (Motion picture). USA: Magnolia Pictures.

Kent, M. L. and Taylor, M. (1998). 'Building Dialogic Relationships Through the World Wide Web.' *Public Relations Review,* 24(3): 321–334.

Kent, M. L. and Taylor, M. (2002). 'Toward a Dialogic Theory of Public Relations.' *Public Relations Review,* 28(1): 21–37.

Kent, M. L. and Taylor, M. (2003). 'Maximizing Media Relations: A Web Site Checklist.' *Public Relations Quarterly,* 48: 14–18.

Kent, M., Taylor, M., and White, W. (2003). 'The Relationship Between Web Site Design and Organization Responsiveness to Stakeholders.' *Public Relations Review,* 29: 63–77.

Kim, J. and Rhee, Y. (2011). 'Strategic Thinking About Employee Communication Behavior (ECB) in Public Relations: Testing the Models of Megaphoning and Scouting Effects in Korea.' *Journal of Public Relations Research,* 23: 243–268.

Kim, S.-Y. and Reber, B. H. (2008). 'Public Relations' Place in Corporate Social Responsibility: Practitioners Define Their Role.' *Public Relations Review,* 34(4): 337–342.

Kim, Y. (2013). 'Strategic Communication of Corporate Social Responsibility (CSR): Effects of Stated Motives and Corporate Reputation on Stakeholder Responses.' June. Paper presented at the annual meeting of the International Communication Association, London.

Kim, Y. and Choi, Y. (2012). 'College Students' Perception of Philip Morris's Tobacco-related Smoking Prevention and Tobacco-unrelated Social Responsibility Programs; a Comparative Study in Korea and the United States.' *Journal of Public Relations Research,* 24: 184–199.

Kjær, P. (2007). "Changing Constructions of Business and Society in the News." In P. Kjær and T. Slaatta (eds), *Mediating Business: The Expansion of Business Journalism,* pp. 159–185. Copenhagen: Copenhagen Business School Press.

Knight, D. (2006). "The SIGMA Management Model." In J. Jonker, and M. de Witte (eds), *Management Models for Corporate Social Responsibility,* pp. 11–18. Berlin: Springer.

Koetsier, J. (2013, March 5). 'Facebook: 15 Million Businesses, Now Companies, and Organizations Now Have a Facebook Page.' Available online at: http://venturebeat.com/2013/03/05/facebook-15-million-businesses-companies-and-organizations-now-have-a-facebook-page/ (accessed 17 August 2014).

Kreps, T. J. (1940). *Measurement of the Social Performance of Business.* US Temporary National Economic Committee, Investigation of Concentration of Economic Power, Monograph No. 7. Washington, DC: US Government Printing Office.

Krishnamurthy, S., Chew, W., Soh, T., and Luo, W. (2007). "Corporate Social Responsibility and Public Relations, Perceptions and Practices in Singapore." In S. K. May, G. Cheney, and J. Roper (eds), *The Debate Over Corporate Social Responsibility*, p. 119–134. New York: Oxford University Press.

Kropp, F., Holden, S. J. S., and Lavack, A. M. (1999). 'Cause-related Marketing and Values in Australia.' *International Journal of Nonprofit and Voluntary Sector Marketing*, 4(1): 69–80.

Kruckeberg, D. (1993). 'Ethical Values Define Public Relations Community.' *PR Update*, 2(2): 1–2.

Kruckeberg, D. and Starck, K. (1988). *Public Relations and Community: A Reconstructed Theory.* New York: Praeger.

Küng, H. (1992). "Why We Need a Global Ethic." In C. Jencks (ed.), *The Postmodern Reader*, pp. 409–416. London: Academy Editions.

Küng, H. (1993). 'Declaration toward a global ethic.' 4 September. Available online at: http://nautilus.org/gps/applied-gps/global-ethics/a-global-ethic/#axzz36baGlcm6 (accessed 5 July 2014).

Kurucz, E. C., Colbert, B. A., and Wheeler, D. (2008). "The Business Case for Corporate Social Responsibility." In A. Crane, A. McWilliams, D. Matten, J. Moon, and D. Siegel (eds), *The Oxford Handbook of Corporate Social Responsibility*, pp. 83–112. Oxford: Oxford University Press.

Kytle, B. and John, G. R. (2005). *Corporate Social Responsibility as Risk Management.* Corporate Social Responsibility Initiative Working Paper Series. Cambridge, MA: John F. Kennedy School of Government.

Lacayo, R. and Ripley, A. (2002). 'Persons of the year 2002.' 22 December, *Time*, 160.

Larrinaga, C. and Bebbington, J. (2001). 'Accounting Change or Institutional Appropriation? A Case Study of the Implementation of Environmental Accounting.' *Critical Perspectives on Accounting*, 12: 269–292.

LeClair, M. S. and Gordon, K. (2000). 'Corporate Support for Artistic and Cultural activities: What Determines the Distribution of Corporate Giving?' *Journal of Cultural Economics*, 24: 225–241.

Ledingham, J. A. (2006). "Relationship Management: A General Theory of Public Relations." In C. H. Botan and V. Hazleton (eds), *Public Relations Theory II*, pp. 465–484. Mahwah, NJ: Lawrence Erlbaum.

Ledingham, J. A. and Bruning, S. D. (1998). 'Relationship Management in Public Relations: Dimensions of an Organization-public Relationship.' *Public Relations Review*, 24(1): 55–65.

Ledingham, J. A. and Bruning, S. D. (2000). "A Longitudinal Study of Organization-public Relationship Dimensions: Defining the Role of Communication in the Practice of Relationship Management." In J. A. Ledingham and S. D. Bruning (eds), *Public Relations as Relationship Management: A Relational Approach to the Study and Practice of Public Relations*, pp. 55–69. Mahwah, NJ: Lawrence Erlbaum Associates.

Lee, S., Hwang, T., and Lee, H. H. (2006). 'Corporate Blogging Strategies of the Fortune 500 Companies.' *Management Decision*, 44(3): 316–334.

Lee, S. T. and Cheng, I.-H. (2011). 'Characteristics and Dimensions of Ethical Leadership in Public Relations.' *Journal of Public Relations Research*, 23(1): 46–74.

"Legacy of Interface" (2011). *Chatahoochee Riverkeeper*. Available online at: www.ucriverkeeper.org/enews/10august2011.html (accessed 1 Julyt 2014).

Legge, K. (1998). "The Morality of HRM." In C. Mabey, D. Skinner, and T. Clark (eds), *HRM: The Inside Story*. London, Sage.

Lehman, G. (2002). 'Global Accountability and Sustainability: Research Prospects.' *Accounting Forum*, 26(3): 219–232.

Lehman, G. (2007). 'A Common Pitch and the Management of Corporate Relations: Interpretation, Ethics and Managerialism.' *Journal of Business Ethics*, 71: 161–178.

Lenhart, A. (2006). 'Bloggers: A Portrait of the Internet's New Storytellers. Pew Internet and American Life Project.' Available online at: www.yourdictionary.com/pew-internet-and-american-life-project-survey (accessed 4 March 2014).

L'Etang, J. (1994). 'Public Relations and Corporate Social Responsibility: Some Issues Arising.' *Journal of Business Ethics*, 13: 111–123.

L'Etang, J. (1995). 'Ethical Corporate Social Responsibility: A Framework for Managers.' *Journal of Business Ethics*, 14: 125–132.

L'Etang, J. (2003). 'The Myth of the "Ethical Guardian": An Examination of its Origins, Potency and Illusions.' *Journal of Communication Management*, 8(1): 53–67.

L'Etang, J. (2006). "Corporate Responsibility and Public Relations Ethics." In J. L'Etang and M. Pieczka (eds), *Public Relations: Critical Debates and Contemporary Practice*, pp. 405–421. Mahwah, NJ: Lawrence Erlbaum Associates.

L'Etang, J., Lugo-Ocando, J., and Ahmad, Z. A. (2014). "Ethics: Corporate Social Responsibility, Power and Strategic Communication." In Ø. Ihlen, J. L. Bartlett, and S. May (eds) *The Handbook of Communication and Corporate Social Responsibility*, pp. 170–187. Malden, MA: Wiley-Blackwell.

Levinas, E. (1966). 'On the Trail of the Other.' Translated by Daniel J. Hoy. *Philosophy Today*, 10(1): 34–45.

Levit, L. (Producer), and Greenwald, R. (Director). (2005). *Wal-Mart: The High Cost of Low Price* (Motion picture). USA: Brave New Films.

Lippmann, W. (1922). *Public Opinion*. New York: Harcourt Brace.

Lips-Wiersma, M. and Morris, L. (2009). 'Discriminating Between "Meaningful Work" and the "Management of Meaning".' *Journal of Business Ethics*, 88(3): 491–511.

Liu, B. F. and Pompper, D. (2012). 'The "Crisis With No Name": Defining the Interplay of Culture, Ethnicity, and Race on Organizational Issues and Media Outcomes.' *Journal of Applied Communication Research*, 40(2): 127–146.

Llewellyn, J. (2007). "Regulation: Government, Business, and the Self in the United States." In S. May, G. Cheney, and J. Roper (eds), *The Debate Over Corporate Social Responsibility*, pp. 177–189. New York: Oxford University Press.

Lourenço, I. C., Branco, M. C., Curto, J. D., and Eugénio, T. (2012). 'How Does the Market Value Corporate Sustainability Performance?' *Journal of Business Ethics*, 108: 417–428.

Luffman, J. (2003). 'Volunteering on Company Time.' *Perspectives on Labour and Income*, 4(4): 5–11.

Luo, X. and Bhattacharya, C. B. (2006). 'Corporate Social Responsibility, Customer Satisfaction, and Market Value.' *Journal of Marketing*, 70(4): 1–18.

Luoma-aho, V., and Vos, M. (2010). 'Towards a More Dynamic Stakeholder Model: Acknowledging Multiple Issue Arenas.' *Corporate Communications: An International Journal*, 15(3): 315–331.

Lyotard, J.-F. (1984). *The Postmodern Condition: A Report on Knowledge* (G. Bennington and B. Massumi, Trans.). Minneapolis, MN: University of Minnesota Press.

Lyotard, J.-F., and Thébaud, J. L. (1985). *Just Gaming* (W. Godzich, Trans). Minneapolis, MN: University of Minnesota Press.

MacLeod, A. (1996). 'In Britain, Ethical Investing Movement Catches Fire; Big Inflows to Wind Fund.' *Christian Science Monitor*. April 17. Available online at: www.csmonitor.com/1996/0417/17092.html (accessed 27 June 2014).

Mahoney, J. (2014). *Teaching Business Ethics in the UK, Europe, and the USA: A Comparative Study*. London: Bloomsbury Academic.

Maignan, I. and Ferrell, O. (2003). 'Nature of Corporate Responsibilities: Perspectives From American, French, and German Consumers.' *Journal of Business Research*, 56: 55–67.

Maignan, I. and Ferrell, O. C. (2004). 'Corporate Social Responsibility and Marketing: An Integrative Framework.' *Journal of the Academy of Marketing Science*, 32: 3–19.

Maignan, I. and Ralston, D. (2002). 'Corporate Social Responsibility in Europe and the US.' *Journal of International Business Studies*, 33(3): 497–514.

Maignan, I., Ferrell, O. C., and Hult, G. T. M. (1999). 'Corporate Citizenship: Cultural Antecedents and Business Benefits.' *Journal of the Academy of Marketing Science*, 27: 455–469.

Márquez, A., and Fombrun, C. J. (2005). 'Measuring Corporate Social Responsibility.' *Corporate Reputation Review*, 7(4): 304–308.

Martinson, D. L. (2004). 'An Essential Component in Teaching Public Relations Ethics.' *Teaching Public Relations Monograph*, 64.

Matten, D., Crane, A. and Chapple, W. (2003). 'Behind De Mask: Revealing the True Face of Corporate Citizenship.' *Journal of Business Ethics*, 45(1–2): 109–120.

Matten, D. and Moon, J. (2004). 'Corporate Social Responsibility Education in Europe.' *Journal of Business Ethics*. 54: 323–337.

May, S. (1993). 'Employee Assistance Programs and the Troubled Worker: A Discursive Study of Power, Knowledge, and Subjectivity.' Unpublished PhD. Dissertation, University of Utah, Salt Lake City.

May, S. (2009). 'CSR Can "Blow Back" If Seen as Market-driven, Researcher Says.' Available online at: www.newswise.com/articles/csr-can-blow-back-if-seen-as-market-driven-researcher-says (accessed 10 June 2014).

May, S. (2011). "Organizational Communication and Corporate Social Responsibility." In O. Ihlen, J. L. Bartlett, and S. May (eds), *The Handbook of Communication and Corporate Social Responsibility*, pp. 87–109. West Sussex: John Wiley & Sons Inc.

McAlister, D. T., Ferrell, O.C., and Ferrell, L. (2010) *Business and Society: A Strategic Approach to Social Responsibility*, 4th edn. Boston, MA: Houghton Mifflin Company.

McDonald, G. M. (2004). 'A Case Example: Integrating Ethics Into the Academic Business Curriculum.' *Journal of Business Ethics*, 54(4): 371–384.

McKinnon, L. M., and Fullerton, J. A. (2014, Summer). 'Public Relations Students' Ethics: An Examination of Attitude and Intended Behaviors.' *Teaching Public Relations*. Available online at: www.aejmc.us/PR/tpr/tpr90su14.pdf (accessed 5 August 2014).

McMillan, S. J., Hwang, J. S., and Lee, G. (2003). 'Effects of Structural and Perceptual Factors on Attitudes Toward the Website.' *Journal of Advertising Research*, 43: 400–409.

McPhail, F. and Bowles, P. (2009). 'Corporate Social Responsibility as Support for Employee Volunteers: Impacts, Gender Puzzles and Policy Implications in Canada.' *Journal of Business Ethics*, 84(3): 405–416.

McVea, J. F. and Freeman, R. E. (2005). 'A Names-and-faces Approach to Stakeholder Management: How Focusing on Stakeholders As Individuals Can Bring Ethics and Entrepreneurial Strategy Together.' *Journal of Management Inquiry*, 14(1): 57–69.

McWilliams, V. and Nahavandi, A. (2006). 'Using Live Cases to Teach Ethics.' *Journal of Business Ethics*, 67(4): 421–433.

Melo, T. and Galan, J. I. (2011). 'Effects of Corporate Social Responsibility on Brand Value.' *Journal of Brand Management*, 18(6): 423–437.

Meyerson, D. E. (2001). *Tempered Radical: How People Use Difference to Inspire Change at Work*. Boston, MA: Harvard Business School Press.

Micklethwait, J. and Wooldridge, A. (2003). *The Company*. London: Weidenfeld & Nicholson.

Miles, R. H. (1987). *Managing the Corporate Social Environment*. Englewood Cliffs, NJ: Prentice-Hall.

Millar, C., Hind, P., and Magala, S. (2012). 'Sustainability and the Need for Change: Organisational Change and Transformational Vision.' *Journal of Organizational Change Management*, 25(4): 489–500.

Milne, M., Kearins, K., and Walton, S. (2006). Creating Adventures in Wonderland? The Journey Metaphor and Environmental Sustainability. *Organization*, 13(6): 801–839.

Mishra, K. E. (2006). 'Help or Hype: Symbolic or Behavioral Communication During Hurricane Katrina.' *Public Relations Review*, 32: 358–366.

Mishra, K., Boynton, L., and Mishra, A. (2014). 'Driving Employee Engagement: The Expanded Role of Internal Communications.' *International Journal of Business Communication*, 51(2): 183–202.

Moberg, D. J. (2006). 'Best Intentions, Worst Results: Grounding Ethics Students in the Realities Of Organizational Context.' *Academy of Management Learning & Education*, 5(3): 207–316.

Molleda, J.-C. and Ferguson, M. A. (2004). 'Public Relations Roles in Brazil: Hierarchy Eclipses Gender Differences.' *Journal of Public Relations Research*, 16(4): 327–351.

Moloney, K. (2000). *Rethinking Public Relations: The Spin and the Substance*. New York: Routledge.

Moloney, K. (2006). *Rethinking Public Relations: PR, Propaganda and Democracy*, 2nd edn. New York: Routledge.

Moneva, J., Archel, B., and Correa, C. (2006). 'GRI and the Camouflaging of Corporate Unsustainability.' *Accounting Forum*, 30(2): 121–137.

Moon, J., Crane, A., and Matten, D. (2005). 'Can Corporations Be Citizens? Corporate Citizenship as a Metaphor for Business Participation in Society.' *Business Ethics Quarterly*, 15(3): 429–453.

Moore, M. (Producer and Director). (1989). *Roger & Me* (Motion picture). USA: Warner Bros.

Moran, G. (1996). *A Grammar of Responsibility*. New York: Crossroads.

Moreno, A. and Capriotti, P. (2009). 'Communicating CSR, Citizenship and Sustainability on the Web.' *Journal of Communication Management*, 13(2): 157–175.

Moreno, A., Zerfass, A., Tench, R., *et al.* (2009). 'European Communication Monitor: Current Developments, Issues and Tendencies of the Professional Practice of Public Relations in Europe.' *Public Relations Review*, 35(1): 79–82.

Morhardt, J., Baird, S., and Freeman, K. (2002). 'Scoring Corporate Environmental and Sustainability Reports Using GRI 2000, ISO 14031, and Other Criteria.' *Corporate Social Responsibility and Environmental Management*, 9(4): 215–233.

Morley, J. R. (Producer), and Spurlock, M. (Director). (2004). *Super Size Me* (Motion Picture). USA: Roadside Attractions.

Morningstar (2010Lessons From Exxon's Valdez spill.' 6 June. Available online at: www.istockanalyst.com/article/viewarticle/articleid/4183157 (accessed 6 July 2014).

Morsing, M., Midttun, A., and Palmas, K. (2007). "Corporate Social Responsibility in Scandinavia: A Turn Toward the Business Case?" In S. May, G. Cheney, and J. Roper (eds), *The Debate Over Corporate Social Responsibility*, pp. 87–104. New York: Oxford University Press.

Morsing, M. and Schultz, M. (2006). 'Corporate Social Responsibility Communication: Stakeholder Information, Response and Involvement Strategies.' *Business Ethics: A European Review*, 15(4): 323–338.

Moss-Coane, M. (Narrator). (2014, June 26). 'Amazon's Feud With Book Publishers' (Radio broadcast episode). In S. Greenbaum (Producer), *Radio Times*. Philadelphia, PA: National Public Radio.

Muller, M. (1974). *The Baby Killer: A War on Want Investigation Into the Promotion and Sale of Powdered Baby Milks in the Third World*. London: War on Want.

Muller, A. and Kolk, A. (2010). 'Extrinsic and Intrinsic Drivers of Corporate Social Performance: Evidence From Foreign and Domestic Firms in Mexico.' *Journal of Management Studies*, 47: 1–26.

"Multi-sited Ethnography Definition" (n.d.). Available online at: http://medanth. wikispaces.com/Multi-Sited+Ethnography (accessed 13 August 2014).

Munemitsu, S. and Knowlton, T. W. (2004). *Rediscovering a Strategic Resource: Your Employees*. New York: TCC Group.

Munshi, D. and Kurian, P. (2005). 'Imperializing Spin Cycles: A Postcolonial Look at Public Relations, Greenwashing, and the Separation of Publics.' *Public Relations Review*, 31: 513–520.

Murphy, P. E. (2005). 'Developing Communicating and Promoting Corporate Ethics Statements: A Longitudinal Analysis.' *Journal of Business Ethics*, 62: 183–189.

Nash, L. (1990). "Ethics Without the Sermon." In W. M. Hoffman and J. M. Moore (eds), *Business Ethics: Reading and Cases in Corporate Morality*, 2nd edn. New York: McGraw-Hill.

National Black Environmental Justice Network (n.d.). 'In the Spotlight: Toxic Wastes and Race.' Available online at: www.nbejn.org/ (accessed 10 February 2014).

Nelson, J. (1989). *Sultans of Sleaze: Public Relations and the Media*. Toronto: Between the Lines Press.

Nelson, K. A. (2004). 'Consumer Decision Making and Image Theory: Understanding Value-laden Decisions.' *Journal of Consumer Psychology*, 13: 316–327.

Nestlé. (n.d.). Nestlé in Society: Creating Shared Value and Meeting Our Commitments. Available online at: www.nestle.com/csv (accessed 22 January 2014).

"Nestlé doesn't Deserve a Break" (2010). Greenpeace. 23 March. Available online at: www.greenpeace.org/international/en/news/features/Nestle-needs-to-give-rainfores/ (accessed 14 July 2014).

Noelle-Neumann, E. (1974). 'The Spiral of Silence: A Theory of Public Opinion.' *Journal of Communication*, 24: 43–51.

O'Connor, A. (2006). 'Alternative Sites of Identification.' *Public Relations Review*, 32: 80–82.

O'Connor, A., Shumate, M., and Meister, M. (2008). 'Walk the Line: Active Moms Define Corporate Social Responsibility.' *Public Relations Review*, 34: 343–350.

O'Dwyer, B. (2003). 'Conceptions of Corporate Social Responsibility: The Nature of Managerial Capture.' *Accountability Journal*, 16(4): 523–657.

O'Higgins, E. (2005). 'Ireland: Bridging the Atlantic.' In A. Habisch and J. Jonker (eds), *Corporate Social Responsibility*, pp. 67–76. Berlin: Springer Verlag.

O'Riordan, L. and Fairbrass, J. (2008). 'Corporate Social Responsibility (CSR): Models and Theories in Stakeholder Dialogue.' *Journal of Business Ethics*, 83(4): 745–758.

Okura, M., Dozier, D., Sha, B., and Hofstetter, R. (2008). 'Use of Scanning Research in decision Making: An Examination of the Environmental Imperative and Power-control Perspective.' *Journal of Public Relations Research*, 21: 1–20.

Olasky, M. N. (1987). *Corporate Public Relations: A New Historical Perspective*. Hillsdale, NJ: Lawrence Erlbaum.

Orts, E. W. and Strudler, A. (2002). 'The Ethical And Environmental Limits of Stakeholder Theory.' *Business Ethics Quarterly*, 12(2): 215–233.

"Our Mission: To Give Everyone the Power to Create and Share Ideas and Information Instantly, Without Barriers" (n.d.). Available online at: https://about.twitter.com/company (accessed 17 August 2014).

"Our work: Forests Program" (n.d.). Available online at: http://ran.org/our-work-for ests-program (accessed 1 March 2014).

"Overview of the UN Global Impact" (2013). Available online at: www.unglobal compact.org/AboutTheGC/index.html (accessed 28 July 2014).

Owen, D. L., Swift, T. A., Humphrey, C., and Bowerman, M. (2000). 'The New Social Audits: Accountability, Management Capture or the Agenda of Social Champions?' *European Accounting Review*, 9(1): 81–98.

Page, A. and Katz, R. A. (2010). 'Freezing Out Ben & Jerry: Corporate Law and the Sale of a Social Enterprise Icon.' *Vermont Law Review*, 35: 211–250.

Painter-Morland, M. (2006). 'Triple Bottom-line Reporting as Social Grammar: Integrating Corporate Social Responsibility and Corporate Codes of Conduct.' *Business Ethics: A European Review*, 15(4): 352–364.

Parsons, P. (2004). *Ethics in Public Relations: A Guide to Best Practice*. London: Kogan Page.

Parsons, T. (1961). "An Outline of the Social System." In T. Parsons, E. A. Shils, K. D. Naegle and J. R. Pitts (eds), *Theories of Society*, pp. 30–79. New York: Free Press.

Partington, R. (2011). 'The Enron Cast: Where Are They Now?'. Available online at: www.efinancialnews.com/story/2011-12-01/enron-ten-years-on-where-they-are-now (accessed 29 June 2014).

Pawlik, J. (2014). 'The Kyosei as CSR Practice in French and English Subsidiaries of Japanese Multinational.' 2 August. Paper presented at the Academy of Management. Philadelphia, PA.

Peloza, J. and Hassay, D. N. (2006). 'Intra-organizational Volunteerism: Good Soldiers, Good Deeds and Good Politics.' *Journal of Business Ethics*, 64: 357–379.

Perera, S. and Pugliese, J. (1998). 'Parks, Mines and Tidy Towns: Enviro-panopticism, "Post" Colonialism, and the Politics of Heritage in Australia.' *Postcolonial Studies*, 1(1): 69–100.

Peterson, D. K. (2004a). 'Recruitment Strategies for Encouraging Participation in Corporate Volunteer Programs.' *Journal of Business Ethics*, 49(4): 371–386.

Peterson, D. K. (2004b). 'The Relationship Between Perceptions of Corporate Citizenship and Organizational Commitment.' *Business and Society*, 43: 296–319.

Phillips, R. (2003). 'Stakeholder legitimacy.' *Business Ethics Quarterly*, 13(1): 25–41.

Pieczka, M. (2006). "Paradigms, Systems Theory, and Public Relations." In J. L'Etang and M. Pieczka (eds), *Public Relations: Critical Debates and Contemporary Practice*, pp. 333–357. Mahwah, NJ: Lawrence Erlbaum Associates.

Pollach, L. (2005). 'Corporate Self-presentation on the WWW: Strategies for Enhancing Usability, Credibility and Utility.' *Corporate Communications: An International Journal*, 10(4): 285–301.

Pompper, D. (2004). 'At the 20th Century's Close: Framing the Public Policy Issue of Environmental Risk.' *The Environmental Communication Yearbook*, 1: 99–134.

Pompper, D. (2011). '"Cheap Labor" Speaks: PR Adjuncts on Pedagogy and Preparing Millennials for Careers.' *Public Relations Review*, 37(5): 456–465.

Pompper, D. (2013). "Volunteerism and Corporate Social Responsibility: Definitions, Measurement, Roles, & Commitment." In L. Lewis, L. Gossett and M. Kramer (eds), *Volunteering and Communication: Studies From Multiple Contexts*, pp. 273–295. New York: Peter Lang Publishers.

Pompper, D. (2014). 'The Sarbanes-Oxley Act: Impact, Processes and Roles for Strategic Communication.' *International Journal of Strategic Communication*, 8(3): 130–145.

Pompper, D. and Crider, D. (2012). "New Media and Symmetry-conservation Duality: As viewed Through the Legal / Public Relations Counselor Relationship Lens." In S. G. Duhé (ed.), *New Media and Public Relations*, 2nd edn, pp. 31–39. New York: Peter Lang.

Pompper, D. and Higgins, L. (2007). 'Corporation Bashing in Documentary Film: A Case Study of News Coverage & Organizational Response.' *Public Relations Review*, 33(4): 429–432.

Post, J. E., Lawrence, A., and Weber, J. (2002). *Business and Society: Corporate Strategy, Public Policy, Ethics*, 10th edn. New York: McGraw-Hill.

Potter, W. (2009a). 'Commentary: How Insurance Firms Drive Debate.' Available online at: www.cnn.com/2009/POLITICS/08/17/potter.health.insurance/index.html (accessed 19 August 2014).

Potter, W. (2009b). 'GOP Fear Tactic From Health Insurance Companies.' Available online at: www.ireport.com/docs/DOC-315401 (accessed 19 August 2014).

Pratt, C. B. (1991). 'Public Relations: The Empirical Research on Practitioner Ethics.' *Journal of Business Ethics*, 10: 229–236.

Pratt, C. B. (1993). 'Critique of the Classical Theory of Situational Ethics in US Public Relations.' *Public Relations Review*, 19: 219–234.

Pratt, C. B. (2003). "Managing Sustainable Development in Sub-Saharan Africa: A Communication Ethic for the Global Corporation." In K. Sriramesh and D. Verčič (eds), *The Global Public Relations Handbook: Theory, Research and Practice*, pp. 441–458. Mahwah, NJ: Lawrence Erlbaum Associates.

Prentice, R. (2003). 'Enron: A Brief Behavioral Autopsy.' *American Business Law Journal*, 40(2): 417–444.

PRSA Commission on Public Relations Education (2012). 'Standards for a Master's Degree in Public Relations: Educating for Complexity.' Available online at: www. commpred.org (accessed 5 July 2014).

"PRSA Member Code of Ethics" (n.d.). Available online at: www.prsa.org/ AboutPRSA/Ethics/CodeEnglish/#.U636nbdOUY0 (accessed 27 July 2014).

Rainey, L. D. (2010). *Confucius and Confucianism: The Essentials*. Oxford: Wiley-Blackwell.

Rämö, H. (2011). 'Visualizing the Phronetic Organization: The Case of Photographs in CSR Reports.' *Journal of Business Ethics*, 104: 371–387.

Ramus, C. A. and Steger, U. (2000). 'The Roles of Supervisory Support Behaviors and Environmental Policy in Employee "ecoinitiatives" at Leading-edge European Companies.' *Academy of Management Journal*, 43: 605–626.

"Ray Anderson Tribute Video" (n.d.). Available online at: www.youtube.com/watch? v=E9T-0bhqOGY (accessed 1 July 2014).

Ready, D. A., Conger, J. A., and Hill, L. A. (2010, June). 'Are You a High Potential?' Harvard Business Review. Available online at: http://hbr.org/2010/06/are-you-a-high-potential/ar/1 (accessed 12 February 2014).

Reber, B. H. and Berger, B. K. (2006). 'Finding Influence: Examining the Role of Influence in Public Relations Practice.' *Journal of Communication Management*, 10(3): 235–249.

Reich, R. B. (2008). 'The Case Against Corporate Social Responsibility.' Available online at: http://papers.ssrn.com/sol3/papers.cfm?abstract_id=1213129 (accessed 18 June 2014).

"Responsibility in the Electronics Industry" (n.d.). *Executive Education in CSR*. Available online at: http://csr.unige.ch/responsibility-in-the-electronics-industry/ (accessed 17 July 2014).

Ricart, J. E., Rodríguez, M. A. and Sánchez, P. (2005). 'Sustainability in the Boardroom.' *Corporate Governance*, 5(3): 24–41.

Robbins, S. S. and Stylianou, A. C. (2003). 'Global Corporate Web Sites: An Empirical Investigation of Content and Design.' *Information & Management*, 40(3): 205–212.

Roberts, J. (2001). 'Corporate Governance and the Ethics of Narcissus.' *Business Ethics Quarterly*, 11(1): 109–127.

Roberts, J. (2003). 'The Manufacture of Corporate Social Responsibility: Constructing Corporate Sensibility.' *Organization*, 10(2): 249–265.

Rodríguez, L. and LeMaster, J. (2007). 'Voluntary Corporate Social Responsibility Disclosure – SEC CSR Seal of Approval.' *Business & Society*, 46(3): 370–385.

Rolland, D. and Bazzoni, J. O. (2009). 'Greening Corporate Identity: CSR Online Corporate Identity Reporting.' *Corporate Communications: An International Journal*, 14(3): 249–263.

Rupp, D. E., Shao, R., Thornton, M. A., and Skarlicki, D. P. (2013). '"Applicants" and Employees' Reactions to Corporate Social Responsibility: The Moderating Effects of First-party Justice Perceptions and Moral Identity.' *Personnel Psychology*, 66(4): 895–933.

Rybalko, S. and Seltzer, T. (2010). 'Dialogic Communication in 140 Characters or Less: How Fortune 500 Companies Engage Stakeholders Using Twitter.' *Public Relations Review*, 36: 336–341.

Sagar, P. and Singla, A. (2004). 'Trust and Corporate Social Responsibility: Lessons From India.' *Journal of Communication Management*, 8(3): 282–290.

Sagawa, S. and Segal, E. (2000). 'Common Interest, Common Good: Creating Value Through Business and Social Sector Partnerships.' *California Management Review*, 42(2): 105–122.

Salazar, J. and Husted, B. (2008). "Principals and Agents: Future Thoughts and the Friedmanite Critique of Corporate Social Responsibility." In A. Crane, A. McWilliams, D. Matten, J. Moon, and D. Siegel (eds), *The Oxford Handbook of Corporate Social Responsibility*, pp. 137–155. Oxford: Oxford University Press.

Samii, R., Van Wassenhove, L. N., and Bhattacharya, S. (2002). 'An Innovative Public Private Partnership: New Approach to Development.' *World Development*, 30(6): 991–1008.

Schmidt, J. (2007). 'Blogging Practices: An Analytical Framework.' *Journal of Computer-Mediated Communication*, 12(4): 1409–1427.

Schneider, S. C., Zollo, M., and Manocha, R. (2010). 'Developing Socially Responsible Behavior in Managers: Experimental Evidence of the Effectiveness of Different Approaches to Management Education.' *The Journal of Corporate Citizenship*, 39: 21–40.

Schramm, W. (1964). *Mass Media and National Development*. Stanford, CA: Stanford University Press.

Schreck, P. (2011). 'Reviewing the Business Case for Corporate Social Responsibility: New Evidence and Analysis.' *Journal of Business Ethics*, 103(2): 167–188.

Schultz, T. (2000). 'Mass Media and the Concept of Interactivity: An Exploratory Study of Online Forums and Reader Email.' *Media Culture & Society*, 22: 205–221.

Scott, P. (2008). 'CSR Assurance: Growth Industry', October 9. Available online at: www.accountancyage.com/accountancyage/features/2227795/csr-assurance-growth-industry (accessed 2 April 2014).

See, G. K. H. (2009). 'Harmonious Society and Chinese CSR: Is There Really a Link?' *Journal of Business Ethics*, 89(1): 1–22.

Seitanidi, M. M. and Crane, A. (2009). 'Implementing CSR Through Partnerships: Understanding the Selection, Design and Institutionalisation of Nonprofit-business Partnerships.' *Journal of Business Ethics*, 85: 413–429.

Seitanidi, M. M. and Ryan, A. (2007). 'Forms of Corporate Community Involvement: From Partnerships to Philanthropy. A Critical Review.' *International Journal of Nonprofit and Voluntary Sector Marketing*, 12: 247–266.

Sen, S. and Bhattacharya, C. B. (2001). 'Does Doing Good Always Lead to Doing Better? Consumer Reactions to Corporate Social Responsibility.' *Journal of Marketing Research*, 38: 225–243.

Sethi, S. P. (1977). *Advocacy Advertising and Large Corporations: Social Conflict, Big Business Image, the News Media, and Public Policy*. Lexington, MA: D. C. Heath.

Shannon, C. E. and Weaver, W. (1949). *The Mathematical Theory of Communication*. Urbana, IL: University of Illinois Press.

Sharma, S., and Ruud, A. (2003). 'On the Path to Sustainability: Integrating Social Dimensions Into the Research and Practice of Environmental Management.' *Business Strategy and Environment*, 12(4): 205–214.

Shen, H. and Kim, J.-N. (2012). 'The Authentic Enterprise: Another Buzz Word, or a True Driver of Quality Relationships?' *Journal of Public Relations Research*, 24(4): 371–389.

Shen, H. and Toth, E. (2008). 'An Ideal Public Relations Master's Curriculum: Expectations and Status Quo.' *Public Relations Review*, 34(3): 309–311.

Shin, J.-H., Heath, R. L., and Lee, J. (2011). 'A Contingency Explanation of Public Relations Practitioner Leadership Styles: Situation and Culture.' *Journal of Public Relations Research*, 23(2): 167–190.

Shishkoff, D. (2013, Summer). 'Cheers & Jeers.' Available online at: http://friendsofa nimals.org/magazine/summer-2013/cheers-jeers (accessed 29 June 2014).

Siegel, D. S. and Vitaliano, D. F. (2007). 'An Empirical Analysis of the Strategic Use of Corporate Social Responsibility.' *Journal of Economics and Management Strategy*, 16: 773–792.

Small, W. (1991). 'Exxon Valdez: How to Spend a Billion and Still Get a Black Eye.' *Public Relations Review*, 17: 9–26.

Smidts, A., Pruyn, A. T. H., and van Riel, C. B. M. (2001). 'The Impact of Employee Communication and Perceived External Prestige on Organizational Identification.' *Academy of Management Journal*, 49: 1051–1060.

Smith, A. (1759). *The Theory of Moral Sentiments*. London: A. Millar.

Smith, M. P. (2012). 'Shareholder Activism By Institutional Investors. Evidence From CalPERS.' *Journal of Finance*, 51: 227–232.

Smith, N. C. (2003). 'Corporate Social Responsibility: Whether or How?" *California Management Review*, 45(4): 52–76.

Smith, S. (1980). "Giving to Charitable Organizations: A Behavioral Review and a Framework for Increasing Commitment." In J. Olsen (ed.), *Advances in Consumer Research 7*, pp. 753–756. Provo, UT: Association for Consumer Research.

Smith, S. M. and Alcorn, D. S. (1991). 'Cause Marketing: A New Direction in the Marketing of Corporate Social Responsibility.' *Journal of Consumer Marketing*, 8: 19–35.

Smudde, P. (2005). 'Blogging, Ethics and Public Relations: A Proactive and Dialogic Approach.' *Public Relations Quarterly*, 50(3): 34–38.

Sockell, D. (2013). 'Corporate Responsibility Should Start in Business School.' *Chronicle of Higher Education*. 15 April. Available online at: http://chronicle.com/article/Corporate-Responsibility/138495/ (accessed 4 September 2014).

Solomon, S. (1981). 'The Controversy Over Infant Formula.' *New York Times*, 6 December, 92.

Soper, S. (2011). 'Inside Amazon's Warehouse.' *Allentown Morning Call*. 18 September. Available online at: http://articles.mcall.com/2011-09-18/news/mc-allentown-amazon-complaints-20110917_1_warehouse-workers-heat-stress-brutal-heat (accessed 1 July 2014).

Soppe, A., Schauten, M., Soppe, J., and Kaymak, U. (n.d.). 'Corporate Social Responsibility Reputation (CSRR): Do Companies Comply With Their Raised CSR Expectations.' Available online at: http://papers.ssrn.com/sol3/papers.cfm?abstract_id=1417995 (accessed 22 March 2014).

Spangler, I. and Pompper, D. (2011). 'Corporate Social Responsibility and the Oil Industry: Theory and Perspective Fuel a Longitudinal View.' *Public Relations Review*, 37(3): 217–225.

Spence, C. (2007). 'Social and Environmental Reporting and Hegemonic Discourse.' *Accounting, Auditing & Accountability Journal*, 20(6): 855–882.

Spreitzer, G. M., DeJanasz, S. C., and Quinn, R. E. (1999). 'Empowered to Lead: The Role of Psychological Empowerment in Leadership.' *Journal of Organizational Behavior*, 20(4): 511–526.

Springett, D. (2003). 'Business Conceptions of Sustainable Development: A Perspective From Critical Theory.' *Business Strategy and the Environment*, 12: 71–86.

Springston, J. K. (2001). "Public Relations and New Media Technology." In R. L. Heath and G. Vasquez (eds), *Handbook of Public Relations*, pp. 603–614. Thousand Oaks, CA: Sage.

Sprinkle, T. (2013). 'Walmart Employees Organize Food Drive… for Other Walmart Employees.' Available online at: http://finance.yahoo.com/blogs/the-exchange/walmart-employees-organize-food-drive-for-other-walmart-employees-191602622.html (accessed 25 December 2014).

Starck, K., and Kruckeberg, D. (2003). 'Ethical Obligations of Public Relations in an Era Of Globalization.' *Journal of Communication Management*, 8(1): 29–40.

Stauber, J. and Rampton, S. (2002). *Trust Us, We're Experts: How Industry Manipulates Science and Gambles With Your Future*. Monroe, ME: Center for Media and Democracy.

Steel, K. (1995). "Managing Corporate and Employee Volunteer Programs." In T. D. Connors (ed.), *The Volunteer Management Handbook*, pp. 259–292. New York: Wiley & Sons.

Stewart, K. J. (2003). 'Trust Transfer on the World Wide Web.' *Organisation Science*, 14(1): 5–17.

Steyn, B. (2007). "Contribution of Public Relations to Organisational Strategy Formulation." In E. L. Toth (ed.), *The Future of Excellence in Public Relations and Communication Management*, pp. 137–172. Mahwah, NJ: Lawrence Erlbaum Associates.

Steyn, B. and Bütschi, G. (2004). 'Theory on Strategic Communication Management is the Key to Unlocking the Boardroom.' *Journal of Communication Management*, 10(1): 106–109.

Stohl, C. (2013). 'Through a Glass Darkly: CSR in the New Media Environment.' September. Keynote session at the 2nd International CSR Communication Conference, Aarhus University, Denmark.

Stone, B. A. (2001). 'Corporate Social Responsibility and Institutional Investment: A Content Analysis Based Portfolio Screening Model for Socially Responsible Mutual Funds.' *Business & Society*, 40: 112–117.

Stoughton, A. M. and Ludema, J. (2012). 'The Driving Forces of Sustainability.' *Journal of Organizational Change Management*, 25(4): 501–517.

Streitfeld, D. (2011). 'Inside Amazon's Very Hot Warehouse.' *The New York Times*. 19 September. Available online at: http://bits.blogs.nytimes.com/2011/09/19/inside-amazons-very-hot-warehouse/?_php=true&_type=blogs&_r=0 (accessed 29 June 2014).

Stuart, H. and Jones, C. (2004). 'Corporate Branding in the Online Marketspace.' *Corporate Reputation Review*, 7(1): 84–98.

Stuart, T. E. (2000). 'Inter-organizational Alliances and the Performance of Firms: A Study of Growth and Innovation Rates in a High Technology Industry.' *Strategic Management Journal*, 21(8): 791–811.

Surma, A. (2005). 'Public Relations and Corporate Social Responsibility: Developing a Moral Narrative.' *Asia Pacific Public Relations Journal*, 5(2): 1–12.

Surma, A. (2006). "Challenging Unreliable Narrators: Writing and Public Relations." In J. L'Etang and M. Pieczka (eds), *Public Relations: Critical Debates and Contemporary Practice*, pp. 41–59. Mahwah, NJ: Lawrence Erlbaum Associates.

"Sustainability Assurance" (n.d.) Standard on Assurance Engagements 3000 (ISAE 3000). Available online at: www.reportingcsr.org/sustainability_assurance-p-211.html (accessed 5 May 2014).

"Sustainability Disclosure Database" (2014). Global Reporting Initiative. Available online at: http://database.globalreporting.org/search (accessed 28 July 2014).

Swift, T. (2001). 'Trust, Reputation and Corporate Accountability to Stakeholders.' *Business Ethics: a European Review*, 10(1): 16–26.

Szykman, L. R., Bloom, P. N., and Blazing, J. (2004). 'Does Corporate Sponsorship of a Socially-oriented Message Make a Difference? An Investigation of the Effects of Sponsorship Identity on Responses to an Anti-drinking and Driving Message.' *Journal of Consumer Psychology*, 14: 13–20.

Tan, S. L. (2000). *Guanxi and Public Relations in Singapore: An Exploratory Study*. Master's thesis, Nanyang Technological University, Singapore.

Taylor, A. (1997). 'Yo, Ben! Yo, Jerry! It's Just Ice Cream! The Celebrated Vermont Do-gooders Seek Global Solutions in Every Spoonful of Their Luscious Products. Meanwhile, Their Business Suffers and Their Shareholders Starve.' *Fortune*, 28 April, 374.

Taylor, M. (2013). "Nongovernmental Organizations (NGOs)." In R. L. Heath (ed.), *Encyclopedia of Public Relations*, 2nd edn., vol. 2, pp. 614–616. Los Angeles, CA: Sage.

Taylor, V. E. and Winquist, C. E. (eds). (2001). *Encyclopedia of Postmodernism*. New York: Routledge.

Tedlow, R. (1979). *Keeping the Corporate Image*. Bingley: Emerald Group Publishing Limited.

Tench, R., Bowd, R., and Jones, B. (2007). 'Perceptions and Perspectives: Corporate Social Responsibility and the Media.' *Journal of Communication Management*, 11(4): 348–370.

Theofilou, A. and Watson, T. (2014). "Sceptical Employees as CSR Ambassadors in Times of Financial Uncertainty." In R. Tench, W. Sun, and B. Jones (eds), *Communicating Corporate Social Responsibility: Perspectives and Practice*, pp. 355–379. Bingley: Emerald Group Publishing Limited.

"Timberland responsibility" (n.d.). Available online at: http://responsibility.timberland. com/service/living-our-values/ (accessed 23 December 2013).

"Top Ten Polluting Industries, Top 5 Toxic Stuff Imperil 125M people" (n.d.). Available online at: www.interaksyon.com/article/46518/lists–top-10-polluting-industries-top-5-toxic-stuff-imperil-125m-people (accessed 16 March 2014).

"Top 100 NGOs" (n.d.). Available online at: http://theglobaljournal.net/top100NGOs/ (accessed 28 February 2014).

Toth, E. L., Serini, S. A., Wright, D. K., and Emig, A. G. (1998). 'Trends in Public Relations Roles: 1990–1995.' *Public Relations Review*, 24(2): 145–163.

Townsley, N. C. and Stohl, C. (2003). 'Contracting Corporate Social Responsibility: Swedish Expansions in Global Temporary Agency Work.' *Management Communication Quarterly*, 16(4): 599–605.

Tschopp, D. (2005). 'Corporate Social Responsibility: A Comparison Between the United States and the European Union.' *Corporate Social Responsibility and Environmental Management*, 12(1): 55–59.

Turban, D. B. and Greening, D. W. (1997). 'Corporate Social Performance and Organizational Attractiveness to Prospective Employees.' *Academy of Management Journal*, 40: 658–672.

Turk, J. V. (ed.) (2006). 'Cultural Values and Beliefs Affecting Public Relations.' In *Public Relations Education for the 21st Century: The Professional Bond*. The Report of the Commission on Public Relations Education. Available online at: www. commpred.org/uploads/report2-full.pdf.

United Nations (2004). Department of Economic and Social Affairs. Division for Sustainable Development, November 9. Available online at: www.un.org/esa/ agenda21/natlinfo/countr/spain/ (accessed 18 June 2014).

"United Nations Framework Convention on Climate Change" (n.d.). Kyoto Protocol. Available online at: http://unfccc.int/kyoto_protocol/items/2830.php (accessed 11 June 2014).

US Department of Labor, Bureau of Labor Statistics (2012). 'Volunteering in the United States – 2012.' Available online at: www.bls.gov/news.release/volun.nr0.htm (accessed 14 September 2013).

van Leeuwen, T. (2005). *Introducing Social Semiotics*. London: Routledge.

van Leuven, J. (1999). 'Four New Course Competencies for Majors.' *Public Relations Review*, 25: 77–85.

van Luijk, H. J. L. (2000). 'In Search of Instruments Business and Ethics Halfway.' *Journal of Business Ethics*, 27: 3–8.

van Luijk, H. J. L. (2001). "Business Ethics in Europe: A Tale of Two Efforts." In R. Lang (ed.), *Wirtschaftsethik in Mittelund Osteuropa*, pp. 9–18. Munich: Rainer Hampp.

Van Manen, M. (1990). *Researching Lived Experience: Human Science for an Action Sensitive Pedagogy*, 2nd edn. Albany, NY: State University of New York Press.

van Oosterhout, J. and Heugens, P. P. M. A. R. (2009). 'Extant Social Contracts in Global Business Regulation: Outline of a Research Agenda.' *Journal of Business Ethics*, 88(4): 729–740.

van Ruler, B. and Verčič, D. (2004). "Overview of Public Relations and Communication Management in Europe." In B. van Ruler and D. Verčič (eds), *Public Relations and Communication Management in Europe: A Nation-by-nation Introduction to Public Relations Theory And Practice*, pp. 1–11. Berlin: Walter de Gruyter.

van Ruler, B. and Verčič, D. (2005). "Reflective Communication Management: Future Ways for Public Relations Research." In P. J. Kalbfleisch (ed.), *Communication Yearbook*, 29, pp. 239–273. Mahwah, NJ: Lawrence Erlbaum Associates.

van Scotter, J. R. and Motowidlo, S. J. (2000). 'Effects of Task Performance and Contextual Performance on Systematic Rewards.' *Journal of Applied Psychology*, 85: 526–535.

Verschoor, C. C. (2005). 'Organizational DNA Should Contain Ethics Component.' *Strategic Finance*, 86(8): 19–21.

Vogel, D. (2005). *The Market for Virtue: The Potential and Limits of Corporate Social Responsibility*. Washington, DC: Brookings Institution.

Votaw, D. (1972). 'Genius Became Rare: A Comment on the Doctrine of Social Responsibility Pt 1.' *California Management Review*, 15(2): 25–31.

Waddell, S. (2000). 'New Institutions for the Practice of Corporate Citizenship: Historical, Intersectoral, and Developmental Perspectives.' *Business and Society Review*, 105(1): 107–126.

Waddock, S. (2004). 'Parallel Universes: Companies, Academics, and The Progress of Corporate Citizenship.' *Business & Society Review*, 109(1): 5–42.

Waddock, S. (2007). "Corporate Citizenship: The Dark-side Paradoxes of Success." In S. May, G. Cheney, and J. Roper (eds), *The Debate Over Corporate Social Responsibility*, pp. 74–86. New York: Oxford University Press.

Wallerstein, I. (1996). "The National and the Universal: Can There Be Such a Thing as World Culture?" In A. King (ed.), *Culture, Globalization and the World-system*, pp. 91–106. Minneapolis, MN: University of Minnesota Press.

Walumbwa, F. O., Wang, P., Wang, H., Schaubroech, J., and Avolio, B. J. (2010). 'Psychological Processes Linking Authentic Leadership to Follower Behaviors.' *The Leadership Quarterly*, 21(5): 901–914.

Wartick, S. L. and Cochran, P. L. (1985). 'The Evolution of the Corporate Social Performance Model.' *Academy of Management Review*, 4: 758–769.

Waters, R. (2005). "The Changing Concerns of Fundraising Ethics: A Five Year Panel Study." In M. L. Watson (ed.), *The Impact of PR in Creating a More Ethical World: Why Can't We All Get Along?* Proceedings of the 8th International Public Relations Research Conference, Miami, Florida, March 10–13, pp. 549. Available online at: www.iprrc.org/docs/IPRRC_08_Proceedings.pdf (accessed 9 June 2014).

"We: Building Stronger Communities" (n.d.). Available online at: www.coca-colacompany. com/sustainability/we-building-strong-communities (accessed 23 February 2014).

Weaver, G. R., Treviño, L. K., and Cochran, P. L. (1999). 'Integrated and Decoupled Corporate Social Performance: Management Commitments, External Pressures, And Corporate Ethics Practices.' *Academy of Management Review*, 42: 539–552.

Webb, M. (2005). 'What Makes a Website Interactive?' Available online at: http://ext337. blogspot.com/2005/02/what-makes-website-interactive.html (accessed 11 May 2013).

Weber, M. (1947). *The Theory of Social and Economic Organization*. Trans. A. M. Henderson and Talcott Parsons. NY: The Free Press.

Weinger, A. (n.d.). 'Corporate Volunteer Grants – What They Are, How They Work.' Available online at: http://nonprofit.about.com/od/fundraising/a/Corporate-Vo lunteer-Grants-What-They-Are-How-They-Work.htm (accessed 1 September 2013).

Welford, R. (2005). 'Corporate Social Responsibility in Europe, North America and Asia: 2004 Survey Results.' *Journal of Corporate Citizenship*, 17: 33–52.

Werther, W. B. and Chandler, D. (2006). *Strategic Corporate Social Responsibility: Stakeholders in a Global Environment*. London: Sage.

"What is Monsanto Doing to Help?" (n.d.). Available online at: www.monsanto. com/improvingagriculture/pages/what-is-monsanto-doing-to-help.aspx (accessed 23 February 2014).

Wheeler, D., Colbert, B., and Freeman, R. E. (2003). 'Focusing on Value: Reconciling Corporate Social Responsibility, Sustainability and a Stakeholder Approach in a Network World.' *Journal of General Management*, 28(3): 1–29.

Whetten, D. A., Rands, G., and Godfrey, P. (2001). "What Are the Responsibilities of Business to Society?" In A. Pettigrew (ed.), *Handbook of Strategy and Management*, pp. 378–408. London: Sage.

White, J. (1999). 'Evaluation must now show it can have an impact.' *PR Week*, 26 March, 13.

Wilcox, D. L., Ault, P. H., Agee, W., and Cameron, G. T. (2000). *Essentials of Public Relations*. Boston, MA: Allyn & Bacon.

Wild, C. (1993). *Corporate Volunteer Programs: Benefits to Business. The Conference Board Report #1029*. New York.

Windsor, D. (2006). 'Corporate Social Responsibility: Three Key Approaches.' *Journal of Management Studies*, 43(1): 93–114.

Witmer, D., Silverman, D., and Gaschen, D. (2009). 'Working to Learn and Learning to Work: A Profile of Service-learning Courses in University Public Relations Programs.' *Public Relations Review*, 35: 153–155.

Wong, Y. H. and Leung, T. K. (eds). (2001). *Guanxi: Relationship Marketing in a Chinese Context*. New York: Routledge.

Wood, D. (1991a). 'Corporate Social Performance Revisited.' *The Academy of Management Review*, 16(4): 691–718.

Wood, D. J. (1991b). 'Social Issues in Management: Theory and Research in Corporate Social Performance.' *Journal of Management*, 17: 383–406.

World Bank (n.d.). 'What We Do.' Available online at: www.worldbank.org/en/about/ what-we-do (accessed 15 June 2014).

World Business Council for Sustainable Development (WBCSD) (2003). *Sustainable Development Reporting: Striking the Balance*. Geneva: WBCSD.

"World Commission on Environment and Development" (1987). Report of the World Commission on Environment and Development: Our Common Future. Available online at: www.un-documents.net/wced-ocf.htm (accessed 31 August 2014).

Wueste, D. E. (1994). "Introduction." In D. E. Wueste (ed.), *Professional Ethics & Social Responsibility*, pp. 1–35. Lanham, MD: Rowman & Littlefield Publishers, Inc.

Yoon, Y., Gürhan-Canli, Z., and Schwarz, N. (2006). 'The Effect of Corporate Social Responsibility (CSR) Activities on Companies With Bad Reputation.' *Journal of Consumer Psychology*, 16: 377–390.

Young, D. and Benamati, J. (2000). 'Differences in Public Web Sites: The Current State of Large US Firms.' *Journal of Electronic Commerce Research*, 1(3): 94–105.

Young-Ybarra, C. and Wiersema, M. (1999). 'Strategic Flexibility in Information Technology Alliances: The Influence of Transaction Cost Economics and Social Exchange Theory.' *Organization Science*, 10: 439–459.

Zambrana, R. E. and Dill, B. T. (2009). *Emerging Intersections: Race, Class, and Gender in Theory, Policy, and Practice*. New Brunswick, NJ: Rutgers University Press.

Zovanyi, G. (1998). *Growth Management for a Sustainable Future: Ecological Sustainability as the New Growth Management Focus for the 21st Century*. Westport, CT: Praeger Publishers.

Zsolnai, L. (2002). "New Agenda for Business Ethics." In L. Zsolnai (ed.), *Ethics in the Economy*, pp. 1–7. Oxford: Peter Lang.

Index